Habeas Corpus

14   And be it further enacted ~~by the authority~~ ~~aforesaid,~~ that all the before mentioned courts of the United States shall have power to issue writs of Scire-facias, ~~subpoena & protestation for witnesses~~ Habeas Corpus, ~~&~~ all other writs not specially provided for by statute, which may be necessary for the exercise of their respective jurisdictions, & agreeable to the principles & usages of law. — And that either of the Justices of the supreme court, ~~●~~ as well as Judges of the district courts, shall have power to grant writs of habeas corpus for the purpose of an enquiry into the cause of commitment. — Provided that writs of habeas corpus shall in no case extend to prisoners in gaol unless where they are in custody under or by colour of the authority of the

81

4

19   United States, or are committed for trial before some court of the same, or are necessary to be brought into court to testify.

Habeas Corpus

Rethinking the Great Writ of Liberty

Eric M. Freedman

NEW YORK UNIVERSITY PRESS

New York and London

NEW YORK UNIVERSITY PRESS
New York and London

Library of Congress Cataloging-in-Publication Data
Freedman, Eric M.
Habeas corpus : rethinking the great writ of liberty /
Eric M. Freedman.
p. cm.
Includes bibliographical references and index.
ISBN 0–8147–2717–4 (cloth : alk. paper)
1. Habeas corpus—United States.   2. Federal government—
United States.   I. Title
KF9011 .F74 2001
347.73'5—dc21   2001003912

New York University Press books are printed on acid-free paper,
and their binding materials are chosen for strength and durability.

Manufactured in the United States of America

10 9 8 7 6 5 4 3 2 1

For M.N.

Contents

Part III

Part IV

Acknowledgments

Like many authors before me, I have found that bringing this book to publication took longer than I had anticipated.

Over the course of the years, many dedicated professional archivists and librarians along with supportive friends and colleagues have provided invaluable assistance and guidance.

It is a pleasure to record my gratitude to Nancy A. Grasser for her devoted secretarial assistance; and to the extremely helpful staffs of: the Deane Law Library of Hofstra Law School, particularly Connie S. Lenz, Daniel L. May, Roberta Roberti, Linda Russo, and Katherine Walkden; the Manuscript Reading Room of the Library of Congress, especially David Wigdor, Ernest Emrich, Jeffrey M. Flannery, and Michael Klein; the Supreme Court of the United States, especially Francis J. Lorson, the Chief Deputy Clerk, and Linda Maslow and Brian Stiglmeier of the Court's Library; the National Archives and Record Administration, particularly Robert Morris and Gregory J. Plunges of the Northeast Region, Robert J. Plowman of the Mid-Atlantic Region, Charles Reeves of the Southeast Region, and W. Robert Ellis of the main library; the Yale Law School Library; the Tarlton Law Library of the University of Texas at Austin, particularly Michael Widener; the Margaret I. King Library of the University of Kentucky, particularly Jeffrey Suchanek; the Bureau of Justice Statistics of the United States Department of Justice, particularly Allen J. Beck; the Forsyth County Public Library in Winston-Salem, North Carolina, particularly Tim Cole; the United States District Court for the Eastern District of Arkansas, particularly Dennis Wysaki; and the Wisconsin State Historical Society, particularly Christine Mak.

I have also benefitted greatly from the generous suggestions and collegial enthusiasm of Anthony G. Amsterdam, Richard B. Bernstein, Paul Finkelman, Richard D. Friedman, Randy Hertz, Peter Charles Hoffer, Wythe Holt, John M. Leahy, James S. Liebman, William E. Nelson, Gerald L. Neuman, William D. Rodgers, Frederick Rowe, Andrew Schepard, and

Larry W. Yackle, and from the much-appreciated logistical support of David A. Diamond, Gail A. Ferris, Jeanne P. Ferris, Roberta Mark, Lisa Polisar, and John Ragsdale. But of course I alone am responsible for the statements of fact and opinion in this volume.

Because of the sustained backing of Dean Stuart Rabinowitz of Hofstra Law School, Hofstra University provided indispensable financial and released-time assistance to this project.

Some of the material in this volume is to be found in my prior essays: *Just Because John Marshall Said It, Doesn't Make It So:* Ex Parte Bollman *and the Illusory Prohibition on the Federal Writ of Habeas Corpus for State Prisoners in the Judiciary Act of 1789*, 51 Alabama Law Review 531 (2000), *Leo Frank Lives: Untangling the Historical Roots of Meaningful Federal Habeas Corpus Review of State Convictions*, 51 Alabama Law Review 1467 (2000), Brown v. Allen: *The Habeas Corpus Revolution That Wasn't*, 51 Alabama Law Review 1541 (2000), *Federal Habeas Corpus in Capital Cases, in* America's Experiment with Capital Punishment: Reflections on the Past, Present and Future of the Ultimate Penal Sanction 409 (James Acker et al. eds.) (Carolina Academic Press, 1998), and *The Suspension Clause in the Ratification Debates*, 44 Buffalo Law Review 451 (1996).

Although those works contain my thinking in more preliminary form, consulting them should in most instances satisfy any of my present readers who may desire more extensive documentation of the points that follow. These pages seek to take account of developments through the spring of 2001.

Finally, as the dedication reflects, my deepest thanks are reserved for my wife, Melissa Nathanson, who in this work, as in all other aspects of my life, has been my partner in the truest sense.

Introduction

In legal terms, habeas corpus is simply the name for the procedure by which a court inquires into the legality of a citizen's detention. But habeas corpus is rarely discussed in merely legal terms. The name carries a special resonance in Anglo-American legal and political history: habeas corpus is universally known and celebrated as the "Great Writ of Liberty."

The reason is straightforward. The availability of habeas corpus means that if an individual is found to have been imprisoned unlawfully the court can release him or her, thus enforcing the rule of law and frustrating governmental oppression. Attempts to extend the range and efficacy of the writ have accordingly been inseparably connected for centuries with attempts to secure justice for those who at any particular moment find themselves execrated by the dominant forces in society.

In America, when a state prisoner files a petition in federal court challenging his or her criminal conviction, the federal court must decide, in the words of the federal habeas corpus statute, whether the prisoner is being held "in custody in violation of the Constitution or law or treaties of the United States."[1]

Thus, federal habeas corpus is closely linked to federalism—which our history has sometimes rightly understood as a device for insuring liberty by dispersing power, and sometimes misunderstood as an excuse for inaction in the face of injustice. Federal habeas corpus insures that, even though the Supremacy Clause of the Constitution already requires state courts to give criminal defendants every protection of the Bill of Rights and federal law,[2] those defendants are also entitled to insist that a federal court review the state court proceedings.[3]

In the context of the history, government, and public passions of the United States—especially with respect to the death penalty—this system of dual safeguards makes sense, implementing the fundamental, and mutually consistent, conceptions of individual liberty and constrained government power that underlie the Constitution.

FIGURE 1
Typical State and Federal Trial and Postconviction Procedure

UNITED STATES SUPREME COURT		
(certiorari)		

UNITED STATES SUPREME COURT
(certiorari)

HIGHEST STATE COURT	HIGHEST STATE COURT	U.S. COURT OF APPEALS
(appeals procedure varies)	(appeals procedure varies)	
INTERMEDIATE STATE APPEALS COURT	INTERMEDIATE STATE APPEALS COURT	
(appeals procedure varies)	(appeals procedure varies)	(appeal as of right after initial showing of merit)
TRIAL COURT	TRIAL COURT	U.S. DISTRICT COURT
TRIAL, SENTENCING, AND DIRECT APPEAL	STATE POSTCONVICTION	FEDERAL HABEAS CORPUS

Those who would limit federal court review of state prisoner convictions, whose views currently find expression in the Antiterrorism and Effective Death Penalty Act of 1996 (AEDPA),[4] too often seek to defend injustice on the basis of federalism—thereby undermining both federalism and justice.

And, hitherto, they have often based their arguments on a misapprehension of the Supreme Court's landmark cases. The principal purpose of this book is to rectify three such errors that have for too long obscured the historical record.

Part I takes up the 1807 case of *Ex Parte Bollman*.[5] The Suspension Clause of the Constitution provides: "The Privilege of the Writ of Habeas Corpus shall not be suspended, unless when in Cases of Rebellion or Invasion the public Safety may require it."[6] In considering the scope of the Clause, the Court and scholars alike have unanimously proceeded on the assumption that the Clause did not originally cover state prisoners seeking a federal writ of habeas corpus.

The basis of this assumption is that, according to language in the *Bollman* opinion, which Chief Justice John Marshall delivered in the course of releasing several of Aaron Burr's coconspirators, Section 14 of the Judiciary Act of 1789[7] did not give federal courts the authority to grant the writ to state prisoners; hence, it was unavailable to those prisoners.

Since the First Judiciary Act is a cornerstone of American jurisprudence (and the idea that it might violate the Suspension Clause has thus been deemed most implausible), acceptance of Marshall's interpretation has served as conclusive evidence for the proposition that the right of state prisoners to obtain federal habeas corpus was not originally protected by the Constitution.

But, I argue, Marshall's interpretation of the act was wrong, and so is any interpretation of the Suspension Clause based upon it. Since the Constitution came into force, the federal courts have had the authority to free state prisoners on habeas corpus, and the Suspension Clause applies as a matter of original intent to any attempt by Congress to limit that authority.

To prove that Marshall's politically convenient dicta in *Bollman*, and thus the implications that have been drawn from them, were simply incorrect, I draw on original sources to show that:

- sensibly read, Section 14 is a grant of authority to the federal courts to grant writs of habeas corpus to state prisoners;
- in any event, no statutory authorization was required, since the federal courts could use the powers granted to them by common law and state law to issue such writs;
- but if Marshall was correct in rejecting both of those positions, then the statute was indeed unconstitutional under the Suspension Clause.

Perhaps because contemporaries recognized how weak *Bollman* was, in several cases first uncovered by my research federal courts simply ignored the opinion, and did issue writs of habeas corpus to state prisoners.

Since Marshall erred in *Bollman* both in reading Section 14 of the Judiciary Act of 1789 as not granting the federal courts the authority to free state prisoners by habeas corpus and in concluding from this supposed absence of statutory authorization that the courts lacked the power, modern courts and scholars should pursue Suspension Clause analyses unbeguiled by his dicta.

The importance of their doing so is illustrated by a case decided on June 25, 2001, just as this volume was going to press (*Immigration and Naturalization Service v. St. Cyr*, 121 S.Ct. 2271 (2001)). The majority of the Court delivered an opinion that was commendable in both technique and result— except when it had to deal with Marshall's *Bollman* opinion.

The issue was whether AEDPA and related immigration statutes had deprived an alien of his pre-existing right to seek habeas corpus review of the Attorney General's decision that she lacked the statutory authority to waive his deportation. Applying much the same method that I employ in Section B of Chapter 4, the Court reached the sound conclusion that the statutes should not be read as depriving the federal courts of their habeas authority.

Critically for our purposes, one basis for this conclusion was an application of the doctrine, first enunciated by Marshall and discussed in Section (B) (6) of Chapter 4, that a court should avoid construing statutes in a way that might make them unconstitutional. In a significant pronouncement, the majority said that if the 1996 statutes were read as failing to carry forward the habeas corpus remedy, there would be a grave Constitutional question as to whether Congress had suspended the writ.

Quite appropriately, the Court seems to have recognized that Marshall's theory—that if Congress suspends the writ by simply failing to grant the courts the right to issue it, citizens are left without a judicial remedy—is untenable as a matter of both policy and history. But the Court did not face up to the implications of its own insight and reject *Bollman*'s dicta. Rather, the majority opinion attributed to Marshall the view that the purpose of the Clause was "to preclude any possibility 'that the privilege itself would be lost' by either the action or inaction of Congress"—an interpretative feat that it accomplished only by truncating the relevant passage of *Bollman*.

Justice Scalia's dissent objected, correctly, that Marshall's position was being distorted by "highly selective quotation," and then, incorrectly, read the Suspension Clause as Marshall had: the Clause is judicially enforceable only if Congress has affirmatively suspended some habeas authority previously granted.

Neither side saw the whole picture, as the historical evidence and legal argument presented in Part I will reveal. The majority got the Constitution right, but Marshall wrong; Justice Scalia got Marshall right, but the Constitution wrong. As a matter of history, Marshall's stated view is clear—the Suspension Clause requires Congress, but not the courts, to provide the habeas remedy in the first instance—but, as a matter of law, it is clearly erroneous.

Part II focuses on two habeas corpus decisions of ongoing importance, *Frank v. Magnum*[8] and *Moore v. Dempsey*.[9] In both cases, defendants who had been sentenced to death in Southern state courtrooms surrounded by hostile mobs brought habeas corpus petitions to the federal courts, and pressed due process claims upon the Supreme Court. But the outcomes were entirely different. The Court refused to intervene in the first case (which resulted in the lynching of an innocent Jew), but granted relief in the second (which resulted in the release of innocent blacks)—asserting all the while that there was no inconsistency between the two decisions.

Both cases arose out of significant national events (the Leo Frank murder trial in one instance, and massive race riots in Elaine County, Arkansas, in the other), and continue to be the subject of conflicting interpretations by those who support broad habeas review (who argue that *Moore* overruled *Frank*) and those who oppose it (who argue that the cases are consistent).

Meanwhile, in the world of historical (as opposed to legal) inquiry, the cases have drawn continuing attention not only because both were major national events, but because they encapsulate a swirl of sexual, racial, religious, and regional tensions in the context of an urbanizing, industrializing, and ethnically diversifying society. Yet legal scholarship has made little use of the historical work that has been done, and none at all of the substantial unmined source material illuminating the cases that is to be found in libraries and archives.

Based on a review of many of these materials, such as draft opinions and Justices' papers (whose publication will, I hope, serve to enrich the ongoing debate over these cases by scholars in both law and history), my own, rather novel, position is that the cases are consistent but support broad habeas corpus review.

Part III refutes the views of those conservative scholars and Justices who have argued that *Brown v. Allen*[10]—which resulted in the denial of habeas corpus in a series of cases displaying all the worst features of Southern justice—represented a revolutionary broadening of the writ, and should be rejected as a modern usurpation of the states' authority.

I explore the question through a detailed examination of the seven surviving sets of papers of the Justices who sat on the case. This review—which includes two sets of notes of the critical Court conference—demonstrates that the Justices did not view themselves as making important new law concerning the scope of the writ. On the contrary, with the exception of Justice Jackson—who, egged on by a series of colorful memos from his law clerk William Rehnquist, wished to make significant cutbacks—they went out of their way to reaffirm the law as it had existed since *Frank* and *Moore*.

Moreover, statistics show that the ruling did not lead to an upsurge in successful petitions; indeed, it may have had the opposite effect. And, despite numerous contemporary legislative and judicial battles over habeas corpus, no one considered the case of major import until the appearance of a Harvard Law Review article ten years later.

I conclude that in attacking *Brown* as the source of the evils they decry, today's antiwrit Justices are attacking a ghost, when what really confronts them is a solid legal cathedral built over many generations by workers who were often at odds on points of decoration but had a common understanding of the contours of the whole edifice.

As Part IV discusses by way of conclusion to this study, federal habeas corpus is not an affront to federalism, but rather implements the theme of checks and balances that pervades our Constitutional structure. Just as the authority of states to provide more Constitutional protections for their citizens than the federal government is willing to recognize is a safeguard of individual liberty, so too is the power of the federal government to enforce federally protected interests against recalcitrant states. That was as true in the early national period, when the states might obstruct international relations by jailing foreign officials, as it has been in the post–Civil War period, when the willingness of the states to enforce the federal Constitutional rights of unpopular criminal defendants has often been in question.

The framers knew well that abuses of governmental power at the expense of individuals would inevitably occur. A vigorous writ of habeas corpus implements one of their key responses—the creation of two levels of government that, in Madison's words, will "control each other," so that "a double security arises to the rights of the people."[11]

Part I

1

Introduction to Part I

As proud heirs to the traditions of English liberty, the framers of the Constitution felt very deeply the importance of habeas corpus as a weapon against tyranny. Hence the Suspension Clause: "The Privilege of the Writ of Habeas Corpus shall not be suspended, unless when in Cases of Rebellion or Invasion the public Safety may require it."[1]

According to firmly entrenched wisdom, this provision was intended to protect only the right of federal—not state—prisoners to seek the writ in federal court.[2] Thus, any such right that state prisoners may have by legislation[3] is purely a matter of Congressional grace, and could be revoked at any time without violating the Suspension Clause.

As the Introduction indicates, I believe that this view is erroneous. The purpose of Part I is to correct it. The origin of the mistake is dicta inserted by Chief Justice John Marshall into *Ex Parte Bollman*.[4] In that case, Marshall discussed Section 14 of the Judiciary Act of 1789,[5] which (with the addition of clause numbers for ease in following the argument), reads:

> *And be it further enacted*, [1] That all the beforementioned courts of the United States shall have the power to issue writs of *scire facias, habeas corpus*, [2] and all other writs not specially provided for by statute, [3] which may be necessary for the exercise of their respective jurisdictions, and agreeable to the principles and usages of law. And that either of the justices of the supreme court, as well as judges of the district courts, shall have power to grant writs of *habeas corpus* for the purpose of an inquiry into the cause of commitment.— [4] *Provided*, That writs of *habeas corpus* shall in no case extend to prisoners in gaol, unless where they are in custody, under or by colour of the authority of the United States, or are committed for trial before some court of the same, or are necessary to be brought into court to testify.[6]

Marshall's opinion includes two key points. First, the proviso "extends to the whole section,"[7]—that is, clause [4] limits both the first sentence of the section (relating to courts) and the second (relating to judges)—with the result that the Act does not (except in very limited circumstances) grant the federal courts the power to issue writs of habeas corpus to state prisoners. Second, except to the extent affirmatively granted by statute, the federal courts lack the power to issue writs of habeas corpus.[8]

The provisions of the First Judiciary Act have long been given special weight in interpreting the Constitution.[9] The idea that the statute might have violated the Suspension Clause by withholding the writ from state prisoners is accordingly thought to be most implausible. On the unexamined assumption that Marshall read Section 14 correctly, the conclusion has been thought to follow that the Clause did not extend to them. This chain of reasoning, however, contains three flaws, each independently fatal to reaching that conclusion.

First, Section 14, read intelligently, does not deny federal courts the power to liberate state prisoners by habeas corpus but instead grants it. Marshall's contrary statement in *Ex Parte Bollman* made political sense but does not make legal sense.

Second, even if the statute did not affirmatively grant the power, the federal courts did not lack it. Common law and state law supplied the necessary authority.

Thus, to arrive at the conclusion that the terms of Section 14 show that the Suspension Clause did not extend to state prisoners, one would have to leap a third set of hurdles: to read the statute as an affirmative statutory preclusion of the writ, and then to demonstrate that, so read, the statute was constitutional. This last position passes the limits of plausibility; if in fact Section 14 not only failed to grant the federal courts habeas corpus jurisdiction over state prisoners but actually denied it, then the statute was indeed unconstitutional.

In the remainder of Part I, I seek to support these propositions as follows.

Chapter 2 recounts the history of the Suspension Clause, in Philadelphia and during the ratification debates. It concludes that there was a broad consensus that the Clause as written would limit legislative interference with the right that both federal and state courts were assumed to possess: to release on habeas corpus both federal and state prisoners.

I then take up *Bollman*. Chapter 3 lays out the legal, political, and factual background to the case, describing the arguments of counsel and the responses provided in Marshall's opinion. It then analyzes the weakness of those responses, which have survived to misdirect modern students only because their practical impact proved to be so slight.

Chapter 4 sets forth the way that *Bollman* should have interpreted Section 14. In making the statutory argument that the proviso limits the power of federal judges, but not federal courts, it relies upon the statutory language, policy considerations, prior legislation, subsequent legislation, the real-world environment in which the legislation was passed, and the appropriateness of a construction that avoids raising doubts as to the statute's constitutionality.

Chapter 5 rebuts the inferences that *Bollman* drew from the first sentence of Section 14: (a) that the Suspension Clause is nothing more than an exhortation to Congress to provide for the writ, so that (b) if Congress failed to do so, the federal courts would lack the jurisdiction to grant it. Reviewing the strong consensus of contemporary jurists concerning the powers the federal courts might exercise by authority of the common law and state law—a consensus that Marshall himself had joined just a few years before—the chapter argues that neither the framers of the Suspension Clause nor those of the Judiciary Act believed that the federal courts would lack habeas corpus powers in the absence of an affirmative statutory grant.

Chapter 6 discusses several previously unpublished rulings by lower federal courts during the early 1800s. In these cases, the courts—seemingly adopting legal theories consistent with the ones presented here—behaved as though Section 14 did not constrain their power to issue the writ of habeas corpus to state prisoners, and sometimes actually discharged such prisoners. Although the cases uncovered so far are too few in number to support any strong conclusions, they do tend to confirm my thesis.

Concluding Part I, Chapter 7 suggests that although—whatever the original intent—the Suspension Clause should protect the writ as it has evolved to date, legal and scholarly arguments would benefit by basing themselves on the most accurate available history. The *Bollman*-derived idea that the federal writ of habeas corpus was not originally available to state prisoners should be discarded.

2

The Origins of the Suspension Clause

A review of the progress of the Suspension Clause as it traveled from the Constitutional Convention in Philadelphia through the state ratification conventions and into the Constitution reveals two salient features: (1) the powerful attachment of all debaters to safeguarding the availability of the writ so as to protect the liberty of individuals against its possible wrongful deprivation by the government, and (2) an ultimate agreement among contemporaries that the Clause as written in Philadelphia accomplished that goal. It is hard to believe that this consensus among otherwise intense adversaries would have existed if they had known how *Bollman* would later read the Clause.

A. *The Suspension Clause in Philadelphia*

As the sources now stand, the history of the Clause at the Convention is sparse but clear.

On August 20, 1787, Charles Pinckney of South Carolina moved that:

> The privileges and benefit of the writ of habeas corpus shall be enjoyed in this government in the most expeditious and ample manner: and shall not be suspended by the legislature except upon the most urgent and pressing occasions, and for a limited time not exceeding ——— months.[1]

The motion was referred without debate to the Committee of Detail.[2]

When the matter returned to the Convention floor on August 28, Madison's notes record that:

> Mr. Pinkney, urging the propriety of securing the benefits of the Habeas corpus in the most ample manner, moved "that it should not be suspended but on the most urgent occasions, & then only for a limited time not exceeding twelve months." Mr. Rutlidge was for declaring the Habeas Corpus inviolable—He did not conceive that a suspension could ever be necessary at the

same time through all the States—Mr. Govr. Morris moved that "The privilege of the writ of Habeas Corpus shall not be suspended, unless where in cases of Rebellion or invasion the public safety may require it." Mr. Wilson doubted whether in any case a suspension could be necessary, as the discretion now exists with Judges, in most important cases to keep in Gaol or admit to Bail. The first part of Mr. Govr. Morris's motion, to the word "unless" was agreed to nem: con: – on the remaining part; N.H. ay. Mass ay. Ct. ay. Pa. ay. Del. ay. Md. ay. Va. ay. N.C. no. S.C. no. Geo. no. [Ayes—7; noes—3.][3]

Luther Martin of Maryland has left us further details of the debate on this last motion (in which he sided with the minority):[4]

> As the State governments have a power of suspending the habeas corpus act [in cases of rebellion or invasion], it was said there could be no good reason for giving such a power to the general government, since whenever the *State* which is invaded or in which an insurrection takes place, finds its safety requires it, *it* will make use of that power—*And* it was urged, that if we gave this power to the general government, it would be an engine of oppression in its hands, since whenever a State should oppose its views, however arbitrary and unconstitutional, and refuse submission to them, the general government may declare it to be *an act of rebellion*, and suspending the habeas corpus act, may *seize* upon the persons of those *advocates of freedom*, who have had *virtue* and *resolution* enough to excite the opposition, and may *imprison* them during its pleasure in the *remotest* part of the union, so that a citizen of Georgia might be *bastiled* in the furthest part of New-Hampshire—or a citizen of New-Hampshire in the furthest extreme to the south, cut off from their family, their friends, and their every connection—These considerations induced me, Sir, to give my negative also to this clause.[5]

The Clause then moved to the Committee of Style and Arrangement, which substituted the word "when" for "where," resulting in the text we have today.[6]

B. The Suspension Clause after Philadelphia

While the foregoing history is generally well known,[7] recent years have given scholars increased access to materials illuminating the debates that took place once the Constitution was released to the public. But, in a development that we should have learned by this time to consider as less surprising than disappointing, the resulting greater volume of the historical record has not been accompanied by any greater insight into the specifics of original intention on matters of particular interest today—as those matters did not happen to be the ones particularly in controversy among the debaters of the time. That fact, however, is itself illuminating. The shared premises of the political opponents may in this instance teach us as much as their disagreements.

The participants were united in their belief that the maintenance of a vigorous writ was indispensable to the political freedom of individuals. Discussions of the Clause revolved about the adequacy of the Constitutional text to achieve the shared goal of liberty preservation.

Specifically, the attacks on the Suspension Clause as it emerged from the Convention fell into two groups.

1. Some debaters used the existence of the Clause to attack the Federalist premise that a Bill of Rights was unnecessary because the proposed federal government would have only those powers specifically delegated to it. These arguments, described in Section 1(A) below, offer little direct illumination on the questions of interest today, but do reveal a strong underlying consensus as to the importance of the writ.

2. As Section 1 (B) below recounts, other debaters attacked the Clause as permitting too much suspension of the writ, to which supporters responded that they, too, expected the Clause to operate so as to protect unpopular characters who might find themselves imprisoned. The supporters of the Clause won this debate, a rare instance in which all parties agreed that the text as written adequately safeguarded a cherished right and that no further protection was required in the Bill of Rights.

As Section 2 below argues, a holistic view of this history would be that almost all of the participants in the ratification debates expected the Clause to protect the independent judicial examination on federal habeas corpus of all imprisonments, state or federal.

1. The Issues

Discussions of the Clause focused on the power of suspension rather than on the nature of the writ—and for good reason: those discussions did not occur in isolation, but rather within the framework of two of the most controversial issues regarding the proposed national government.

A. THE ISSUE OF DELEGATED POWERS

It is familiar history that, in response to the attack that the Constitution as it emerged from the Convention lacked a Bill of Rights, the Federalists argued, among other things, that the document did not need one, since every power not explicitly granted to the national government was withheld from it.

Thus, for example, in No. 84 of *The Federalist* Alexander Hamilton contended that there was no need for a Bill of Rights, since under the proposed Constitution "the people surrender nothing; and as they retain everything they have no need of particular reservations."[8] He continued by urging that the inclusion of a Bill of Rights in the Constitution:

> would even be dangerous. . . . For why declare that things shall not be done which there is no power to do? Why, for instance, should it be said that the liberty of the press should not be restrained, when no power is given by which restrictions may be imposed? I will not contend that such a provision would confer a regulating power; but it is evident that it would furnish, to men disposed to usurp, a plausible pretense for claiming that power. They might urge with a semblance of reason that the Constitution ought not to be charged with the absurdity of providing against the abuse of an authority which was not given, and that the provision against restraining the liberty of the press afforded a clear implication that a power to provide proper regulations concerning it was intended to be vested in the national government.[9]

The structure and substance of the Suspension Clause enabled opponents of the proposed Constitution to respond that the government was in fact not one of delegated powers. This issue, rather than that of the scope of the writ, dominated much of the debate over the Clause.

Thus, for example, John Smilie drew the attention of the Pennsylvania ratifying convention to the clauses "expressly declaring that the writ of *habeas corpus* and the trial by jury in criminal cases shall not be suspended or infringed," and asked:

> How indeed does this agree with the maxim that whatever is not given is reserved? Does it not rather appear from the reservation of these two articles that everything else, which is not specified, is included in the powers delegated to the government?[10]

Similarly, a prominent Anti-federalist pamphleteer in New York wrote:

> We find they have . . . declared that the writ of habeas corpus shall not be suspended, unless in cases of rebellion. . . . If every thing which is not given is reserved, what propriety is there in [the exception]? Does this constitution any where grant the power of suspending the habeas corpus. . . ? It certainly does not in express terms. The only answer that can be given is, that these are implied in the general powers granted.[11]

In short, as Patrick Henry observed, the statement that the writ of habeas corpus should not be suspended except in certain cases meant that it could be suspended in the ones not covered; the fact that the affirmative grant of power to do so was not contained in the Constitution, but needed to be implied, "is destructive of the doctrine advanced by the friends of that paper."[12]

The Federalist response was to deny any inconsistency, claiming (with considerable plausibility in light of the Convention proceedings described above) that, despite its negative phraseology, the Clause was in fact a grant of power to the federal government. Thus, the Federalist pamphleteer A Native of Virginia explained:

> that as the Congress can claim the exercise of no right which is not expressly given them by this Constitution; they will have no power to restrain the press in any of the States; and therefore it would have been improper to have taken any notice of it.

Habeas corpus, on the other hand, presented a different case, one which "corroborates this doctrine." With respect to that issue:

> The Convention were sensible that a federal government would no more have the right of suspending that useful law, without the consent of the States than of restraining the liberty of the press: But at the same time they knew that circumstances might arise to render necessary the suspension of the habeas corpus act, and therefore, they require of the States, that they will vest them with that power, whenever those circumstances shall exist.[13]

In short, since the Suspension Clause was a grant of power to the federal government (albeit an appropriately circumscribed one), it did not represent a violation of the underlying principle that any power not explicitly granted to the federal government was withheld from it.

For our purposes, the key point is that the Anti-federalists' attack was not on the scope of the writ being protected by the Suspension Clause. They approved of that (as did the Federalists, of course). The Anti-federalist argument, rather, was that the same protections should have been given explicitly to other rights—hence the need for a bill of rights.[14]

Thus, behind the disagreements over the delegated powers issue as it relates to the Clause lie much more significant agreements: that a vigorous writ was a key safeguard of liberty, and that the writ protected by the proposed text was one broad enough to serve that purpose.

B. THE ISSUE OF THE DANGER OF TYRANNY

The second major point of the opponents of the Suspension Clause was that its grant of power to the federal government was a dangerous one. This argument took place within the framework of a universal agreement among all political debaters that, because human nature is inherently power seeking, any grant of authority to government officeholders must be scrutinized with extreme care as they will inevitably attempt to misemploy the authority.[15] In the words of a delegate to the North Carolina ratifying convention, "It is well known that men in power are apt to abuse it, and extend it if possible."[16]

As the account given above indicates, a proposal for an outright ban on suspensions of the writ was defeated in Philadelphia, on the explicit premise that there were certain circumstances under which the exercise of this power would be appropriate. This decision of the Convention, which Luther Martin promptly made public, drew a good deal of fire during the ratification debates.

The gist of the attack was that "[t]he Congress will suspend the writ of *habeas corpus* in case of rebellion; but if this rebellion was only a resistance to usurpation, who will be the Judge? the usurper."[17] Accordingly, various commentators (including Thomas Jefferson in private correspondence)[18] suggested that the proposed Constitution be rewritten to avert this danger.[19]

The Federalists' response was that they shared the goals of their opponents—which were fully implemented by the Constitutional text. Thus, in a speech to the Maryland legislature reporting on his doings as a Convention delegate (and responding to the views of Luther Martin), James McHenry said:

> Public safety may require a suspension of the Ha: Corpus in cases of necessity: when those cases do not exist, the virtuous Citizen will ever be protected in his opposition to power, 'till corruption shall have obliterated any sense of Honor & Virtue from a Brave and free People.[20]

As subsequent developments show, it seems fairly clear that the Federalists won this debate.

2. The Ratification Process

As they ratified the proposed Constitution, a number of states passed sets of amendments that they wished to see incorporated; James Madison collated these, and those that had achieved a reasonable degree of consensus among the states eventually became the Bill of Rights. There were explicit safeguards for numerous rights—from freedom of press and religion, to protections for the civil jury trial and a ban on cruel and unusual punishments—that the Anti-federalists had warned would be in jeopardy under the Constitution as originally proposed, and the entire project thus represented a repudiation of the Federalist position that those and other rights had already been sufficiently protected. But with respect to habeas corpus, events fell out in precisely the opposite pattern.

However odd the notion may appear to modern lawyers, contemporaries all assumed that the state courts would be able to issue writs of habeas corpus to release those in federal custody.[21] Nor did anyone question the authority of the federal courts to issue the writ to state prisoners. With one minor exception,[22] the states did not propose any further protection for habeas corpus during the ratification process, and nothing on the subject appears in the Bill of Rights. A fair conclusion is that the ratification debates had convinced all parties that the Clause as written would meet the aims they agreed that they shared: to safeguard a critical mechanism for protecting the liberties of those who might fall afoul of the organs of power. Certainly, there was no debater who suggested that state sovereignty might somehow operate to limit the rights of individuals to vindicate their right to freedom from unlawful restraint.

The Federalists were not worried about preserving state sovereignty— neither in the sense of the dignity of the states as against the federal government, nor in the sense of preserving the rights of statewide majorities to act as they pleased toward their own citizens. With regard to the first, it was the overabundance of reserved power in the states that led to the need to write the Constitution in the first place.[23] With regard to the second, checking the excesses of local majorities (like Rhode Island's) that might act oppressively toward local minorities (like creditors) was a major Federalist goal. Indeed, by:

> the 1780s many Americans had concluded that their popular state assemblies[,] . . . alarmingly, had become a major threat to minority rights and individual liberties and the principal source of injustice in the society.[24]

As for the Anti-federalists, their contributions to the debate over the Clause clearly show that they, unlike some modern Supreme Court Justices,[25] were not worried about whether the states would sufficiently retain their sovereign rights to imprison or execute people. Rather, they were concerned that federal power might be exerted so as to keep unpopular prisoners—rightly or wrongly branded by the authorities as criminals—from vindicating their rights to freedom. From the Anti-federalist point of view, a power in the general government to release state prisoners would be an example of federalism as a preserver of individual liberty—an instance of the virtue of a federal, as opposed to a national, government.[26]

That both sides ultimately agreed that the Clause as drafted met the goals that they proclaimed in common—as evidenced by the lack of any effort to amend it during the ratification process—suggests that all parties read it as protecting broadly against Congressional interference with the power that federal and state courts were each assumed to possess: to order the release on habeas corpus of both federal and state prisoners.

3

The Opinion in *Ex Parte Bollman*

A. *The Political Background*

Ex Parte Bollman was decided against the backdrop of the upheaval in American politics that followed the Presidential election of 1800. The key two effects for our purposes of the historic victory of Thomas Jefferson and his Republicans in that election were:

- The elevation of Secretary of State John Marshall to the Chief Justice-ship, and to the titular leadership of the judicial branch, now the Federalists' last bastion; and
- Connectedly, the ruling in *Marbury v. Madison*,[1] in which Marshall read Section 13 of the Judiciary Act as conferring authority on the Supreme Court to exercise original mandamus powers, and then held the section unconstitutional because it expanded the original jurisdiction of the Supreme Court beyond the limits laid down in Article III of the Constitution. Thus Marshall was able to write an opinion lambasting his successor, James Madison, for not delivering to the Federalist William Marbury the commission for the office of Justice of the Peace to which the Adams Administration had appointed him in its last hours (and that Secretary of State Marshall had probably lost himself in the confusion), while not issuing an order that the Jefferson Administration would surely have ignored.

When the Jefferson Administration completed its first term in office, Vice President Aaron Burr (whose poisoned relationship with Jefferson had led to his being brusquely removed from the second-term ticket, and who was facing charges in New York and New Jersey for murder as a result of having killed Alexander Hamilton in a duel) found it prudent to travel west.[2] There, he was said to have plotted to separate some of the country's newly acquired western territories from their allegiance to the United States. Among his alleged coconspirators were Samuel Swartwout and Dr. Erick Bollman. In December, 1806, they were seized by General James

Wilkinson, the United States Army commander in New Orleans (who had himself been involved in Burr's plans), and summarily transported by warship to Baltimore via Charleston—in defiance of writs of habeas corpus granted by federal judges in New Orleans[3] and Charleston.[4]

The prisoners arrived in Washington, on Friday, January 23, 1807. That afternoon, as Jefferson met with Bollman to learn his version of the events,[5] one of the President's leading Senate allies—seeking to insure that Bollman and Swartout would not obtain any further pesky writs of habeas corpus—introduced legislation to suspend the writ for three months and to keep the two imprisoned. Convening in closed session, the Senate passed the measure with only a single dissenting vote, but by Monday, January 26, the atmosphere had cooled and the House by a vote of 113–19 bluntly rejected the proposal as unworthy of consideration.[6]

On the following day, the United States attorney moved the Circuit Court for the District of Columbia for an arrest warrant in order to have the pair committed to stand trial on a charge of treason.[7] A politically divided bench granted the motion.[8]

The prisoners then applied to the United States Supreme Court for a writ of habeas corpus. As Justices Johnson and Chase expressed doubts as to the Court's jurisdiction, Chief Justice Marshall set that preliminary question down for a full argument,[9] which took place with almost the entire Congress present as spectators.

B. Arguments of Counsel

The Attorney General, who apparently did not doubt the Court's power to grant the writ, "declined arguing the point on behalf of the United States."[10] In fact, he told the bench that if it should determine "to issue a writ of Habeas Corpus he should cheerfully submit to it."[11] Thus, the Justices heard argument only from petitioners' counsel, principally from Robert Goodloe Harper, a prominent Federalist politician. Having announced the division of his presentation into the questions (1) whether "this court has the power generally of issuing the writ," and, if so, (2) whether the fact of the circuit court's having committed the prisoners barred the issuance of the writ,[12] Harper proceeded as follows.[13]

(1)(A). First, he argued:

The general power of issuing this great remedial writ [of habeas corpus] is incident to this court as a supreme court of record. It is a power given to such a court by the common law. [A court that] possessed no powers but those given by statute . . . could not protect itself from insult and outrage. . . . It could not imprison for contempts in its presence. It could not compel the attendance of a witness. . . . These powers are not given by the constitution, nor by statute, but flow from the common law. . . . [T]he power of issuing writs of *habeas corpus*, for the purpose of relieving from illegal imprisonment, is one of those inherent powers, bestowed by the law upon every superior court of record, as incidental to its nature, for the protection of the citizen.[14]

Harper supported this argument with a survey designed to show "that all the superior courts of record in England," whether or not they had any criminal jurisdiction or statutorily granted habeas jurisdiction, "are invested by the common law with this beneficial power, as incident to their existence."[15] As an example providing "a conclusive authority in favour of the doctrine for which we contend," he cited a case that would have been very familiar to his audience as a monument to English liberty, *Bushel's Case*,[16] in which the court of common pleas (which had no statutory habeas corpus jurisdiction) employed its common law habeas corpus powers to release a juror who had been imprisoned because—contrary to evidence that the trial judge considered convincing—he had dared to vote to acquit William Penn on a charge of unlawful preaching.

Harper then asked whether the American people had not "as good a right as those of England to the aid of a high and responsible court for the protection of their persons?"[17]

(1)(B). Turning to Section 14, Harper first argued that the first sentence contained "two distinct provisions," viz., clause [1] and the remainder of the sentence.[18] The authority to issue writs of habeas corpus, he argued:

is positive and absolute; and not dependent on the consideration whether they might be necessary for the ordinary jurisdiction of the courts. To render them dependent on that consideration, would have been to deprive the courts of many of the most beneficial and important powers which such courts usually possess.[19]

In other words, the federal courts had the authority to issue writs of habeas corpus when appropriate whether or not there was an underlying action over which they had subject matter jurisdiction—a point of some importance to the *Bollman* prisoners, since, other than the habeas corpus application itself, there was no action pending in the Supreme Court.

(1)(C). Harper next addressed the problem posed by *Marbury*, namely, that the final sentence of Section 13 of the Judiciary Act[20]—which bore an uncomfortable resemblance to the first sentence of Section 14—had been held unconstitutional as an attempt to confer upon the Court original jurisdiction in violation of the limitations on that jurisdiction contained in Article III of the Constitution.[21] Harper asserted that Section 14's grant of habeas jurisdiction was not subject to this objection because "the object of the habeas corpus now applied for, is to revise and correct the proceedings of the court below."[22] Hence, the current proceedings were appellate, and fell within the class of cases in which Congress had plenary power over the Court's jurisdiction.[23] Moreover, Harper urged, the Court had in fact granted relief on similar facts twice before. In *United States v. Hamilton*,[24] which arose out of the Whiskey Rebellion, Hamilton, who "had been committed upon the warrant of the District Judge of Pennsylvania, charging him with High Treason," brought a habeas corpus petition to the Supreme Court challenging the sufficiency of the evidence against him. Rejecting the government's defense that the decision of the District Judge could be revised only on the "occurrence of new matter" or a "charge of misconduct," the Court had ordered that Hamilton be admitted to bail.[25] And just the previous year, the Court had decided *Ex Parte Burford.*[26] There, Burford, confined in the District of Columbia under a commitment charging that he was "an evil doer and disturber of the peace," had petitioned the Supreme Court for a writ of habeas corpus. Since the Court was "unanimously of opinion, that the warrant of commitment was illegal, for want of stating *some good cause certain, supported by oath,*" it had ordered the prisoner discharged.[27]

(2)(A). As to the issue of whether the prior commitment of the prisoners by the circuit court barred issuance of the writ, Harper appealed strongly to this latter precedent, and urged that the whole purpose of habeas corpus was to reexamine the legality of commitments, even where they had been ordered by courts of competent jurisdiction.[28]

C. Marshall's Response

(1)(A). Marshall's opinion begins by rejecting Harper's argument that all courts of record have inherent habeas corpus powers and disclaiming "all jurisdiction not given by the constitution, or by the laws of the United States":

> Courts which originate in the common law possess a jurisdiction which must be regulated by the common law . . . but courts which are created by written law, and whose jurisdiction is defined by written law cannot transcend that jurisdiction. It is unnecessary to state the reasoning on which this opinion is

founded, because it has been repeatedly given by this court; and with the decisions heretofore rendered on this point, no member of the bench has, even for an instant, been dissatisfied. . . . The inquiry therefore on this motion will be whether by any statute, compatible with the constitution of the United States, the power to award a writ of habeas corpus, in such a case as that of Erick Bollman and Samuel Swartwout, has been given to this court.[29]

(1)(B). Marshall accepted Harper's assertion that clause [1] of Section 14 is independent of the remainder of the first sentence, but did so in a way from which the field has yet to fully recover.

(i) He began by quoting the Suspension Clause and suggesting that, "acting under the immediate influence of this injunction," the First Congress:

> must have felt, with peculiar force, the obligation of providing efficient means by which this great constitutional privilege should receive life and activity; for if the means be not in existence, the privilege itself would be lost, although no law for its suspension should be enacted.[30]

Thus, the statute should receive a robust reading.

(ii) Marshall next observed that, since the restriction in clause [3] (i.e., "which may be necessary for the exercise of their respective jurisdictions") plainly did not apply to the second sentence of Section 14, if it were to be applied to clause [1], the result would be that individual judges would have more power than courts, which "would be strange."[31]

(iii) Moreover, Marshall continued, in a lengthy passage, to apply the restriction in clause [3] to clause [1] would render it meaningless, since, in light of the limited jurisdiction of the federal courts, there would never be any occasion to issue the writ if it could be done only in cases in which it is "being merely used to enable the court to exercise its jurisdiction in causes which it is enabled to decide finally,"[32] with one exception.

That exception, he wrote—the only power "which on this limited construction would be granted by the section under consideration"—would be the power "of issuing writs of *habeas corpus ad testificandum,*" that is, ones designed to bring witnesses before the court. But the "section itself proves that this was not the intention of the legislature," because that variety of the writ was the subject of its own special provision, namely the proviso in clause [4].[33]

He continued:

> This proviso extends to the whole section. It limits the powers previously granted to the courts. . . . That construction cannot be a fair one which would make the legislature except from the operation of a proviso, limiting the express grant of a power, the whole power intended to be granted.[34]

Therefore, Marshall concluded, Section 14 allowed a federal court to make "an inquiry into the cause of commitment" by federal authorities regardless of whether or not there was an underlying litigation pending before it.

(1)(C). Having decided that the Court had statutory authority to issue the writ, Marshall turned to the constitutional issue framed by *Marbury* and, accepting Harper's argument, ruled in a few terse sentences that the jurisdiction "which the court is now asked to exercise is clearly *appellate*. It is the revision of a decision of an inferior court, by which a citizen has been committed to gaol."[35]

(2)(A). On the question of whether the previous commitment of the prisoners by the Circuit Court was a bar to the issuance of the writ, Marshall accepted as "conclusive" Harper's argument, and acknowledged *Hamilton* as authoritative.[36]

Accordingly, in proceedings stretching over five days, the Supreme Court proceeded to examine the merits. The "clear opinion of the court," Marshall said, is:

> that it is unimportant whether the commitment be regular in point of form, or not; for this court, having gone into an examination of the evidence upon which the commitment was grounded, will proceed to do that which the court below ought to have done.[37]

With the prisoners present,[38] the Court "fully examined and attentively considered," on an item-by-item basis, "the testimony on which they were committed," held it insufficient, and ordered their discharge.[39]

D. Analysis

(1)(A). Marshall's claim that the Court had "repeatedly" explained the reasoning behind the proposition that courts created by written law could exercise only the powers explicitly granted by such laws was false.[40] "Where this reasoning had been given Marshall was not able to say, not because he had no time to collect the citations, but because there were none to collect."[41]

(1)(B). The bottom-line conclusion that clause [1] of Section 14 is not limited by the remainder of the sentence is correct, but for the reasons stated by counsel, not those stated by Marshall. And the difference has significant practical consequences. Harper's policy-based rationale was based on the sound observation that there might be numerous cases, e.g., a service member arrested for debt in defiance of a federal statute or a foreign seaman imprisoned contrary to the terms of a treaty,[42] in which the issuance of a writ of habeas corpus might be appropriate to vindicate federal interests, regardless of whether the custodian were state or federal.[43] In contrast, Marshall's cramped statutory reading has the effect that Harper described: "to deprive the courts of many of the most beneficial and important powers which such courts usually possess."[44]

(i). Marshall's suggestion that Congress could suspend the writ by doing nothing at all would certainly have come as a shock to all of the debaters over the Suspension Clause whose positions were described in Chapter 2 above, particularly since suspension of the writ in England or its colonies had required an affirmative Act of Parliament.[45]

According to *Bollman*, the Constitution as it emerged from Philadelphia did not preserve a preexisting writ from suspension, but only whatever writ Congress might choose to vouchsafe in the future. In light of the tenor of the ratification debates—in which both sides vied in expressions of their appreciation for the importance of the writ—it seems hard to believe that if any substantial body of opinion had shared Marshall's view the writ would not have been preserved by an amendment in the Bill of Rights, just as the right to a jury trial was.

But the ratifiers saw no need to do this because, since "the writ was not constitutionally granted in positive terms in many state constitutions, and [was] only recognized indirectly by a limitation placed upon the authority to suspend its operations," they naturally assumed "that the non-suspension clause in the federal document also functioned in oblique fashion, implicitly conferring the right of the privilege."[46]

(ii). Marshall's reasoning that clause [1] of Section 14 could not be read more restrictively than the second sentence of the section, since it would be "strange" to read the statute as granting more power to individual judges than to courts, is sound. Indeed, the actual holding of the case—the perfectly reasonable conclusion that the Judiciary Act gave the Court jurisdiction over the proceedings before it—might appropriately have rested on this ground.

(iii). However, the heart of the *Bollman* opinion for present purposes is not its holding, but rather its proclamation that the proviso in clause [4] of Section 14 (the limitation on granting the writ to those in state custody) "extends to the whole section," that is, restricts the exercise of power both by courts and by their individual judges.[47]

This statement is a classic example of *obiter dictum*—a statement unnecessary to the decision of the case before the court, and therefore not entitled to legal weight in the future. *Bollman* involved federal, not state, prisoners and, indeed, ones who secured their release after full judicial investigation into the justification for their confinement.

The appearance of Marshall's pronouncement in the opinion is perhaps best explained by a perceived political need for federal judges to appear solicitous of state prerogatives. Particularly in the wake of the results of the election of 1800 and the 1805 attempt to impeach Justice Chase,[48] strong considerations of political prudence suggested that Marshall do everything possible to minimize the opportunities for confrontations between the federal and state judicial systems. As so often, he "was doing what was politically smart and institutionally essential."[49]

In any event, the *Bollman* opinion is the mirror image of the *Marbury* opinion. In *Marbury*, Marshall wrote a decision spiked with harsh dictum, but did not order the Jefferson Administration to deliver Marbury's commission. In *Bollman*, Marshall ordered the Jefferson Administration to release the prisoners, but wrote a decision softened with placatory dictum.

Legally, however, the reasons given by Marshall for his statements are weak. Whether or not he was correct in his position that only the writ of habeas corpus *ad testificandum* would remain if the first sentence were construed as authorizing merely ancillary uses of the writ (i.e., its use only in cases over which the federal court otherwise had jurisdiction),[50] there is no logical connection between this observation and the conclusion that the proviso governs the entire section.

Moreover, as fully set forth in Chapter 4 below, strong arguments of statutory construction affirmatively support the contrary reading.

(1)(C); (2)(A). The ruling that the Court's habeas jurisdiction was appellate rather than original was certainly important to John Marshall—it enabled him to meet the immediate political imperative of releasing Bollman and Swartout from Republican hands while leaving *Marbury* intact—but, while it led the Supreme Court into a variety of doctrinal muddles,[51] it may have had little actual impact on prisoners.[52] In practice, state prisoners received as full a review by writ of error on direct appeal as federal prisoners did through habeas corpus.[53]

As the proceedings on the merits in *Bollman* show, the Court conducted habeas review with scant concern for whatever factual or legal conclusions may have been reached below.[54] Similarly, the lower federal courts in exercising their original habeas jurisdiction were not bound by custodians' returns to their writs, but commonly conducted evidentiary hearings to examine the substantive legality of detentions. This took place most frequently in the context of challenges to military enlistments, where the return to the writ would invariably be that the alleged soldier had regularly enlisted, and the court would conduct an evidentiary hearing to determine whether, for example, he had been drunk or underage at the time.[55]

Thus, to take a typical instance, on December 31, 1827, George Peters submitted a petition to the United States District Court for West Tennessee setting forth that he was being held by Captain Robert Sands, on the claim "that your petitioner has been enlisted in the United States Army for five years."[56] But:

> your petitioner most positively avers that if he has enlisted it was done at a time when he was wholly incapable of transacting business or understanding it by reason of intoxication.

The court issued the writ as requested, and, having the parties before it, listened to full evidentiary presentations by both sides. Whereupon, it concluded:

> that at the time the said Peters enlisted, he was not in a state of mind which would make his contracts binding—but the undersigned is satisfied at the same time that the conduct of Captain Sands was entirely honorable and correct as it appeared in evidence that a stranger would be unable to detect the alienation of the said Peters' mind altho' it might exist at the time of conversation.

Accordingly, the court ordered "that the said Peters be discharged from the Service of the United States, and that his enlistment be taken for nothing."

For prisoners, then, *Bollman* may have represented a Cheshire cat guarding the jailhouse door. Although it did have a body real enough to bar state prisoners' access to the federal courts, particularly the lower federal courts, from time to time,[57] it was largely insubstantial as a practical matter even before it was mooted by the statutory expansion of the writ in 1867 to cover state prisoners generally.[58] That may be one reason it was subject to so little testing that would have exposed its weaknesses and forestalled its transformation into what it has now become—a lingering grin that survives to disorient today's travelers in the woods of doctrine.

4

Bollman's Errors—I

A. The Background of the First Judiciary Act

As Chapter 2 has described, the path of political wisdom in the debates over the Suspension Clause lay in presenting the habeas corpus powers of the federal judiciary as having not been unduly constricted. The path of political wisdom in the debates over the First Judiciary Act lay in presenting the habeas corpus powers of the federal judiciary as having not been unduly enlarged.

The reason for this reversal is simple enough. As a result of fears expressed during the ratification process over the expansive Constitutional language regarding federal judicial authority, there was heavy political pressure on the First Congress to limit the scope of the federal court system. Because so many of their constituents "desired significant restrictions upon, or elimination of portions of, national-court jurisdiction," the challenge facing the members of the First Congress—overwhelmingly ardent Federalists— "was to cater to these demands without seriously crippling the national judiciary." They accomplished this by writing a statute that "was as astute politically as it was legally. It was an ingenious collection of compromises, using both tight, detailed wording and broad, open-ended wording in different places."[1]

In the case of federal habeas corpus for state prisoners, the authors wrote a statute containing the appearance rather than the substance of a limitation on federal court authority. This argument rests upon two pillars. In the present state of our knowledge, the first of these is the more solid, but further scholarship may well change that situation.

First, as this chapter argues, assuming that the provisions of the Judiciary Act exhaustively set forth the habeas corpus powers of the federal courts, *Bollman* misread the statute in a way that wrongly narrowed those powers.

Second, there are sound reasons to believe that the assumption just set forth is wrong, and that the framers of the Judiciary Act expected the federal courts to have powers additional to those specifically set forth by statute, powers derived from the common law and from state law. The next chapter presents this argument.

B. Misinterpreting the Statute: Why the Section 14 Proviso Applies to Judges, Not Courts

As already indicated, the first two sentences of Section 14 distinguish between courts (i.e., tribunals composed of a quorum of their members) and judges (i.e., individual members of those tribunals).[2] In those two sentences, the section authorizes first courts and then individual judges to issue writs of habeas corpus. It then contains a proviso, clause [4], saying that the power generally extends only to prisoners in federal custody. *Bollman* stated in dictum that "the proviso extends to the whole section," i.e., that it limits the power of both courts and individual judges.[3]

This interpretation of the statute has little to recommend it. Soundly read, the proviso limits judges but not courts. This conclusion finds support in at least six considerations.

1. Language

First, while the argument to be drawn from the language of the section is not particularly compelling in either direction, it would certainly be most natural to attach a proviso to the sentence that immediately precedes it, rather than the two that do.

In this connection, I invite the reader to examine the Frontispiece, which is a photoreproduction from the collections of the National Archives of a manuscript of Section 14 in the handwriting of Oliver Ellsworth. Although I do not put any heavy weight on this consideration, it was my subjective feeling after seeing the original that the period followed by a dash at the end of the first sentence was intended to definitively close the thought it contained, while the single space underline after the second sentence and before the third is almost in the nature of a ligature.

2. Policy

Second, the framers—beginning with Oliver Ellsworth, a leader both in the adoption of the Constitution and in the drafting of the First Judiciary Act who was later to serve as Chief Justice[4]—were plainly aware that state authorities could obstruct national policy, especially in foreign affairs. Thus, for instance, in *Waters v. Collot*,[5] the Supreme Court of Pennsylvania refused to order the discharge of the defendant in a state civil suit alleging that, as Governor of Guadeloupe, he had improperly confiscated plaintiff's brig. (He was eventually freed after the government of France complained to the government of the United States). Under my interpretation of Section 14, he would have been able to seek habeas corpus from the federal courts; under *Bollman*'s he would not. Since rectifying situations like this was one key reason for adopting the Constitution altogether,[6] a statutory interpretation that would have Congress denying the federal government the ability to protect its interests is profoundly implausible.

Moreover, as examples both before and after *Bollman* illustrate, the results could be thoroughly mischievous. In *Ex Parte Caberra*, for instance, Pennsylvania brought criminal charges against a secretary to the Spanish legation, notwithstanding his diplomatic immunity. Two federal judges thought the state's conduct indefensible, but held that they lacked jurisdiction to remedy it, with Justice Bushrod Washington pointedly lamenting the restrictions put upon the court's power by the proviso.[7] Similarly, *Elkison v. Deliesseline*[8] dealt with a South Carolina statute providing that any free colored person serving as crew member aboard a ship arriving from another state or country "shall be seized and confined in gaol until such vessel shall clear out and depart from this state." Ruling on a motion for habeas corpus submitted by a British seaman so confined, Justice William Johnson, sitting on circuit, ruled that, although the statute was unconstitutional under the Commerce Clause and was "an express violation of the commercial convention with Great Britain of 1815," he was prevented by the proviso from granting the writ.[9]

The results in the purely domestic context were no less inimical to the rule of law, as *Ex Parte Dorr*[10] persuasively shows. Following Dorr's Rebellion, Thomas Dorr was sentenced by Rhode Island to life imprisonment. Counsel wished to seek review by writ of error of the legal point whether treason could be committed against a state. But Rhode Island blocked counsel from having access to Dorr, "in consequence of which his authority could not be obtained for an application for such a writ." Counsel accordingly sought habeas corpus from the Supreme Court to bring Dorr before it, so that counsel could ascertain his wishes, and, if so advised, pursue the appellate remedy that Dorr concededly had available. But the Court ruled that the proviso to Section 14 forbade issuance of the writ, thereby rewarding Rhode Island's behavior.

It strains credulity that a Congress dominated by Federalists would have wished a statute it crafted to lead to results like these.

3. Previous Legislation

Third, in considering what Section 14 means, it makes sense to consider the legislative context in which its drafters acted. The founding generation well knew that "the power of individual judges, out of term, to issue the writ," had been "the immediate incitement for the most significant habeas corpus legislation ever enacted,"[11] the English Habeas Corpus Act of 1679,[12] which was widely influential throughout the United States.[13] The English Act had been largely inspired by the ordeal of Francis Jenkes, who was imprisoned for making a speech urging that a new Parliament be called. When he sought his release by habeas corpus from the Lord Chief Justice, "his lordship denied to grant it, alledging no other reason but that it was vacation"; when he sought his release by habeas corpus from the Lord-Chancellor, that officer refused on the same grounds, with the ultimate result that Jenkes languished in jail for some months.[14] In response to this case, the "principal new substantive right created by the 1679 act was the power it gave selected judicial officers to issue the writ of habeas corpus 'in the vacation time and out of term' (§ 3)."[15]

This episode reinforced a basic principle that was clear throughout the period of more than a century and a half between the planting of the English colonies and the framing of the Judiciary Act: all superior courts of record had inherent common-law power to issue writs of habeas corpus;[16] but individual judges lacked that power, and so legislation was needed to confer it.

4. Subsequent Legislation

Fourth, efforts to increase federal habeas authority in the years immediately after the Judiciary Act focused on judges, not courts. In 1790, Attorney General Edmund Randolph (who had been a delegate to Philadelphia), responding to a request from the House of Representatives to propose improvements in the judicial system, suggested as statutory amendments:

> every district judge shall moreover have the same power to issue writs of *habeas corpus*, returnable in vacation before himself, as in session returnable to the court;

and

> every circuit judge shall moreover have the same power to issue writs of
> *habeas corpus*, returnable in vacation before himself as a circuit judge, or be-
> fore any other judge of his circuit, who shall happen to be within the district,
> as the circuit court has to issue such writs returnable to the court.[17]

The clear meaning of this proposal is that legislation was needed because (contrary to the interpretation that would later be adopted in *Bollman*), the habeas
powers of individual judges were more constricted than those of courts.[18]

5. Practicalities

Fifth, an additional consideration of some force emerges from a review of
the early court records. The proposed reading of the proviso makes practical
and political sense. A very great deal of the work of the early federal judiciary was done by judges acting in their individual capacities, in chambers
or during vacation, not while sitting on courts formally assembled during
regularly stated terms with a full quorum. Hence, to place a limitation on
the power of individual judges and require that the sensitive decision to release a state prisoner be made only by a full court was to impose a real restraint on judicial authority.

This argument finds support in two propositions, each of which has substantial evidentiary support.

First, the sessions of full courts were limited to defined and relatively
short periods fixed by statute. And, in light of the difficulties of traveling in
the early United States, it was sometimes "impossible for the justices to hold
the circuit court as required by [the Judiciary Act of 1789],[19] which gave
rise to complaints."[20] Prior to 1802,[21] the absence of a Supreme Court Justice meant that there was no "court" in session.

The record of the United States Circuit Court for the District of Maryland offers an example of what this might mean in practice. Although the
court was formally called into session on 75 days prior to 1802, it sat as a
"court" on only 59 of those days, since it lacked a quorum on the remainder.[22] The reading of the proviso to Section 14 of the Judiciary Act urged
here would mean that state prisoners would have been able to obtain habeas
corpus only on the latter occasions. So, for instance, a state prisoner seeking
habeas corpus after the close of the November, 1797, term would not have
been able to obtain it until the court reconvened as such a year later in
November, 1798; similarly, a prisoner detained after the two days of that

session would not have been able to secure habeas corpus for another year, until November, 1799.

Second, in cases where the proviso on any reading was plainly inapplicable (i.e., with respect to persons held under federal authority) individual judges routinely issued writs of habeas corpus and granted or denied discharges from custody as warranted:

> The reason of this is, that when a case of unlawful imprisonment, under color of legal process or legal authority exists, there is a necessity for prompt and speedy action; and hence the party is entitled to be heard before a single judge, without waiting a regular session of a court, which might be months distant, and at a point remote from the place of the imprisonment of the party applying for deliverance.[23]

Thus, my reading of Section 14 is meaningful in that it has Congress restricting a practice that we know actually existed.

The record of the Circuit Court for the District of Georgia seems typical, although perhaps better documented than most.[24] There, judges issued chambers orders:

- requiring a creditor to show cause why his debtor should not be discharged pursuant to federal statute from the prison where he was being held under civil process issuing from a federal court;[25]
- discharging a petitioner from custody after a factual determination that "he is a free person of colour";[26]
- releasing "a Negro woman" who had been seized by state authorities and turned over to the federal marshal on suspicion of having been "imported into the United States contrary to law,"[27] but who turned out to be "a free British subject" and resident of Jamaica;[28]
- freeing prisoners who had been committed to the federal authorities by the state ones to stand trial for a larceny allegedly committed "on board of an American vessel lying along side of and fastened to a wharf in the port of Havanna";[29]
- discharging from custody an alleged debtor to the United States on the grounds that the distress warrant was for considerably more than the evidence suggested he owed;[30]
- releasing a prisoner, who had seemingly been held on a charge of theft from the mails, on the presentation of evidence "that the Packet taken from the Post office was not against the Will of the officers of the Post office [in] that the packet had been put upon the floor with old news-

papers from whence it was taken," so that although the prisoner may have done something "very improper," it had not been criminal.[31]

In short, a reading of the proviso to Section 14 under which, *pace* Marshall, it applies exclusively to the second sentence, i.e., to limit the actions of judges in chambers and out of term, would be a meaningful one.

6. Constitutionality

Sixth, the statutory reading advocated here is strengthened to the extent that Congress might be constrained by the Constitution from eliminating federal court habeas corpus jurisdiction over state prisoners, since it is a deeply rooted rule—originating in a pre-*Bollman* opinion by Marshall[32] and based largely upon presumed Congressional intent—that statutes are to be construed in a way that avoids calling their constitutionality into question.[33]

In this case, as the Suspension Clause debates presented in Chapter 2 support, there is certainly substantial reason to believe that if the statute had the restrictive effect Marshall claimed, it violated the Clause.[34] While no case has yet surfaced of a state prisoner litigating this proposition during the 1807–1867 period when it presented a viable legal issue, not even Marshall's precatory theory of the Clause[35] would have been sufficient to justify an affirmative statutory preclusion of the right of state prisoners to test the federal validity of their detentions.[36]

The significant possibility that *Bollman's* reading makes Section 14 unconstitutional provides a strong legal reason why that reading is wrong. It may also provide a practical reason why some courts faced with situations to which the *Bollman* dictum might actually have been applicable simply ignored the case.[37]

In short, the sensible reading of Section 14 of the First Judiciary Act is as a grant of power to the federal courts, although not federal judges, to issue writs of habeas corpus to all prisoners, state and federal alike.

5

Bollman's Errors—II

Even if Marshall's reading of Section 14 in *Bollman* as withholding from the federal courts the power to issue writs of habeas corpus to state prisoners were correct, it would by no means follow that those courts lacked the power. As suggested in Chapter 3, Marshall's statement that courts created by written law could exercise only the powers explicitly granted by such laws was simply an *ipse dixit* conveniently brought forth for the occasion. Although the proposition sounds unremarkable to modern ears—accustomed to the now-received notion that the jurisdiction of the federal courts is limited to that explicitly granted by statute—it was at odds with the contemporary legal consensus. And Marshall knew this as well as anyone. Just seven years before *Bollman*, he had written:

> My own opinion is that our ancestors brought with them the laws of England both statute and common law as existing at the settlement of each colony, so far as they were applicable to our situation. That on our revolution the preexisting law of each state remain so far as it was not changd either expressly or necessarily by the nature of the governments which we adopted.
>
> That on adopting the existing constitution of the United States the common & statute law of each state remain as before & that the principles of the common law of the state woud apply themselves to magistrates of the general as well as to magistrates of the particular government. I do not recollect ever to have heard the opinions of a leading gentleman of the opposition which conflict with these. Mr. Gallatin in a very acute speech on the sedition law was understood by me to avow them. On the other side it was contended, not that the common law gave the courts jurisdiction in cases of sedition but that the constitution gave it.[1]

The views set forth in the second paragraph would certainly support the position that no statute of Congress was needed to give the federal courts authority to issue the writ of habeas corpus. And Marshall's words also indicate where that authority might be found instead: in the common law or in state law.

1. Common Law

As William R. Casto accurately states, the Judiciary Act was written in a world in which all lawyers:

> believed that the common law existed independently from the state. Neither kings nor legislators nor even judges were necessary to create the common law. Instead, it was part of the law of nature [having] an existence outside and independent of the court.[2]

Statutes, of course, might be part of this existing law, but they did not define or exhaust it; rather, they would be absorbed into its overall fabric. Thus, to apply Casto's description to the present subject, "under this almost Platonic vision of the common law," the contours of habeas corpus had an objective reality that courts would strive to define for themselves largely undisturbed by the views of Convention delegates, legislators, or even previous judges' decisions that might on further reflection appear to misrepresent "the true common law."[3]

These ideas seem at best naive today. But they were natural ones in the environment—very different than today's—from which they came: a substantially nonhierarchical judicial world in which all judges were trial judges, seeking, with counsel, to find (rather than make) the law, in a country in which opinions were written rarely, and were, like state statutes, extremely difficult to find in print.[4]

Although historians disagree over what members of the Philadelphia Convention may have thought about the precise role that common law would play in the federal courts generally, they have long been in accord that the Convention's solicitude for habeas corpus led it to anticipate that the federal courts would exercise common-law powers in that field at least.[5] The debates over the Judiciary Act provide no enlightenment on this issue.[6] But the robust discussion of a similar question may be illuminating.

There is good evidence that the framers of the Judiciary Act expected that the federal courts would exercise common-law criminal jurisdiction. The June 12, 1789, draft of the Act granted to district courts (in Section 10) and circuit courts (in Section 11) "cognizance of all crimes & offences that shall be cognizable under the authority of the United States *& defined by the laws of the same*," but the Senate struck out the language I have italicized.[7] The best historical scholarship suggests that this was done as a stopgap measure, until Congress should enact a federal crimes bill.[8] But:

the implication is earthshaking. No matter how little common-law jurisdiction Congress may have expected to exercise as a stop-gap measure, there seemed to be no doubt that the federal courts . . . could exercise such power.[9]

Yet the framers of the Judiciary Act maintained a discreet statutory silence on the issue or, at best, intimated their view by indirection in such a way as to not "wave a red flag before opponents."[10]

It was left to the courts to implement the intentions of the framers of the Act. And so they did in several key cases.[11] For example, in *Williams' Case*,[12] Oliver Ellsworth—the leading drafter of the Judiciary Act, who was then Chief Justice—upheld on circuit a common-law prosecution charging an American citizen with waging war on a friendly power. And in *United States v. Ravara*:[13]

> distinguished counsel for Ravara did not dispute that the circuit court had jurisdiction under the act to entertain a criminal prosecution applying federal common law; instead . . . the argument was about how that common law was to be determined.[14]

Further, Justice William Paterson, another of the leading framers of the Judiciary Act, has left us a substantial draft opinion upholding federal common-law criminal jurisdiction on a basis very similar to that advanced by Marshall as he approved of *Williams' Case* in the first quotation of this chapter.[15]

Eventually, more than twenty years after the passage of the Judiciary Act and in a different historical context, the Supreme Court, in a Marshall opinion, repudiated the concept of common-law crimes.[16] But however sound that decision may have been on policy grounds,[17] the members of the First Congress would not have anticipated it,[18] but rather expected the courts as a matter of course to supplement the statute with the common law.

If the Congress thought it could legislate through silence or near-silence a controversial extension of the criminal powers of the federal courts, it is certainly plausible that—in a climate hostile to such extensions—it would not feel obliged to be particularly explicit in the noncontroversial area of habeas corpus,[19] trusting the courts to do the right thing by reading Section 14 as working no diminution of the federal courts' common-law habeas powers.

2. State Law

The Judiciary Act also left open by silence the question of the extent to which the lower federal courts were to have the powers of the corresponding state courts. Indeed, there are two early cases in the United States District Court for the Eastern District of Pennsylvania in which petitioners who were being held on federal criminal charges sought habeas corpus relief under Pennsylvania's state habeas corpus statute without mentioning the Judiciary Act at all.[20] While in those particular instances the petitioners, who were not represented by counsel, may simply have been copying an inapplicable state form,[21] the episodes have value in alerting us to the important question of whether the federal courts could add state-law powers to the ones granted them by federal law.

The states generally had well-developed bodies of habeas corpus law. For example, the detailed and emphatic Pennsylvania statute cited by the Eastern District petitioners contains explicit provisions regarding the powers of judges to issue the writ in vacation.[22] Even adopting my limited reading of the proviso to Section 14, individual federal judges during vacation could not utilize the authority of that section to release state prisoners. Thus, the ability to exercise such power under the authority of state law would be of some practical significance.

At the moment, however, we simply do not know enough to come to a firm conclusion as to whether federal judges believed themselves to have state-law habeas corpus powers, and further historical research is plainly called for.

We do know that in the period of interest to us the lower federal courts had adopted state forms of practice on a widespread basis.[23] Indeed, from the beginning, procedures in the lower federal courts have been a confusing blend of independently federal and state-derived practices.

Section 17 of the Judiciary Act, enacted on September 24, 1789, provided that:

> all the said courts of the United States shall have power . . . to make and establish all necessary rules for the orderly conducting business in the said courts, provided such rules are not repugnant to the laws of the United States.[24]

Section 2 of the Process Act, enacted five days later, on September 29, 1789, provided that:

> until further provision shall be made, and except where by this act or other statutes of the United States is otherwise provided, the forms of writs and executions, except their style, and modes of process and rates of fees, except fees to judges, in the circuit and district courts, in suits at common law, shall be the same in each state respectively as are now used or allowed in the supreme courts of the same.[25]

For unrelated political reasons, this statute was very controversial, and Congress several times extended it for only one additional year.[26]

Eventually, Congress passed the Act of May 8, 1792, which provided:

> That the forms of writs, . . . except their style and the forms and modes of proceedings in suits [at] common law shall be the same as are now used in the said courts respectively in pursuance of the act [of September 29, 1789] . . . except insofar as may have been provided for by [the Judiciary Act], subject however to such alterations and additions as the said courts respectively shall in their discretion deem expedient, or to such regulations as the supreme court of the United States shall think proper from time to time by rule to prescribe to any circuit or district court concerning the same.[27]

But this statute simply increased the chaos at ground level:

> The conformity thus called for in actions at law was a static conformity. The state practice as of September 29, 1789 was to be followed, regardless of changes that the states might thereafter have made. Further the conformity statute made no provision for states subsequently admitted to the union; in those states the federal court could follow whatever procedure it chose. The rule-making power, though utilized in admiralty and equity, was not employed in actions at law, where the Court considered it its duty "to yield rather than encroach" upon state practice.[28]

In response to these difficulties, Congress provided by statute in 1828 that:

> procedure in the federal courts sitting in the original states was still to conform to the 1789 procedure, while procedure in states subsequently admitted was to conform to the 1828 state procedure.[29]

In other respects, notably the grant of power to the courts to make "such alterations and additions as the said courts respectively shall in their discretion deem expedient," the language of the 1792 Act remained unchanged.[30]

It makes sense to speculate that, under these circumstances, a court in the habeas corpus context might consider its state law powers additive of its federal ones. Given the ample judicial freedom available in an utterly amorphous legal situation, a court could very plausibly deem itself authorized to rely on state law to justify the issuance of a writ calling for production of a prisoner, even if the ultimate substantive decision as to whether the commitment was legal would necessarily be controlled by federal law.[31] This line of thinking draws support from the fact that in dealing with the similar problem of the extent to which, notwithstanding the rule of static conformity, later state acts ameliorating imprisonment for debt applied in federal courts, the Supreme Court seems to have concluded that the federal scheme implicitly allowed federal courts and judges to exercise the additional discharge powers conferred by state statutes where they could "be executed just as conveniently and properly, by the federal courts and judges, as they can be by the state courts or judges"[32]—a description that would certainly apply to habeas corpus.

But the hypothesis must remain tentative until we unearth cases in which explicit reliance was had on state law to justify the issuance of writs unauthorized (or thought to be unauthorized) by Section 14. And such cases remain to be found.

We can, however, say with some confidence that Marshall's assertion in *Bollman* that the federal courts could exercise no "jurisdiction not given by the constitution, or by the laws of the United States"[33] was an inaccurate description of original intent.

6

Some Suggestive Court Decisions

Early jurists did in fact sometimes act as though only individual judges, and not courts, were bound by the proviso to Section 14. Concededly, the cases are neither sufficiently numerous nor sufficiently unambiguous to carry alone the burden of supporting my arguments. That is hardly surprising. After all, *Bollman* was the law from an early date. Moreover, the substantive federal rights that state prisoners might have had to vindicate in federal court were few.[1] And, finally, there is almost surely additional historical evidence to be found. Nonetheless, the cases I have uncovered are at least suggestive. They not only provide examples of courts acting in ways that would not have occurred if the proviso in Section 14 "extends to the whole section," but, to the extent that their rationales can be inferred, seemingly doing so on the basis of theories that comport with the ones presented so far.

One of the better-documented cases is that of George Daze (also referred to as George Stouts).[2] In May, 1814, he presented to United States District Court for the Eastern District of Pennsylvania a petition setting forth that he was "an enlisted seaman in the service of the United States," currently "in confinement in the debtors apartment of the City and County of Philadelphia" by virtue of an execution (a copy of which is attached to the petition) issued on a state court judgment for debt; that "by the provisions of an Act of Congress approved the 11th of July 1798," he was "exempted from all personal arrests for any debt or contract";[3] and praying for "a Habeas Corpus directed to the keeper of the debtors apartment that he may be discharged according to Law."

Of course, if the *Bollman* reading of Section 14 were correct, the court would have had no power to grant this petition, since the petitioner did not fall within the terms of the proviso. In fact, the court promptly issued the requested writ, requiring the keeper of the debtors apartment to produce Mr. Daze "forthwith."[4]

It appearing from the keeper's return to the writ that the petitioner had correctly set forth the cause of his detention, the court rendered an endorsement order the same day, May 27, 1814: "Discharged. The Act of Congress forbids arrests of persons lawfully engaged in *naval* Service."

I have also found two other cases that appear to have involved similar facts, although the documentation is less clear. In an April, 1832, case, Samuel Miller filed a petition on behalf of George Richards.[5] It alleged that the latter was a serving United States marine who had been arrested on a civil process for debt arising out of a state court action and was in custody of the keeper of the Philadelphia debtors apartment; it sought his release pursuant to the same Act of Congress as in the *Daze* case just described. The District Court for the Eastern District of Pennsylvania issued a writ requiring the keeper to produce Richards at a hearing, but the court records have not yielded an order discharging the prisoner from custody. Thus, there is no proof—only a most plausible guess—that one was in fact issued.

Similarly, a May 9, 1822, case from the Circuit Court for the District of Maryland reads in full as follows:

James D. Snow }
v. } Habeas Corpus
William Brown }
William Handell }
    Discharged by the Court from the cause of action upon which they were detained in prison, and delivered to the custody of Captain James D. Snow.[6]

Here, although the court's action is clear, we must supply, first, the inference (based upon their release to a Captain who had petitioned on their behalf) that the prisoners were military men and, second, the inference (based upon the use of the phrase "cause of action") that they were being held on state civil process.

In any event, there were verifiably instances in which the federal courts would utilize the writ of habeas corpus to protect federal interests from state ones, statute or no. In a case arising in the Circuit Court for the Southern District of New York in 1800, Comfort Sands was subpoenaed to appear as a witness.[7] "[I]n coming from his place of Residence on Long Island to the City of New York to attend as a Witness in consequence of the service of the Subpoena aforesaid," he was, "in contempt of the authority of the Court and in breach of the privileges of the said Witness taken and arrested by the Sheriff of the City and County of New York and is now in his custody upon a writ" issued by the state courts to enforce a civil judgment. On being so advised, the federal court peremptorily:

ordered that as the arrest of the said Comfort Sands upon the process aforesaid being a direct breach of his priviledges as a witness is illegal . . . he therefore be discharged forthwith from the custody of the said Sheriff.

It is implicit in this order that the court (which included Justice Bushrod
Washington, who later sat on *Bollman*) did not consider itself restricted by
the proviso to Section 14, since the decree was that Sands be discharged
from state custody, not that he be brought in to federal court to testify.
Rather, the court plainly drew its conception of itself and its privileges entirely from the common law.[8]

In a similar case that commenced on June 22, 1811, Joseph Cobb complained to the Circuit Court for West Tennessee that while attending court
as a witness he had been arrested by the Sheriff of Davidson County "by
virtue of a writ of capias ad respondendum issued from the Circuit Court of
Davidson County at the Suit of Jenkin Whitesides against him in alleged
trespassing."[9] The court granted Cobb a rule directing the Sheriff to show
cause why Cobb should not be released. However, on hearing argument on
July 17, the court "ordered that the said rule be discharged." The reason for
this disposition does not appear. Possibly, however, the court found Cobb's
allegations to be factually unsubstantiated. If it had believed itself without
jurisdiction to order his release, it presumably would not have granted the
rule in the first place.[10]

A case of yet another type came before the United States District Court
for the Southern District of Georgia on February 12, 1830, under the cap-
tion *U.S. v. Desfontes & Gaillard*.[11] As reported by the District Judge:

> The French Counsel petitioned for and obtained Habeas Corpus to bring be-
> fore me the prisoners alleging that by the treaty between the Governments of
> France and America[12] they ought to be delivered up as deserters. The persons
> named in the Writ were this day brought before me with the cause of their ar-
> rest and detention. By this return it appears that Gaillard was assaulted and
> beat by Desfontes on board of the Venus a French Merchant Vessel now in
> this Port and for which offence the one was committed to take his trial at the
> ensuing Term of the Court of the State of Georgia having cognizance of the
> offence and the other as the prosecutor and witness according to the State
> Laws, both being unable or unwilling to give bail for their appearance in the
> State Court. Mr. Leake for the Counsel of France now moves for their dis-
> charge. These prisoners do not appear to be deserters. They are prisoners of
> the State of Georgia charged with a violation of the law of that State. I have
> carefully examined the Treaty between the American and French govern-
> ments and the Act of Congress produced in argument[13] and I am satisfied

that I have not the power to discharge the Prisoners. Let them both be returned to the prison from whence they were brought.

Although the statement "I have not the power to discharge the Prisoners," might at first glance suggest otherwise, the most reasonable reading of this ruling is as one on the merits, i.e., that the prisoners are not deserters under the treaty and for that reason not entitled to their discharge, rather than one of jurisdiction, i.e., that whether or not they fall within the terms of the treaty, the court has no power to release them. After all, if the latter meaning were intended, there would have been no reason to discuss the terms of the treaty at all. But the fact of the court's feeling itself free to examine the merits necessarily implies that it was not constrained by the proviso to Section 14, but would, if it had believed the terms of the treaty so required, have issued an order releasing the prisoners from state custody. And although the court's allowance of a writ of habeas corpus to bring the sailors into court to testify as to their status was not inconsistent with Section 14, the grant of such an order of discharge would have been.

In short, there are some early cases showing state prisoners successfully invoking federal habeas corpus jurisdiction—and even going on to success on the merits—in circumstances under which the federal courts could not have proceeded at all if, as *Bollman* stated, they were bound by the limitations of the proviso to Section 14. This adds some support to the idea that it was not in fact the courts, but only their individual judges, who were restricted—either because, as a matter of statutory interpretation, the proviso had nothing to do with courts, or because courts were thought to have additional powers independent of federal statute that enabled them to grant the writ to state prisoners regardless of the terms of the Judiciary Act.

7

Conclusion to Part I

One could certainly argue that even if the claims made so far are correct they are of purely academic interest. To be sure, the "fact" that Congress effectually withheld the federal writ from state prisoners in 1789 has been a premise of substantially all judicial and academic writing on the Suspension Clause. But, on the other hand, the statutory grant of jurisdiction has been unambiguous since 1867, and, even before then, as we have just seen, courts sometimes managed to solve the Section 14 problem.

Most critically, the Court in *Felker v. Turpin* in 1996, even while repeating the erroneous statement that state prisoners had no right to the federal writ under Section 14,[1] assumed "that the Suspension Clause of the Constitution refers to the writ as it exists today, rather than as it existed in 1789."[2]

This assumption would be an entirely sound one for reasons of law and policy regardless of the state of our historical knowledge.[3] Indeed, legal theories too closely tied to current scholarship—whether the field be eugenics,[4] economics,[5] child psychology,[6] or history[7]—may suffer for it.[8]

Still, to the extent that legal arguments are going to be based on history, it does seem to be reasonable to insist that "they get the facts right."[9] In the case of the Suspension Clause, the Justices are more likely to reach an appropriate interpretation if they are aware that their *Felker* assumption is not based on a frail, lawyerly "arguendo," but is, rather, firmly based on a robust historical record. In order that their structures of reasoning be solidly grounded, courts and scholars alike need to begin with a recognition that Chief Justice Marshall erred in *Bollman* both in reading Section 14 of the Judiciary Act of 1789 as not granting the federal courts the power to free state prisoners by habeas corpus, and in concluding from this putative lack of statutory warrant that they lacked the power.

Once the site has been cleared of the Potemkin village of Marshall's pronouncements, the foundations of the American habeas corpus structure become clearly visible: Since the Constitution came into force, the federal courts have had the authority to free state prisoners on habeas corpus, and the Suspension Clause applies as a matter of original intent to any attempt by Congress to limit that authority.

Part II

8

Introduction to Part II

The landmark decisions in *Frank v. Magnum*[1] and *Moore v. Dempsey*,[2] in which seemingly indistinguishable facts led to starkly distinguishable outcomes,[3] lie at the heart of the current controversy over the appropriate scope of federal habeas corpus review of state criminal convictions.

In both cases, unpopular defendants tried in mob-dominated Southern courtrooms in the wake of murders that had shattered the local community brought federal habeas corpus petitions and urged the Supreme Court to rule that egregious due process violations had been responsible for their convictions and death sentences. And, indeed, both cases displayed many of the features that, as we shall see again in Parts III and IV, were common to death penalty cases then and remain so now: incompetent defense counsel, prosecutorial misconduct, public passion, juror partiality, and intense political pressure on all the actors.[4] But the Court denied relief in *Frank* and granted it in *Moore*.

In recent times, those who support broad federal habeas corpus review of the constitutionality of state convictions have generally taken the view that the cases are inconsistent. *Frank*, they say, unjustifiably narrowed the scope of the federal courts' habeas corpus investigations by mandating deference to states' procedurally adequate mechanisms for the correction of error in criminal trials no matter how wrong the outcome of the procedures; it was rightly overruled by *Moore*, which called for a searching inquiry into the facts underlying petitioners' Constitutional claims.[5]

Those seeking to limit habeas corpus have argued that the cases are consistent, and that the Court should adhere to the doctrine that they perceive as governing both. For conservatives, *Frank* did indeed set forth a rule that federal habeas courts should give heavy deference to state proceedings. In their view, the rule was (and is) correct, and *Moore* applied it—although, because of the extreme inadequacy of the state's review process in that particular case, the result was a victory for the petitioners.[6]

This debate about the past—which intensified in the run-up to the enactment of AEDPA,[7] limiting the right of state prisoners (especially Death Row inmates) to obtain federal habeas corpus review of their convictions—is taking place with a sharp eye on the present and near future. One key statutory revision made by AEDPA was to require some increased degree of respect by federal habeas corpus courts for prior state proceedings challenging the same conviction. But the precise contours of this requirement remain cloudy.[8]

Meanwhile, *Frank* and *Moore* have been the subject of continuing investigation by historians. But, with rare exceptions,[9] legal scholars have not benefitted from this work, much less from the previously unexamined archival material that is available to illuminate the cases.

This Part seeks to make a contribution to the integration of historical and legal knowledge. Using previously unutilized historical materials, it provides the first comprehensive account of the procedural steps in the cases. It then draws on this investigation to reach a novel legal conclusion: *Frank* and *Moore* are consistent, and both require in-depth federal habeas corpus review of state prisoner convictions. The differing outcomes of the cases reflect no more than differing discretionary determinations in specific factual settings.

More broadly, I suggest a reconciliation between the historical and legal modes of explaining legal decisions. From a realistic or "historical" perspective, outcomes result from the subjective motivations of individual judges. From a formalistic or "legal" perspective, the outcome of a later case results from the application or nonapplication of the rule laid down by an earlier case. My claim is that, while the identity and motivation of legal decision makers critically affect the outcome of cases at the time they are decided, in the long run the influence of legal opinions is likely to depend on their intellectual merits. Leo Frank, his lawyers, and the Justices who decided his case are now dead. Their personal traits were important in determining why the Supreme Court ruled as it did during their lifetimes. But Frank's enduring importance, to history as well as to law (not to mention to the next prisoner who seeks to invoke it to save his life), will be doctrinal—and specifically, in my view, in its mandate for the searching federal habeas corpus review of state convictions.

Chapter 9 describes the first portion of the legal proceedings in *Frank*, and Chapter 10 takes up the story from his filing of a federal habeas corpus petition. After Chapter 11 sets forth a transitional chronology, Chapters 12–14 provide an account of the legal proceedings in *Moore*, on state direct appeal, state collateral review, and federal habeas corpus.

Chapter 15, after considering and rejecting the legal explanations that have so far been offered for the outcomes, argues that both decisions relied upon the same quite broad rule. Both cases recognized that federal courts reviewing state convictions on habeas corpus had the power to go behind the record of the state court proceedings and conduct a factual inquiry into the existence of a Constitutional violation; they differed only as to whether that power should have been exercised in the situation at hand. This consistency has been obscured by the dramatic facts and manifest injustice of *Frank*—whose real-world outcome was that an innocent Jew was lynched. But it was in *Frank*, not *Moore*, that the Supreme Court first recognized the legal and practical imperative of a federal habeas corpus review that "look[s] through the form and into the very heart and substance of the matter."[10]

Noting the obvious importance of the differing identities of the Justices who decided the two cases, the remainder of Chapter 15 concludes Part II by offering some thoughts on the utility and limits of the legal and historical modes of explaining the outcome of cases. My somewhat counterintuitive suggestion is that the "historical" perspective has more explanatory power as a short-run matter and the "legal" one more over the longer term. The immediate political considerations and passions that seem so critical in explaining the outcome of any controversial case at the moment it is decided are short-term, albeit real. But as they pass into history, opinions also pass increasingly beyond such explanations and ever deeper into the realm of legal doctrine, where they live or die (to the benefit or detriment of future litigants) by their legal power.

Thus, showing that decided cases are or are not legally sound has practical importance. And it is why, in the words of Justice Holmes—who wrote the dissent in *Frank* and the majority opinion in *Moore*, and would, I think, support the conclusions reached here—the law offers all of its acolytes:

> the secret isolated joy of the thinker, who knows that, a hundred years after he is dead and forgotten, men who never heard of him will be moving to the measure of his thought—the subtile rapture of a postponed power.[11]

9

The Legal Proceedings in *Frank*:
The First Round

Because of its prominence as a national news event, its resonance in the areas of sexual, racial, and religious relations, and its historical
significance in helping launch the Anti-Defamation League of B'nai Brith
and relaunch the Ku Klux Klan,[1] Leo Frank's story has been told many
times—in historical works,[2] in plays,[3] and in at least one novel.[4] In keeping
with the concerns of this book, the focus of the account contained in this
chapter and the next is on the history of the litigation that culminated in
the United States Supreme Court, a history that has not been comprehen-
sively documented by previous authors.

At around 3:00 A.M. on April 27, 1913, a black night watchman at the
National Pencil Factory in Atlanta found the badly mutilated corpse of 13-
year-old Mary Phagan, a white employee. A few days later, the police arrested Leo M. Frank. The plant's superintendent and part-owner, Frank was
a rising member of the Jewish community who had been elected president
of the local B'nai Brith the previous year.

As the investigation unfolded, it generated new revelations—reliable
and unreliable—on a daily basis, including many centering around Jim
Conley, a black employee of the plant, who was to become Frank's chief ac-
cuser but who was almost certainly the actual killer.[5] These were broadcast
for months by sensational newspaper stories that roiled public passions
throughout the South.

The prosecution team at trial was led by Solicitor Hugh M. Dorsey, who
would later be one of the state's counsel in the Supreme Court, and, on the
strength of his success—however unethically achieved[6]—be twice elected
Governor of Georgia. The defense was conducted by prominent—albeit ineffective[7]—local trial lawyers, one of whom was Dorsey's brother-in-law.
Four weeks of testimony, highlighted by the accounts of Conley and Frank
himself, were followed by several days of floridly oratorical summations

whose progress was monitored by a demonstrative crowd of several thousand gathered inside and outside the courtroom.[8]

In this atmosphere, the editors of the three Atlanta papers wrote to the trial judge urging him to take precautions against the possibility of mob violence if Frank should be acquitted; the judge accordingly met with counsel in chambers, and secured an agreement that only Dorsey—and not Frank or any of his lawyers—would be present when the verdict was returned. Within sight of the jury, the judge also discussed security arrangements with the commanding officer of the National Guard and the Police Chief.

When the jury announced its verdict, an enormous din erupted from the crowd outside; the windows had to be shut so that the juror's responses could be heard when they were polled individually.[9] Frank, who had reportedly been confident of an acquittal is said to have exclaimed on hearing of the verdict, "My God . . . even the jury was influenced by that mob."[10] The following day, the judge—still fearing public violence—secretly convened the principals in the case and sentenced Frank to death.

Frank's lawyers issued a statement saying that, in light of "the temper of the public mind," the proceedings had been "a farce, and not in any way a trial," since it "would have required a jury of Stoics, a jury of Spartans to have withstood this situation,"[11] and announced that they would appeal.

The first step was a motion for a new trial. The original motion, filed on August 26, 1913 (the day after the verdict and the day of sentencing), contained only a few bare-bones sentences; but these included assertions that "the verdict is contrary to the evidence," and "against the weight of the evidence,"[12] which were sufficient to trigger the judge's review of those issues.[13] As eventually amended, the motion included more than one hundred grounds of error.[14] Most of these related to evidentiary rulings,[15] particularly ones admitting testimony that Frank had in various instances engaged in sexual activity with other women in the factory;[16] some attacked various prosecution arguments as prejudicial;[17] a few challenged the refusal of particular jury instructions;[18] and two alleged that specific jurors had formed fixed opinions of Frank's guilt prior to trial.[19]

As to the issues that eventually were before the Supreme Court of the United States in its *Frank* case, the grounds also included:

> several raising the contention that defendant did not have a fair and impartial trial, because of alleged disorder in and about the court-room including manifestations of public sentiment hostile to the defendant sufficient to influence the jury.[20]

The Supreme Court continued, accurately:

> In support of one of these, and to show the state of sentiment as manifested, the motion stated: "The defendant was not in the court room when the verdict was rendered, his presence having been waived by his counsel. This waiver was accepted and acquiesced in by the court, because of the fear of violence that might be done the defendant were he in court when the verdict was rendered." But the absence of the defendant at the reception of the verdict, although thus mentioned, was not specified or relied upon as a ground for a new trial.[21]

The government responded to the new trial motion with affidavits from eleven of the twelve jurors (the twelfth being out of town on business) attesting to their impartiality, asserting that they had made up their minds strictly on the evidence presented, and affirming their continued agreement with the verdict they had reached.[22]

The trial judge denied the motion for a new trial. In the course of addressing the assertion that the verdict was against the weight of the evidence, he stated, as Frank's lawyers recounted to the Georgia Supreme Court:

> that the jury had found the defendant guilty; that he, the judge, had thought about this case more than any other he had ever tried; that he was not certain of the defendant's guilt; that with all the thought he had put on this case he was not thoroughly convinced whether Frank was guilty or innocent, but that he did not have to be convinced; that the jury was convinced; that there was no room to doubt that; that he felt it his duty to order that the motion for new trial be overruled.[23]

Today at least, the weight of the historical record supports the view that the judge believed that Frank was probably innocent but feared an outbreak of mob violence if he granted a new trial—which would in any event take place while the public was still aroused—and hoped that there would be a reversal in the Georgia Supreme Court, leading to an eventual new trial in a calmer atmosphere. Indeed, one Atlanta newspaper predicted editorially that the judge's expression of doubt would have just this effect.[24]

On appeal, Frank's lawyers argued that the judge's remarks showed that he had "failed to sanctify the verdict by exercising that discretion which the law demands," but rather had "put forward the discretion of the jury as an excuse for not exercising his own."[25]

But the Georgia Supreme Court rejected the argument; it ruled that a trial court's:

legal judgment [is] expressed in overruling the motion . . . and, if there is sufficient evidence to support the verdict, this court will not interfere because of the judge's oral expression as to his opinion.[26]

With respect to the manifestations of public hostility, the court wrote that, in light of the conflicting evidentiary presentations of the two sides on the motion, the judge "was authorized to find from the evidence that only two instances occurred within the hearing or knowledge of the jury," and those two, it held, were "insufficient to impugn the fairness of the trial."[27]

The court then turned to the tumult during the polling of the jury:

> In order that the occurrence complained of shall have the effect of absolutely nullifying the poll of the jury taken before they dispersed, it must appear that its operation upon the minds of the jury, or some of them, was of such a controlling character that they were prevented, or likely to have been prevented, from giving a truthful answer to the questions of the court. We think that the affidavits of jurors submitted in regard to this occurrence were sufficient to show that there was no likelihood that there was any such result.[28]

Rejecting also the instructional[29] and evidentiary[30] arguments on state-law grounds, the court affirmed the conviction, although two dissenting justices argued at length that the testimony of Conley and others "tending to show independent acts of lasciviousness on the part of Frank or improper conduct of his with other parties at other times, was inadmissible," and "certainly calculated to prejudice the defendant in the minds of the jurors, and thereby deprive him of a fair trial."[31]

While awaiting this decision, which they anticipated would be favorable, Frank's attorneys had been vigorously engaged in further investigation, resulting in a great deal of new evidence supporting their case and undermining the veracity of the prosecution's witnesses.

After they presented this in an "extraordinary motion for a new trial" based on newly discovered evidence,[32] the prosecution induced some of its recanting witnesses to return to their original accounts and attacked some of the other new evidence as having been obtained by bribery. Following an evidentiary hearing, a newly seated judge denied the motion, an action that the Georgia Supreme Court in due course routinely affirmed as not constituting an abuse of discretion.[33]

Separate counsel representing Frank also filed a motion to set aside the verdict as a nullity on the theory that the state and federal constitutions had been violated by his absence from the courtroom at the time of its rendition.[34] This motion was made on April 16, 1914, at about the same time as the one based on the new evidence. Demurring, the state argued, among other things, that the challenge should have been included in Frank's original motion for a new trial.[35] The Georgia Supreme Court, rejecting Frank's claim that its prior decisional law was to the contrary, accepted this argument and held that imposing such a procedural requirement was consistent with the state and federal constitutions.[36] On November 18, 1914, the Georgia Supreme Court denied Frank a writ of error for the purpose of pursuing the federal issues to the United States Supreme Court.[37]

On November 21, 1914, Frank's counsel applied to Justice Lamar, the Circuit Justice for the Fifth Circuit, for the same relief.[38] He denied it on November 23, in a memorandum opinion which stated:

> The decision of the Supreme Court of Georgia in this case holds that, under the laws of that State where a motion for a new trial was made and denied, the defendant could not thereafter make a motion to set aside the verdict on the ground that he was not present when it was returned by the jury. That ruling involves a matter of State practice and presents no Federal question. The writ of error is therefore denied.[39]

Frank then exercised his right to apply to another Justice for the writ of error. Justice Holmes denied the application on November 25, 1914.[40] His memorandum opinion stated:

> I understand that I am to assume that the allegations in the motion to set aside are true. On these facts I very seriously doubt if the petitioner has had due process of law—not on the ground of his absence when the verdict was rendered so much as because of the trial taking place in the presence of a hostile demonstration and seemingly dangerous crowd, thought by the presiding Judge to be ready for violence unless a verdict of guilty was rendered. I should not feel prepared to deny a writ of error if I did not consider that I was bound by the decision of the Supreme Court of Georgia that the motion to set aside came too late . . . I think I am bound by this decision even if it reverses a long line of cases and the Counsel for petitioner were misled to his detriment, which I do not intimate to be my view of the case. I have the impression that there is a case in which the ground that I rely on as showing want of due process of law was rejected by the Court with my dissent, but I have not interrupted discussion with Counsel to try to find it, if it exists.[41]

According to Holmes, this memorandum was written:

> for any of our Judges in case he applied to another as he had a right to. To my surprise the mem. was published and as it seems the case had excited much

attention though I never had heard of it the papers talk about it and I get letters from sensitive females crying for mercy. . . . I am somewhat annoyed at the publication as I wrote what was intended only as a suggestion to my brethren if any of them could see a way to giving relief.[42]

At this point, Frank's counsel, Louis Marshall (the President of the American Jewish Committee and a prominent Constitutional lawyer who was serving *pro bono publico*), applied to the full Court for the writ of error.[43] Justices Holmes and Hughes, it subsequently transpired, favored granting the writ[44] but it was denied on December 7, 1914, without recorded dissent.[45]

10

The Legal Proceedings in *Frank*: Federal Habeas Corpus

On December 17, 1914, Frank filed a petition in the United States District Court for the Northern District of Georgia seeking a writ of habeas corpus.[1] The principal contention was that his absence from the courtroom at the rendition of the verdict was, under the circumstances, a denial of due process but the petition also asserted that the "trial did not proceed in accordance with the orderly processes of the law . . . because [it was] dominated by a mob which was hostile to me, and whose conduct intimidated the Court and jury," in violation of Fourteenth Amendment due process and equal protection.[2]

As Marshall had anticipated,[3] the District Court denied the application. Its opinion, issued on December 21, 1914, reviewed the prior course of proceedings and continued:

> If this writ should issue . . . the only thing the Court here could do would be to hear evidence and determine whether this applicant had been denied the equal protection of the laws and due process of law, and consequently should be discharged. It seems to me that this would be the exercise by this Court of supervisory power over the action of the State courts in a manner not warranted by the Constitution or the Laws of the United States. Also the Court would be considering the matter . . . in the face of the decisions of two Justices of the Supreme Court—indeed of the entire Court—to the effect . . . that no Federal question remained for consideration or now exists in the case.[4]

Frank then applied to Justice Lamar for a certificate of probable cause to appeal. On December 28, 1914, Justice Lamar granted the application.[5] His printed opinion provided to counsel recited the procedural history, and then continued as follows—with the omission of the bracketed phrase, which he had stricken from his typed draft:[6]

[T]he application for the certificate is not to be determined by any views which may be held as to the effect of the final judgment of the State Supreme Court refusing a New Trial, [or by the effect of the Supreme Court of the United States refusing a writ of error to review the judgment refusing to Set Aside the verdict,] but by considering whether the nature of the constitutional right asserted in the absence of any decision expressly foreclosing the right to an appeal, leaves the matter so far unsettled as to constitute probable cause justifying the allowance of the appeal. The Supreme Court of the United States has never determined whether, on a trial for murder in a State court, the due process clause of the Federal Constitution guarantees the defendant a right to be present when the verdict is rendered. Neither has it decided the effect of a final judgment refusing a New Trial in a case where the defendant did not make the fact of his absence when the verdict was returned a ground of the Motion, nor claim that the rendition of the verdict in his absence was the denial of a right guaranteed by the Federal Constitution. Nor has it passed upon the effect of its own refusal to grant a writ of error in a case where an alleged jurisdictional question was presented in a Motion filed at a time not authorized by the practice of the State where the trial took place. Such questions are all involved in the present case, and since they have never been settled by any authoritative ruling of the full court . . . the appeal [is] allowed.[7]

The parties filed simultaneous briefs on the merits.[8] Marshall began with the disorderly conditions at trial[9] and stressed throughout that their result was that Frank was not tried by a "court" in the legal sense.[10] Thus, he stated a "jurisdictional" claim (that is, one raising fundamental issues, especially Constitutional ones) which was cognizable on habeas corpus,[11] as opposed to a "merely legal claim" (that is, one not implicating basic concerns of substantive or procedural fairness) which was subject to Supreme Court review only by writ of error.[12]

Marshall wrote:

There was no longer a court or a jury. They were as though they had never been. There ceased to be a trial or a hearing, or an opportunity to be heard. For all practical purposes, the court might as well have handed the appellant over to the tender mercies of the boisterous bystanders who were clamoring for his blood. . . .[13]

Marshall was, nonetheless, careful to conclude by assuring the Court that the appropriate relief was retrial, not release.[14]

On the procedural issues, Marshall argued that the District Court had "entirely misconceived"[15] the significance of Frank's recent efforts to obtain a writ of error from the Justices:

The reason for the denial of a writ of error by this Court, and its several members, was not that a Federal question was not involved in the case, but that the Supreme Court of Georgia put its decision upon two grounds, (1) that the Fourteenth Amendment to the Constitution was not violated, and (2) that in any event it was too late to raise that question. . . . [Since] each of the grounds was a sufficient basis . . . , this Court held [that] a writ of error . . . would not lie. Our hope was, to satisfy the Court that the two grounds stated were not independent of one another, but interdependent, and amounted, in substance, to a determination . . . that, by his non-action or ac-quiescence [appellant] had waived a constitutional right which, it had been held by this Court, could not be waived expressly. It is evident, however, that the view prevailed here, that the Supreme Court of Georgia, whether right or wrong, had determined that the proper remedy was a motion for a new trial, and not a motion to set aside the verdict.

Our present proceeding, an application for a writ of *habeas corpus*, is . . . based upon the proposition that, because the appellant was . . . deprived of due process of law, . . . the court had lost jurisdiction.

That presents a proposition which is not affected by State practice. The case is in the precise situation that it would have been if no timely proceeding had been attempted in the State courts of Georgia. . . . In that event, the bare question presented in this proceeding would have been, Did the court possess jurisdiction to pronounce sentence of death? That is the exact condition that now exists. That is the same question which must now be answered. . . . [A]ppellant's unavailing attempts in the State court for relief . . . cannot make that a legal judgment which was before a nullity.[16]

For the government, Dorsey argued that, in light of Frank's failure to submit the state's rebuttal affidavits from the jurors, and the asserted inad-missibility of oral evidence in habeas corpus proceedings to show a lack of jurisdiction in the convicting court, the factual determinations of the state courts should be presumed correct.[17] Further, inasmuch as Frank had al-ready obtained rulings from the state courts on every issue presented, those rulings should be considered *res judicata*.[18] Even if not so considered, he continued, the errors alleged were not fundamental enough to justify habeas relief.[19] This argument in various forms occupied much the greater part of his brief; the argument that Frank was precluded by the denial of the writ of error was made briefly and awkwardly.[20]

On April 19, 1914,[21] over the dissent of Justices Holmes and Hughes, the Court affirmed the denial of the writ. All the Justices agreed on several critical points:

1. The District Court did have the authority to hold a hearing "to test the jurisdiction of the state court." Indeed, the opinion described as one of the "established rules and principles" the proposition:

> that it is open to the courts of the United States upon an application for a writ of *habeas corpus* to look beyond forms and inquire into the very substance of the matter, to the extent of deciding whether the prisoner has been deprived of his liberty without due process of law, and for this purpose to inquire into the jurisdictional facts, whether they appear upon the record or not.[22]

Given the meaning of "jurisdictional" in the law of habeas corpus as noted above, this statement of the District Court's investigatory authority was of considerable importance.

2. The determinations of the state courts were not *res judicata*,[23] nor were Frank's claims precluded by his prior unsuccessful applications for a writ of error.

While it seems clear enough from the editorial change made in his draft opinion allowing the appeal that Justice Lamar had originally entertained some doubts on this subject, the point was rejected without explicit discussion, a course doubtless facilitated by the weakness of Dorsey's brief on the issue. Although the Court cited the relevant cases, it silently confined them to their facts, merely observing that

(a) habeas corpus review should ordinarily follow writ of error review;[24] and

(b) the writ of habeas corpus "cannot be employed as a substitute for the writ of error," a reiteration of the uncontested and uncontroversial distinction between "[m]ere errors in point of law, however serious," which could only be reviewed by writ of error, and the fundamental or "jurisdictional" (particularly Constitutional) claims cognizable on habeas corpus.[25]

In thus reaffirming its pre-1892 practice,[26] the Court sent a significant, albeit silent, message. The decision to review the merits necessarily implied that, just as Marshall had argued, writ of error proceedings would not be preclusive of later habeas corpus review, at least where the Court had found itself unable to reach the federal merits due to an adequate and independent state ground.

More broadly, the Court's decision to reach the merits was an important data point in the line of developments by which the writ of error (a writ of right) gradually began to lose importance in favor of the expanding writ of certiorari (a discretionary writ). Because the Court had justified its preference for writ of error over habeas corpus review in the post-1892 period on the grounds that the former was available as of right, the erosion of the writ of error "expanded the use and widened the scope of habeas corpus review."[27]

3. Frank's challenge to his absence from the verdict did not rise to the level of a Constitutional claim.[28]

4. There was no merit to the assertion that the Ex Post Facto clause was violated by the alleged change of view on the part of the Georgia Supreme Court respecting the appropriate procedure for bringing that challenge.[29]

5. Perhaps most critically, the Justices also agreed that "if a trial is in fact dominated by a mob, so that the jury is intimidated and the trial judge yields . . . there is, in that court, a departure from due process of law."[30]

The crucial disagreement was what showing a habeas corpus petitioner had to make for a successful invocation of the District Court's conceded authority to determine whether the trial court had "in fact" been intimidated. The majority wrote that the facts concerning this issue as found by the state court of last resort:

> must be taken as setting forth the truth of the matter, certainly until some reasonable ground is shown for an inference that the court which rendered it was wanting in jurisdiction, or at least erred in the exercise of its jurisdiction; and . . . the mere assertion by the prisoner that the facts of the matter are other than the state court upon full investigation determined them to be will not be deemed sufficient to raise an issue respecting the correctness of that determination.[31]

The dissent began its analysis by elaborating on the whole Court's common understanding that the District Court did have the power to conduct an independent fact review:

> The only question before us is whether the petition shows on its face that the writ of habeas corpus should be denied, or whether the District Court should have proceeded to try the facts.

> We have held in a civil case that it is no defence to the assertion of the Federal right in the Federal court that the State has corrective procedure of its own— that still less does such procedure draw to itself the final determination of the Federal question. *Simon v. Southern Ry.*, 236 U.S. 115, 122, 123 [1915]. We see no reason for a less liberal rule in a matter of life and death. When the decision of the question of fact is so interwoven with the decision of the question of Constitutional right that the one necessarily involves the other, the Federal court must examine the facts. *Kansas Southern Ry. v. C.H. Albers Commission Co.*, 233 U.S. 573, 591 [1912].[32] *Nor. & West. Ry. v. Conley*, . . .

236 U.S. 605, [609-610] [1915].[33] Otherwise, the right will be a barren one. It is significant that the argument for the State does not go so far as to say that in no case would it be permissible on application for *habeas corpus* to override the findings of fact by the state courts. . . . If, however, the argument stops short of this, the whole structure built upon the state procedure and decisions falls to the ground.[34]

Observing that the petition showed "the judgment of the expert on the spot, of the judge whose business it was to preserve not only form but substance, to have been that if one juryman yielded to the reasonable doubt he himself later expressed in court as the result of most anxious deliberation, neither prisoner nor counsel would be safe from the rage of the crowd," the dissent found "the presumption overwhelming that the jury responded to the passions of the mob," and the allegations of the petition of sufficient gravity that the District Court should have held a hearing, "whatever the decision of the state court may have been."[35]

"[I]t is our duty," Justices Holmes and Hughes concluded, "to declare lynch law as little valid when practiced by a regularly drawn jury as when administered by one elected by a mob intent on death."[36]

In the aftermath of the Court's decision, Justice Holmes was uncharacteristically direct as to its effect on him, alluding to the distressing facts of the case in a number of letters,[37] chafing at the conflict between the demands of law and those of justice,[38] and describing his opinion as "a dissent as to which I feel a good deal."[39]

Holmes was, in fact, feeling somewhat "tired and discouraged" at the time, around his 74th birthday on March 8, 1915, remarking on the "impalpable soft approaches of the enemy," death, and taking comfort in his continuing speed at writing opinions as evidence that he was keeping the enemy at bay.[40] He could not "help wondering whether our judicial protection of bills of rights against legislation may not be nearing its end. On the one hand I seem to see and I lament the weakening of the realizing senses that the fundamentals of personal liberty are worth fighting for, and on the other I see great danger" as the "judicial notion of freedom of contract" thwarts economic experimentation.[41]

For their part, once the Court's opinion came down Frank's lawyers immediately began working for executive clemency, co-ordinating a massive legal and press campaign (which ultimately resulted in some 100,000 letters being written to the Governor of Georgia) designed to secure a commutation to life imprisonment.[42] On June 21, 1915—having first made elaborate arrangements to move Frank secretly to a distant prison for his protection against an outburst of violence—Governor Slaton issued his commutation order, the bulk of which consisted of a detailed review of the unreliability of the evidence against Frank.[43] Outraged, violent anti-Semitic mobs ravaged the state for more than a week.[44]

Shortly afterwards, Frank wrote a warm letter to Justice Holmes:

> I feel that you, as Judge, do not look for thanks. Yet, I cannot but feel profoundly gratified, that . . . you, and Justice Hughes diagnosed the situation with rare insight and sagacity.

After recounting the "deplorable" protests that had greeted the news of the commutation—sparked by "these same people, this same crowd, the same shouts and threats, which pervaded the atmosphere of my trial," thus verifying "that my trial could not have approximated justice"—Frank closed by expressing "confident trust" in his ultimate vindication, and looking forward to the day when, "with liberty + honor restored," he could have the pleasure of greeting Holmes in person.[45]

Writing to a correspondent the day he received this letter, Holmes observed that it was "very well written, with a surprising moderation of tone," and vowed to keep it.[46] Less reliably, he is reported to have remarked that "a man who could write to him so sensitively as Frank couldn't have raped and murdered a girl."[47]

A month later, Frank was abducted from prison in a well-organized operation led by eminent citizens and lynched in Mary Phagan's hometown.[48]

11

From *Frank* to *Moore*

Frank's tragic aftermath aroused strong feelings throughout the country.

Louis D. Brandeis, then in private practice, had already expressed concern about the case.[1] Writing to Senator George Sutherland after its denouement, he referred to the "occurrences in the Frank case" as having "subjected the reputation of the Courts to severe strain" and urged Sutherland to prevent a repetition.[2] The Executive Committee of the American Bar Association, at a meeting at which William Howard Taft was present, adopted a resolution condemning Frank's "willful and deliberate murder . . . in a spirit of savage and remorseless cruelty, unworthy of our age and time," as "an act of wanton savagery . . . well calculated to promote lawlessness and anarchy."[3]

Within Georgia, however, popular opinion supported the lynch mob, not the Governor. The prevailing view at the time was "that mob violence protected society from both lawbreakers and a criminal justice system that failed to carry out its mandate." But this attitude broke up with surprising rapidity over the following decade under the influence of a coalition of anti-lynching activists comprising "white businessmen dedicated to economic progress, white reformers animated by a vision of Christian social justice, and black activists committed to color-blind justice."[4] Among this group was the Governor, Hugh M. Dorsey.[5]

The same years saw a number of changes in the composition of the Supreme Court—including the appointments of Brandeis, Sutherland, and Taft—with the results indicated in Table 1. Thus, four of the eight Justices who would be deciding *Moore* had ascended the bench since *Frank*. But one of these was a replacement for one of the dissenters in that case, and the most salient factor influencing the appointments of Taft, Sutherland, and Butler had been their perceived skepticism regarding the validity of economic regulations under the Due Process Clause, rather than their views on individual rights.[6]

Perhaps, as Brandeis suggested later, the importance of the change was not so much the identity of the appointees as their relative newness to the

TABLE 1

The *Frank* Court (April 19, 1915)	The *Moore* Court (February 19, 1923)
Edward D. White, C.J.	William Howard Taft, C.J. (Seated October 3, 1921)
Joseph McKenna	Joseph McKenna
Oliver Wendell Holmes	Oliver Wendell Holmes
Willis Van Devanter	Willis Van Devanter
James C. McReynolds	James C. McReynolds
Joseph R. Lamar	Louis D. Brandeis (Seated June 5, 1916)
Charles E. Hughes	George Sutherland (Seated October 2, 1922)
William R. Day	Pierce Butler (Seated January 2, 1923)
Mahlon Pitney	[Vacant][7]

bench; specifically, it may be that the raw realities of Southern justice would come as a greater shock to the newer Justices than to those who had been seeing similar scenarios regularly presented for (and denied) review. But then, one could with equal plausibility adopt the opposite hypothesis—that Justices who had more recently lived outside the ivory tower of the Court would be more familiar with the realities of the world, and more cynical about it. Indeed, as it turned out, one of the only two recorded dissenters in *Moore* was George Sutherland, who had recently joined the Court from a litigation practice.[8] And in our own day, it would seem that the increased misgivings over time of Justices O'Connor, Stevens, and Blackmun regarding the death penalty were the result of greater and greater exposure to specific instances of injustice coming before them judicially.[9]

Of more immediate relevance to *Moore*, perhaps it is of significance that the problem of lynching continued to gnaw at the national conscience. Although lynchings had been declining steadily between 1900 and 1917:

> World War I disrupted the status quo. Black men returned from military service were far less willing than they had once been to accept quietly the indignities of Jim Crow. Whites met their new assertiveness with increased violence. The number of black lynchings, down to only 36 in 1917, leaped to 76 in 1919.[10]

Moreover, around the country "city after city exploded in the worst racial conflicts that the country would ever see"[11]—race riots in which the death toll (overwhelmingly among blacks) ran into the hundreds.[12]

In this atmosphere, the NAACP launched a high-profile (although ultimately unsuccessful) campaign in Washington for federal antilynching legislation that ran almost continuously from 1919 through 1923, increasing public awareness of profound societal problems yet unremedied.[13] "The agitation for a federal anti-lynching law," a contemporary observed, "may be another symptom of the flux in social consciousness that accounts partially for the development from *Frank v. Magnum* to *Moore v. Dempsey.*"[14]

12

The Legal Proceedings in *Moore*:
The State Criminal Proceedings

Underlying *Moore* is not a single crime but a massive race riot that took place in the fall of 1919 in Phillips County, Arkansas, near the town of Elaine.[1] How the outbreak originated was sharply disputed at the time,[2] and remained so for generations.[3] The local white establishment called the events an "insurrection"—the product of an organization of violent radicals and the machinations of an unscrupulous charlatan who duped blacks into joining[4]—whose object, fortuitously disrupted before it could come to fruition, was a general massacre of whites by blacks. In the words of the Committee of Seven, a quasi-official group of prominent local citizens who investigated the outbreak:

> The present trouble with the Negroes in Phillips county is not a race riot. It is a deliberately planned insurrection of the Negroes against the white[s], directed by an organization known as the "Progressive Farmers' and Household Union of America," established for the purpose of banding Negroes together for the killing of white people.[5]

The NAACP took the view, which is supported by modern scholarship, that the violence was an effort by whites to revenge and deter legal attacks on an entrenched system of peonage.[6]

The events took place, moreover, within the context not only of bloody race riots throughout the country but of the "Red Scare": class-based strife was manifesting itself in violent disputes over working conditions, and in vigorous advocacy—and even more vigorous suppression—of radical political and economic views.[7] Thus, as the riot was beginning, a lawyer seeking to meet with the tenant farmers in the neighborhood was seized by vigilantes who claimed to have taken from him literature of the Industrial Workers of the World (IWW), as well as of the Progressive Farmers' Union. After being held in jail for a month—partly for his own protection from lynching—he was released, but, to appease the mob, indicted for barratry (a charge that was dropped the following year). Following the disturbances, the Arkansas authorities sought, by complaint to the Post Office and by state court injunction proceedings, to prevent the circulation of newspapers containing "untrue and seditious" accounts of the Elaine riot and other contentious episodes.[8]

Meanwhile, between 200 and 250 blacks and at least four whites had been killed in the violence before order was eventually restored by federal troops. No whites faced criminal charges growing out of the upheaval, but 122 blacks were indicted, 73 of them for murder. Ultimately, 67 blacks were sentenced to prison terms and 12 to death, all for the murder of whites.[9]

The death sentences were returned within six weeks of the riot in a series of trials in each of which jury deliberations lasted less than ten minutes:

TABLE 2
The Elaine Riot Capital Cases, 1919

Defendant	Date Convicted	Victim	Jury Deliberations	
Ware Defendants				
Ed Ware	Nov. 18	W. D. Adkins	4 minutes	
William Wordlow	Nov. 4	W. D. Adkins	9 minutes	
Albert Giles	Nov. 4	James A. Tappan	6 minutes	Joint
Joe Fox	Nov. 4	James A. Tappan	6 minutes	trial
John Martin	Nov. 4	W. D. Adkins	Unknown	Joint
Alf Banks, Jr.	Nov. 4	W. D. Adkins	Unknown	trial
Moore Defendants				
Frank Hicks	Nov. 2	Clinton Lee	8 minutes	
Frank Moore	Nov. 2	Clinton Lee	7 minutes	Joint
Ed Hicks	Nov. 2	Clinton Lee	7 minutes	trial
J. E. Knox	Nov. 2	Clinton Lee	7 minutes	Joint
Paul Hall	Nov. 2	Clinton Lee	7 minutes	trial
Ed Coleman	Nov. 2	Clinton Lee	7 minutes[10]	

The remaining 67 sentences resulted from guilty pleas entered, perhaps prudently, after these trials had taken place.[11]

In December, the defendants sentenced to death filed motions for new trials.[12] The primary grounds were:

1.

[They are all] negro[es] of the African race, and . . . at the time of the returning of . . . [the] indictment and trial . . . bitterness of feeling among the whites of . . . [the] county, against the negroes, especially against the defendant[s] was . . . at the height of intensity . . . [and] co-extensive with the county . . . ; [t]hat during . . . [their] confinement . . . [they] were frequently subjected to torture, for the purpose of extracting from . . . [them] admission[s] of guilt—as were others then also in custody, to force them to testify against defendant[s] . . . ; [t]hat while . . . [they were] . . . confined, several hundred white men of said county, assembled at or near the court house and jail, for the purpose of mobbing . . . [them], and were only prevented from doing so . . . by the presence of United States soldiers . . . ; [t]hat the indictment was returned . . . by . . . [a] grand jury composed wholly of white men . . . ; [t]hat . . . without ever having been permitte[d] to see or talk with an attorney, or any other person, in reference to . . . [their] defense, . . . [they were] carried from the jail to the Court room and put on trial—the court appointing an attorney for them—before a jury composed wholly of white men . . . ; [t]hat the excitement and feeling against the defendant[s] among the whites of said county was such that it was impossible to obtain any unprejudiced jury of white men to try . . . [them]—and that no white jury, . . . [even if] fairly disposed, would have had the courage to acquit . . . [them] . . . ; [t]hat the trial proceeded without consultation on . . . [their] part with any attorney, without any witnesses in . . . [their] behalf and without an opportunity on . . . [their] part to obtain witnesses or prepare for defense. . . ; [t]hat no evidence was offered in . . . [their] behalf; . . . [t]hat the jury . . . returned . . . within about three to six minutes, with a verdict of guilty against the defendant[s]. . . . Defendant[s], therefore, say[] that . . . [they were] convicted and sentenced to death without due process of law. . . .

2.

[N]o negro has been appointed a jury commissioner, or selected to serve as a juror, either grand or petit, for more than thirty years . . . ; that they are excluded therefrom solely on account of their race and color . . . ; that the defendants have thus been . . . deprived of their rights under the Constitution of the United States, and especially the 14th Amendment . . . [and are] denied the equal protection of the law. Defendant[s] further say[] that while it is true, as . . . [they are] now advised, that the proper . . . time to have objected . . . would have been before trial—yet . . . [they] knew nothing of . . . [their] right[] to raise any objection[] . . . and . . . [were] not advised in that regard . . . and that . . . [they], therefore, feel that . . . [their] objection, taken at this time should prevail to the extent of securing them a new trial.[13]

Annexed as exhibits were two affidavits, both from prisoners under death sentences as a result of the *Ware* trials. One, from Alf Banks, Jr., stated that while confined prior to trial:

I was frequently whipped with great severity, and was also put into an electric chair and shocked, and strangling drugs would be put to my nose to make me tell things against others . . . [they] tortured me so that I finally told them falsely that what they wanted me to say was true and that I would testify to it. . . . As they were taking me to the Courtroom, they told me if I changed my testimony or did not testify as I had said, when they took me back, they would skin me alive. I testified as I had told them. . . . It was not true; it was false. . . . I would never have testified falsely as I did if I had not been made to [d]o it.[14]

The other, from William Wordlow, stated:

[In jail,] I was not permitted to . . . do anything towards preparing any defense. While in custody there, I was frequently taken from the cell, blindfolded, whipped and tortured to make me tell things I did not know, and furnish false information, and testify against others of the negroes. . . . To escape from the torture, I finally said what they wanted me to say. . . . All that I said against [defendants] . . . was forced. I do not know of any negro who killed or advised or encouraged the killing of either Mr. Adkins, Mr. Lee, Mr. Tappan or anyone else, and would not have voluntarily testified that I did. As I was taken to the court-room, I was given to understand that if I did not testify as they had directed, I would be killed.[15]

The motions were summarily denied the day they were filed,[16] and all the defendants appealed from the denials as part of their direct appeals.

On appeal, the Arkansas Supreme Court divided the cases into two groups, as shown in Table 2 above. In one opinion, it reversed the convictions of the *Ware* defendants and remanded for new trials because the juries had simply rendered general guilty verdicts, failing to abide by a state statute requiring them to "find by their verdict whether [the defendant] be guilty of murder in the first or second degree."[17]

With respect to the *Moore* defendants, the court, in another opinion, first ruled that the allegations of racial discrimination in jury selection had come too late.[18] It then continued:

It is now insisted that, because of the incidents developed at the trial and those recited in the motion for new trials, and the excitement and feeling growing out of them, no fair trial was had, or could have been had, and that the trial did not, therefore, constitute due process of law.

It is admitted, however, that eminent counsel was appointed to defend appellants, and no attempt is made to show that a fair and impartial trial was not had, except as an inference from the facts stated above; the insistence being that a fair trial was impossible under the circumstances stated.

We are unable, however, to say that this must necessarily have been the case. The trials were had according to law, the jury was correctly charged . . . and the testimony is legally sufficient to support the verdicts returned. We cannot, therefore, in the face of this affirmative showing, assume that the trial was an empty ceremony, conducted for the purpose only of appearing to comply with the requirements of the law, when they were not in fact being complied with. . . .

We have given these cases the careful consideration which their importance required, but our consideration is necessarily limited to those matters which are properly brought before us for review, and . . . the judgments must be affirmed.[19]

Purely for exhaustion purposes, but expecting that the real contest would come on federal habeas corpus, counsel filed petitions for certiorari.[20]

13

The Legal Proceedings in *Moore*: The State Collateral Proceedings

As the cases of the *Moore* defendants languished, the retrials of the *Ware* cases got under way; this time, they were litigated far more aggressively than before. Counsel filed motions seeking:

(a) removal of the prosecutions to federal court on the grounds that there had been no blacks summoned to serve on either the grand or trial juries and the defendants could not receive the equal protection of the laws in the state court.[1]

(b) a change of venue. "Apparently because of fear of retaliation [counsel] could only get four blacks to testify in support of the motion for a change of venue," which was denied after a hearing lasting an hour and a half.[2]

(c) to quash the indictments and the venire because, in violation of the Equal Protection Clause, no blacks had been included. These motions were also denied.[3]

In three separate trials, all six *Ware* defendants were convicted once more, notwithstanding the testimony of two of them that they had previously been tortured.

On appeal, the Arkansas Supreme Court again reversed and remanded for a new trial. In an opinion issued on December 6, 1920, it held:

(a) that the denial of the removal petition had been proper, since no state law prevented blacks from enforcing their civil rights;

(b) over one dissent, that the "lower court did not abuse its discretion" in rejecting the motion for a change of venue after hearing the testimony of the witnesses;

(c) but that, under controlling federal authority, the defendants had been entitled to present evidence in support of their claims of racial discrimination in jury selection.[4]

Meanwhile, on October 11, the United States Supreme Court had denied the certiorari petition of the *Moore* defendants[5]—whose identical claim had been rejected because it was made too late.[6]

This action led to various lobbying efforts aimed at persuading the Governor to grant or deny the defendants clemency. Elaine's local American Legion post opposed clemency on the ground that:

> when the guilty Negroes were apprehended, a solemn promise was given by the leading citizens of the community, that if these guilty parties were not lynched, and let the law take its course, that justice would be done and the majesty of the law upheld.[7]

Supporting this position, five of the members of the Committee of Seven wrote the Governor:

> With all the provocation, our people refrained from mob violence. The reason they did this was that this Committee gave our citizens their solemn promise that the law would be carried out. This Community can be made a model one so far as resorting to mob violence is concerned, but should the Governor commute any sentence of these Elaine rioters, this would be difficult, if not impossible.[8]

On November 15, the Governor announced that he had decided to deny clemency, in recognition of the fact that the community "had refrained from mob violence" on the basis of "the definite promise to the people of Phillips County [by the Committee of Seven] that the law would be enforced and that there would be no outside influence permitted to interfere. . . ."[9]

Eventually, an execution date was set for June 10, 1921.[10] Then, a potentially fatal roadblock suddenly appeared in the path to obtaining federal habeas relief: the District Judge was out of town until after the scheduled execution date. On June 8, counsel in desperation turned to the state system, and filed petitions for writs of habeas corpus in the Pulaski County Chancery Court consisting essentially of the petitions they had been planning to file in federal court.[11]

Frank Hicks's petition (which was "exactly alike as to form and substance" as the one filed on behalf of the other petitioners)[12] annexed two new affidavits. In one, sworn to on May 18, 1921, George Green stated that he had testified against Frank Hicks, but:

> I now state and swear positively, that the testimony was false from beginning to end, and that I testified as I did because I was compelled to do so. . . . I was not whipped, but a great many of the Negroes there in jail with me were whipped. . . . [I]n order to avoid such punishment I finally agreed to testify to

anything that they wanted me to say. . . . At the same time I was indicted for the murder of Clinton Lee, and they told me that if I would testify against Frank Hicks and then plead guilty, that they would get the court to make it light on me. I later pleaded guilty to murder in the second degree and was sentenced to six years in the penitentiary. . . . I was not guilty of having anything to do with the killing of Clinton Lee or anyone else. . . .[13]

The second affidavit, also sworn to on May 18, 1921, was from John Jefferson. He stated that he had testified in both *Moore* trials, but had done so falsely because of threats of whipping and execution, and eventually, despite his innocence, in order "to save my own life," had pleaded guilty to the second degree murder of Clinton Lee (receiving a five-year sentence).[14]

In a third affidavit of the same date Walter Ward stated that, arrested for the killing of Clinton Lee, he had been whipped until:

they nearly killed me. I was also put in an electric chair, stripped naked and the current turned on to shock and frighten me. They also put up my nose some kind of strangling drugs to further torture and frighten me.

As a result, he testified falsely "in the case against Frank Moore and others," and, having been:

told that if I did not plead guilty I would be sent to the electric chair and in order to save myself further torture and to save my life I plead guilty to murder in the second degree, and was sentenced to 21 years in the penitentiary. I was not guilty.[15]

In response to the petitions, the chancellor, John E. Martineau, ordered the warden to produce the prisoners before him on June 10, and stayed the executions.[16] The Attorney General on June 9 filed an application for a writ of prohibition with the Arkansas Supreme Court, which, over the objections of the Chief Justice, set the matter down for argument on June 13, leaving the stay in place.[17]

Although there were early signs that the defendants' vivid accounts were beginning to undermine the public's hitherto-solid support for the state's handling of the riots,[18] the Arkansas Supreme Court was uninterested in the substance of their grievances. When counsel:

argued on behalf of the condemned men that the state's evidence in the original trials had been secured through torture, in violation of due process, Chief Justice McCulloch stopped him in mid-argument. Such contentions, he said, were irrelevant to the issue of the chancery court's jurisdiction to issue the writs and the injunction.[19]

On June 20, the court issued a unanimous opinion granting prohibition. It held that under state law the chancellor clearly lacked jurisdiction over the proceeding, and continued with a discussion of counsel's contention:

> that the provision of the Constitution with reference to due process of law and the federal statutes prescribing the remedies whereby the Constitutional guaranty may be enforced must be read into the state laws so that the pre-scribed remedies may be afforded in the state courts.[20]

The court rejected the argument that *Frank* supported this conclusion, and held that the federal habeas corpus statute applied only to the federal courts, while the Due Process Clause did not reach the arrangements that a state chose to make for the distribution of judicial business within its own court system.[21]

Although it commented, "[w]hat the result would be of an application to a federal court under the statute referred to and upon the facts stated in the petition we need not inquire," the court strongly hinted that such an application would be meritless under *Frank*.[22] (Contrary to Justice Holmes's later suggestion,[23] the passage certainly does not appear to be meant as encouragement for the prisoners to pursue federal relief.)

Since Circuit Justice Van Devanter was unavailable at his vacation home in Canada, counsel were given a choice of Justices in Washington to whom to present an application for a writ of error.[24] Unsurprisingly, they picked Justice Holmes—who denied the application on August 4.[25]

Counsel then followed up with a certiorari petition.[26] But, quite apart from its dubious probabilities of success,[27] this petition would not operate as a stay.[28] With a new execution date set for September 23, and the Court in recess until October, the prisoners were once more facing the electric chair.

14

The Legal Proceedings in *Moore*: The Federal Habeas Corpus Proceedings

On September 21, 1921, two days before their scheduled executions, the *Moore* defendants filed habeas corpus petitions in the United States District Court for the Eastern District of Arkansas.[1]

These petitions alleged that on September 30, 1919, while "petitioners and a large number of the members of their race were peaceably and lawfully assembled in their church house at or near Hoop Spur . . . white persons began firing guns . . . for the purpose of breaking up said meeting," and that in the resulting melee W. A. Adkins, one of the raiders, "was killed either by members of his own party or by some other person unknown."[2] News of the killing "spread like wild fire," through the region, and early the next day numerous white men formed themselves into posses and:

> began the indiscriminate shooting down of Negroes, both men and women, particularly the posse from the State of Mississippi, who shot down in cold blood innocent Negro men and women, many of whom were at the time in the fields picking cotton.

Clinton Lee, whom petitioners were convicted of killing, was one of these white men, whose activities were supported by public officials and the press as an effort to quell an "uprising of the Negroes . . . or insurrection." Finally, "a company of soldiers was dispatched to the scene of the trouble who took charge of the situation and finally succeeded in stopping the slaughter."

Having been charged with murder, the petition continued, the petitioners were incarcerated "together with a large number of their race, both men and women." A "committee of seven . . . leading . . . business men and officials . . . was selected for the purpose of probing into the situation." This group examined those incarcerated, and if the prisoners failed to give satisfactory evidence, they would be sent out and certain of their keepers would take them to a room in the jail w[h]ich was immediately adjoining, and a part of the Court-house building where said Committee was sitting, and torture them by beat-ing and whipping them with leather straps with metal in them, cutting the blood at every lick until the victim would agree to anything their torturers demanded of them; [and] to further frighten and torture them, [there was] an electric chair, into which they would be put naked and the current turned on to shock and frighten them into giving damaging statements against them-selves and others; also strangling drugs were put up their noses for the same purpose and by these methods and means false evidence was extorted from Negroes to be used and was used against your petitioners.

After the committee had published its conclusion that the tumult had not been a race riot, but rather "a 'deliberately planned insurrection of the Ne-groes against the Whites'," a mob:

of hundreds of men . . . marched to the County jail for the purpose and with the intent of lynching your petitioners . . . and would have done so but for the interference of United States soldiers and the promise of some of said Committee and other leading officials that if the mob would stay its hand they would execute those found guilty in the form of law.

The petitioners then recounted how the attorney who had been consulting with them on attacking the sharecropping system had been incarcerated for a month and eventually, with the assistance of the same judge who was to try them, spirited out of town "so as to avoid being mobbed."[3]

Resuming the main thread of the narrative, the petitioners continued with the allegations "that a grand jury was organized composed wholly of white men, one of whom . . . was a member of the said Committee . . . and many of whom were in the posses"; that the grand jury heard false tes-timony—extracted by torture—and indicted them for the murder of Clin-ton Lee, "a man petitioners did not know, and had never, to their knowl-edge even seen"; that they were brought into the trial courtroom on No-vember 3, 1919,

and were informed that a certain lawyer was appointed to defend them [who] did not consult with them, took no steps to prepare for their defense, [and] asked nothing about their witnesses, though there were many who knew that petitioners had nothing to do with the killing. . . .[4]

After a "joint trial before an exclusively white jury," in which only the state presented evidence—consisting of testimony that "was wholly false" and had been extracted by torture, death threats, and promises of leniency—

"the jury retired just long enough to write a verdict of guilty of murder in the first degree . . . —not being out exceeding two or three minutes. . . ."[5]

All during this trial and those of the other defendants:

> large crowds of white people bent on petitioners' condemnation and death thronged the courthouse and . . . the attorney appointed to defend them knew that the prejudice against them was such that they could not get a fair and impartial trial . . . yet he filed no petition for a change of venue[;] . . . all, Judge, jury and counsel were dominated by the mob spirit . . . so that if any juror had had the courage to . . . vote for an acquittal, he, himself, would have been the victim of the mob. . . .

If counsel had objected to the government's testimony on the grounds that it was extorted by torture, he would have suffered the same fate.

The court "lost its jurisdiction by virtue of such mob domination," and, although "carried through in the apparent form of law, . . . the verdict of the jury was really a mob verdict, . . . returned because no other verdict would have been tolerated." Indeed, "the entire trial, verdict, and judgment" were simply the implementation of the prior extralegal investigation and conclusions of the Committee of Seven.

After an attack on the all-white jury system,[6] the petitioners recounted the protests of the American Legion post and others to:

> show that the only reason the mob stayed its hand, the only reason they were not lynched was that the leading citizens of the community made a solemn promise to the mob that they should be executed in the form of law.

They added that the setting of their execution date the previous June had been to deter the mob from lynching the *Ware* defendants as they came up for retrial in May,[7] and concluded "that the mob spirit, mob domination, is still universally present in Phillips County."[8]

Thus, petitioners:

> were deprived of their rights and are about to be deprived of their lives in violation of Section 1 of the 14th Amendment of the Constitution of the United States and the laws of the United States enacted in pursuance thereto, in that they have been denied the equal protection of the law, and have been convicted, condemned, and are about to be deprived of their lives without due process of law.[9]

In a significant strengthening of the factual case that they had previously presented, the petitioners annexed the affidavits of two men who had been special agents of the Missouri-Pacific Railroad at the time of the riot, T. K.

Jones and H. F. Smiddy (later a local law enforcement officer), who was in the automobile with Clinton Lee when he was killed. Both men had assisted the Committee of Seven in its investigation and they provided detailed accounts of the whippings and other tortures they had personally inflicted, as well as eyewitness corroboration for almost all of the petitioners' other major allegations—including the allegation of actual innocence.[10]

In response to this petition, the state tersely demurred, on the basis "that the said petition does not allege facts sufficient to entitle the petitioners to the relief prayed for," and moved for dismissal.[11]

In view of the significant consequences of the decision to adopt this course (which will become clear in the description of the Supreme Court argument below), it seems worthwhile pausing to wonder why it was made. Quite possibly, the simple answer is that this was the most viable tactical choice. Apart from the reality that any hearing—which would take place under the eyes of a well-informed press—would be at best highly embarrassing to the state, its counsel surely had every reason to believe that an unbiased federal judge would find the factual allegations of the petition to be true.[12] Hence, the government's most plausible strategy—and a reasonable one in view of *Frank*—was to attempt to win on the law.

In any event, the District Court, having heard oral argument on the dismissal motion, granted it in a summary order, and issued a certificate of probable cause to appeal.[13]

The bulk of the appellants' brief to the United States Supreme Court was devoted to a forceful discussion of the facts. Indeed, even the relatively few pages headed "The Law" concluded:

> If this Court on reading this petition, these affidavits and this record is not satisfied that if there ever was a case in which *habeas corpus* should be granted this is the case, no argument of counsel will convince them, and we submit with confidence that either *habeas corpus* should be granted in this case or *habeas corpus* is not a practical remedy for such outrages as the evidence in this case discloses.[14]

The strictly legal discussion consisted primarily of attempts to distinguish *Frank* on various grounds:

(a) "[T]he thing which distinguishes this case from the *Frank* case is that the Supreme Court of Arkansas did not pass on the question whether the allegations in the motion for a new trial . . . were true or not. The court assumed that they were true, and said it did not follow from them that the trial was *necessarily* unfair."[15]

(b) In *Frank*, those factual allegations of the petitioner which were found by the Georgia Supreme Court to have been supported by the facts—his absence from the verdict and two "expressions of feeling by spectators during the trial [which were] promptly repressed by the court"—did not, "in the opinion of the [U.S. Supreme Court] majority show such mob control of the court as denied the defendant due process of law."[16] But the "[v]ery far different . . . facts in this case" do make that showing.[17]

(c) By statute, the appellate jurisdiction of the Supreme Court of Arkansas in criminal cases is limited to matters of law.[18] "In the case at bar, the question whether the circumstances surrounding the trial were such as to render impossible a righteous verdict was primarily a question of fact. Hence the Supreme Court could not, without exceeding its jurisdiction, reverse the action of the circuit court in refusing a new trial."[19]

In *Frank*, the Court decided:

> that, in a situation like that now presented, a State cannot be said to have deprived an accused person . . . due process of law if it has provided an independent tribunal for the examination of his complaint and this tribunal, sitting in an atmosphere free from the allegedly disturbing elements, has held the complaint unfounded.

But the Arkansas statutory scheme "has made no provision of this kind," leaving an applicant for a new trial:

> nothing but the empty right to have the facts upon which his application is based passed upon by the very judge whose conduct is complained of, and that, too, only at a time when the adverse influences . . . must still be operative with all their force.[20]

Indeed, the brief suggested that "the Supreme Court of Arkansas was itself influenced by the same feeling that influenced the leaders of society throughout the region where these tragedies occurred."[21]

The state filed its brief simultaneously.[22] In addition to setting out the *Frank* opinion practically verbatim,[23] this argued that the issues being presented to the Court had been before it previously on the unsuccessful application to Justice Holmes for a writ of error,[24] so that "[a]ppellants are merely attempting to use a writ of habeas corpus to review alleged errors of law of the State Courts," contrary to *Frank's* holding that habeas corpus "*cannot be employed* as a substitute for the writ of error."[25] Petitioners would be entitled to habeas corpus only if the record were to "show on its face that the trial court was under the influence of mob domination . . . to such an extent that the effect thereof wrought a disillusion [*sic*] of the court."[26] In addition, several of the affidavits annexed to the petition (i.e., those of officers Jones and Smiddy described above) had never been before the state courts, and:

> [t]o sustain appellants' application . . . [on] said affidavits, would open an avenue for every person charged with a crime, to wait until he had exhausted his remedies in the State Courts [and] then open his masked batteries on the State Courts.[27]

Our knowledge of the oral argument has been greatly enhanced by the research of Professor Richard C. Cortner, who uncovered two illuminating letters at the Wisconsin State Historical Society.[28] The first, from an NAACP official to local counsel, summarizing the report of another NAACP official who was present, recounts:

> [T]he worthy Attorney General of Arkansas, Mr. Utley, in his nasal twang, set out . . . to argue the case before the Supreme Court as though he were talking to a petit jury in Phillips County. He started off by telling the court that it could do nothing else than throw out the cases because the attorneys for the appellants had made an error in attempting to bring the cases to that tribunal on a Writ of Habeas Corpus instead of on a Writ of Error. Mr. Justice Holmes sharply reprimanded Attorney General Utley at that point asking him in amazement if the Attorney General meant to say that since the members of the jury, the presiding judge and every person involved in the trial had figuratively and almost literally pistols pressed against their breasts demanding conviction of the defendants, the court had no right to inquire into whether or not the men had had a fair trial. All the Attorney General could do was to hastily disclaim any such statement which he did in a very embarrassed manner.
>
> The only comment of any of the justices which savored of unfavorable opinion was that of Mr. Justice McReynolds from Tennessee. He said that undoubtedly the men had not received a fair trial but that he was not at all sure that the attorneys had properly handled the case. The cases lie "on the laps of the gods", but we here feel very optimistic as to the decision. I hope that we shall not be disappointed.[29]

The second is from one of the counsel who argued the case for petitioners to the author of the previous letter:

> I feel very hopeful for a reversal. The indications which I observed from the Court's remarks, made me feel that they were convinced of the equity of our

plea. The only remark made during the whole proceeding which could be construed as in any way raising a question as to the possible outcome was made by Justice [Mc]Reynolds. He said that it appeared to be a rotten deal and that the only question was as to whether it was in their power to give the relief prayed for. Justice Holmes inquired of the Assistant Attorney General from Arkansas in this manner, "You do not contend that if the whole affair was a mere sham, that however regular the proceedings may have been, this Court would be deprived of the right of going into the case and granting the relief?."

Just as [cocounsel] was concluding, Justice Holmes said to him, "Your contention is that the whole procedure was one dominated by a mob and that the conditions surrounding the trial [were] such as to render the whole trial a nullity, and that under the decisions of this Court in such cases, we have the jurisdiction and it is our duty to give relief." Judge Taft said to the attorney representing the State, during the argument, "Yes, but you demurred to the petition thereby admitting the allegations of the bill."

From this you will see that the indications were that the Court was not in sympathy with the claimof the State.

. . . In the limited time [allowed for my argument], I endeavored to get a mental picture in the minds of the Court as to the exact conditions in Arkansas. I told the Court that conditions had grown up there that were worse than before the Civil war; that I spoke from my knowledge gained during my 12 years experience as a legal representative of the Department of Justice. I then gave them an insight as to the brutality administered to the prisoners and then wound up with the treatment that was accorded my son, and the conduct of the Judge in getting him away from Helena; all showing that the conditions were such that it was preposterous to have imagined a fair trial was had.

I referred to the fact that wholesale murders on the part of the whites were committed by the killing of some 200 innocent Negroes, and that not a single indictment had been returned; that if the influence of those in control of the Court was such as to prevent an indictment, the same influence was sufficient to indict and condemn the Negroes that they had marked for execution.

[Cocounsel] told the Court that if the record did not warrant the relief demanded, that part of the Constitution should be eliminated as it would mean nothing. [He] feels, as I do, very sanguine of success.[30]

After argument, Holmes circulated a draft opinion that is substantially the one that was eventually published, having drawn minimal editorial comment from those prepared to join it.[31]

Justice Van Devanter, who was home ill,[32] wrote to Chief Justice Taft:

I sent the opinion in the Arkansas habeas corpus case to Justice McReynolds. I could not well read the changes suggested, but they were read to me, and I rather doubt that there is enough in them to have any particular trouble about them. As you say, the opinion has been framed on a line which makes it almost impossible to write in anything that is worth while; and the more I think about it the more I am disposed to believe that the opinion will not constitute an unhappy precedent.[33]

Except for Brandeis,[34] no majority Justice ever suggested, either on or off the bench, so far as I am aware, that *Moore* represented an alteration in the law of habeas corpus. In particular, Holmes, the central figure in this drama, who had freely expressed his distress over *Frank*,[35] said virtually nothing about *Moore* in his correspondence, even while discussing other cases decided at the same time.[36]

In any event, the published *Moore* opinion, representing the views of six Justices, consists principally of a summary of the allegations of the petition and a statement of the procedural history. Virtually the whole of its legal analysis is this:

> In *Frank v. Magnum* . . . it was recognized that if in fact a trial is dominated by a mob so that there is an actual interference with the course of justice, there is a departure from due process of law. . . . We assume in accordance with that case that the corrective process supplied by the state may be so adequate that interference by *habeas corpus* ought not to be allowed. It is certainly true that mere mistakes of law in the course of a trial are not to be corrected in that way. But if the case is that the whole proceeding is a mask —that counsel, jury and judge were swept to the fatal end by an irresistible wave of public passion, and the State Courts failed to correct the wrong, neither perfection in the machinery for correction nor the possibility that the trial court and counsel saw no other way of avoiding an immediate outbreak of the mob can prevent this Court from securing to the petitioners their constitutional rights. . . .
>
> We shall not say more concerning the corrective process afforded to the petitioners than that it does not seem to us sufficient to allow a Judge of the United States to escape the duty of examining the facts for himself when if true as alleged they make the trial absolutely void.[37]

The dissent, written by Justice McReynolds and joined by Justice Sutherland, said that the "right and wholesome" doctrine of *Frank*, reached "after great consideration," should be applied rather than being put aside in favor of "the views expressed by the minority of the Court in that cause."[38] On reviewing the record—including the low character of the affiants relied upon, the two prior applications to the Court,[39] the fact that the American Legion and other protests to the Governor came a year after trial, and the actions of the Arkansas Supreme Court in twice reversing the convictions of the *Ware* defendants—the dissent found itself:

> unable to say that the District Judge, acquainted with local conditions,[40] erred when he held the petition for the writ of *habeas corpus* insufficient. His duty was to consider the whole case and decide whether there appeared to be substantial reason for further proceedings.[41]

After the decision, which "produced relatively few editorial comments in the national press,"[42] the momentum behind the Elaine riot cases began to dissipate. The *Ware* defendants were released after a court ruling that the prosecution had delayed too long in bringing them to trial.[43] In light of this development, and with neither side eager to actually push the federal habeas proceedings to a hearing,[44] much less to undergo a possible retrial of the underlying charges, a series of negotiated arrangements led to a gubernatorial order commuting the sentences of the *Moore* defendants to twelve years' imprisonment, and then to another, in January 1925, releasing them.[45]

15

Frank v. Moore: The Legal and Historical Explanations

Legal scholars have long differed irreconcilably in their explanations of the disparate outcomes of *Frank* and *Moore* in the Supreme Court of the United States. There are three leading theories.

Paul M. Bator, a conservative Harvard Law School professor whom we shall see again in Part III, argued that the *Moore* "case is entirely consistent with *Frank*." He claimed that Frank lost because:

> the prisoner's allegations were considered by the Georgia Supreme Court under conditions which were concededly free from any suggestion of mob domination and found by that court, on independent inquiry to be groundless,

while

> in *Moore*, unlike in *Frank*, the state supreme court did not conduct any proceedings or make any inquiry into the truth of the allegations of mob domination, and made no findings with respect to them.

Thus, *Frank* presented a situation in which the state courts had delivered "reasoned findings rationally reached through fair procedures," resulting in "a reasoned probability that justice was done," while in *Moore* there was:

> a conclusory and out-of-hand rejection by a state court of a claim of violation of federal right, without any process of inquiry being afforded at all, [which] cannot insulate the merits of the question from the federal habeas court.[1]

To Bator, then, the cases spoke to the scope of federal habeas corpus review,[2] and were consistent.

To Gary Peller, a Georgetown law professor whose views are closely aligned with those of Justice Brennan, in contrast, the two cases dealt with the substantive requirements of due process. In *Frank*:

[b]y allowing a procedurally adequate state *appellate* hearing to satisfy due process requirements, the Court reduced constitutional claims available to a state prisoner on direct Supreme Court, or habeas, review.

In *Moore*, "the due process doctrine of *Frank* was overturned," and the Court held that "regardless of the nature of the state's appellate review," an allegation of a mob-dominated trial stated a claim under the Due Process Clause. Thus, the "dispositive difference between *Frank* and *Moore* was the Court's view of the requirements of the due process clause," with *Moore* returning "due process law to its pre-*Frank* state."[3]

Criticizing both of these views, Professor James S. Liebman of Columbia Law School, today's best-known scholar of habeas corpus, finds that from "*Frank* to *Moore*, it was not habeas corpus or due process that changed, but rather federal question appellate review." In *Frank*, the question of mob domination was treated as one of fact, and therefore not to be reviewed in a federal appellate court, on direct appeal or by habeas corpus, whereas in *Moore* the majority accepted the view that Justice Holmes had articulated in his *Frank* dissent and characterized the issue as a "mixed question"; then, applying in the criminal context a doctrine of appellate review it had already articulated in the realm of economic liberties, it granted de novo review.[4]

While each scholar's perspective captures important aspects of the cases, none is fully explanatory. Bator's view ignores the fact that, even in *Frank*, it was agreed on all hands that, regardless of the state processes, the federal court *could* examine the merits; the disagreement was over whether it *should* do so. Peller fails to recognize that all Justices in both cases agreed that actual mob intimidation of a jury was a due process violation; and his additional statement that *Moore* returned due process law to its pre-*Frank* state on this point is unsupported by the authority cited.

Liebman, perhaps misled by Holmes's elaboration for rhetorical reasons in *Frank* of a point on which there was actually no disagreement,[5] fails to recognize that all Justices considered the issue of mob domination to be one of fact.[6] Moreover—in the most important holding of *Frank*, whose poor reputation among friends of habeas corpus surely owes more to the drama of the surrounding facts than to the legal doctrine it articulated—all the Justices recognized the power of the District Court to conduct an independent investigation of the facts.[7] But in neither *Frank* nor *Moore* was the Court engaged in appellate review of lower court findings of fact; in both, it was reviewing the summary dismissal of a petition and deciding whether there should be a hearing—a purely legal question.[8]

And to that purely legal question of when the District Court should exercise its conceded power, the answer was frustrating but clear: it depends. More formally, the Court unanimously agreed in *Frank* that the decision to invoke the power to conduct a plenary hearing was a discretionary one. One factor in the exercise of discretion was to be the procedural rigor of the state's appellate process. Another was to be the outcome of that process. For the majority, the completeness of the record supplied by the petitioner was another. Others were left unstated, but plainly existed.[9]

The Supreme Court split in *Frank* occurred only when, proceeding on a de novo basis,[10] it applied its discretion to the particular situation at hand. The majority believed that, on balance, a hearing should not be held; the dissenters believed the opposite. The split was not over the rule but over its application.

This explanation is consistent with the known facts. It is consistent with the language of *Frank*, and with the arguments counsel made in that case. It is consistent with the state's concession on oral argument in *Moore* that the District Court could inquire into the facts.[11] It is consistent with both opinions in *Moore*—the majority, which reiterates and applies the rule that a corrective state appellate process is one factor to be considered, but holds that other circumstances had greater weight in the case at hand[12]—and the dissent, which states that the duty of the District Judge "was to consider the whole case and decide whether there appeared to be substantial reason for further proceedings."[13]

All the Justices in *Moore* not only stated but acted as though they were simply applying the established law. And that phenomenon makes sense if one takes the established law as being that the decision at hand was discretionary. Of course, on that view, the *Moore* Court would have been applying the established law even if every Justice on it would have decided *Frank* the other way. This might suggest as an objection to my argument that the rule it proposes is so broad as to be meaningless. But that is not an objection to the accuracy of the rule. Although it certainly does indicate that the standard is one that may be less than useful for predictive purposes, that is true as well of many other legal norms on which important decisions may turn. For instance, the basic legal measure of whether or not someone acted negligently is simply whether he or she exercised "the level of care customarily exercised by an ordinarily prudent person."

Still, if an amorphous legal standard is an unsatisfying explanation for why one case came out one way and another seemingly identical case came out differently, is there a better explanatory tool available?

A few months after *Moore* was decided, Felix Frankfurter asked Justice Brandeis[14] how it had come about that "the Frank case was departed from." The Justice replied, "Well—Pitney was gone, the late Chief was gone, Day was gone—the Court had changed."[15]

Without recorded pause, he continued with some general ruminations, not seemingly linked to *Moore* in particular:

Pitney had a great sense of justice affected by Presbyterianism but no imagination whatever. And then he was much affected by his experience & he had had mighty little. . . .

The new men—P. B. [Pierce Butler] and Sanford—are still very new. It takes three or four years to find oneself easily in the movements of the Supreme Court. Sanford's mind gives one blurs; it does not clearly register. Taft is the worst sinner in wanting to "settle things" by deciding them when we ought not to, as a matter of jurisdiction. He says, "we will have to decide it sooner or later and better now." I frequently remind them of [the] Dred Scott case—Sutherland also had to be held in check. McR. [McReynolds] cares more about jurisdictional restraints than any of them—Holmes is beginning to see it.

Of course there are all sorts of considerations that affect one in dissenting—there is a limit to the frequency with which you can do it, without exasperating men; then there may not be time, *e.g.* Holmes shoots down so quickly & is disturbed if you hold him up;[16] then you may have a very important case of your own as to which you do not want to antagonize on a less important case etc. etc.

McR. is a very extraordinary personality—what matters most to him are personal relations, the affections. He is a *Naturmensch*—he has very tender affections and correspondingly hates. He treated Pitney like a dog—used to say the cruelest things to him. . . . But no one feels P's sufferings more now, not as a matter of remorse but merely a sensitiveness to pain. He is a lonely person, has few real friends, is dilatory in his work.[17]

What is revealing here, of course, is the extent to which Brandeis locates the influences affecting the work of the Court almost everywhere but in legal considerations.[18] And, indeed, an explanation that emphasizes the ephemeral contingencies of quotidian reality may come closest to capturing as accurately as we can why a particular court decision turned out as it did.

Yet the adventitious features of decisions and decision makers are just the factors that the rules of legal discourse prohibit from being used as explanatory factors.[19] And these rules serve important values: they force legal argument to rest on generally accessible data and facially neutral considerations.

Moreover, such a paradigm responds to the powerful instinct—shared by pigeons[20] and people alike,[21] and doubtless particularly strong in legal actors—to find that the forces exercising power in one's environment are rational, predictable, and perhaps controllable.

Perhaps the way to give both the aleatory and rational factors their due is to view the matter from the perspective of the future. As time passes, the force of contingent contemporary pressures fades, and legal rules must prove their merits on other grounds. At the time it is rendered, the immediate personal and political context of any Supreme Court opinion will naturally have primacy in the understandings of contemporary actors. But the individuals involved—the litigants, the lawyers, and even the scholars—will die. And as the passions and memories of the contemporary context fade, they will have less and less influence on the opinion's survival, which will depend increasingly on its intellectual and practical power as a tool of persuasion in the context of new controversies. In short, what is left will be legal argument.

Thus, to say that one legal theory or another provides a more persuasive explanation for the differing outcomes of *Frank* and *Moore* is to say a good deal, even if one is thinking historically. For it is that explanation—and not the one closer to capturing the texture of the contemporary events of the past in the Brandeis sense—that is likely to have the most impact on the future.

This insight, however, may be of limited use to legal actors who consider the brevity of their own lifespans, particularly to those legal actors who must put bread on the table through legal practice while awaiting the vindication of history. Fortunately, even over the shorter term, law is at least an element in outcome of decisions, and therefore entitled to some predictive weight. And even the broadest of legal rules gain predictive power as they are applied in decided cases to specific fact patterns, and as their underlying principles are explored through legal and public dialogue.

To be sure, at the time a case is decided, no legal actor—not even the judge making the ruling—can know with precision just how decisive legal principles were to the decision.[22] In the field of habeas corpus, it may well be that most accurate way to predict outcomes over the past 15 years would have been uniformly to place the bet that the petitioner would lose,[23] just as it may be that the most statistically accurate way to predict the outcome of cases in general would be to bet on a victory for the party with the most money. But over time law, as a human creation, changes. And it changes because of the efforts of individuals to persuade judges through the use of rational arguments—including cogent historical arguments. Thus, historical accuracy matters not just to history, and not just to law as an academic field, but to the course of future events.

Returning to the subject at hand, an examination that integrates historical evidence and legal argument leads to the conclusion that the power of a federal habeas corpus court to conduct an independent investigation of the facts claimed to render a state conviction unconstitutional was firmly established by *Frank* and strengthened by *Moore*.

Part III

16

Introduction to Part III

Notwithstanding the deep historical roots of the searching review on federal habeas corpus of state criminal convictions, opponents of the practice seek to undermine its legitimacy by portraying it as a recent innovation. To do so, they have seized upon a remarkably unlikely target, *Brown v. Allen*.[1] Crediting a law review article by Professor Paul M. Bator of Harvard, who was introduced in the last chapter, they have sought to suggest that this 1953 case—in which all relief was denied to the state prisoners before the Court, even though each of them had been sentenced to death and presented extremely sympathetic claims on the merits—revolutionized the ability of the federal courts to examine the constitutionality of state criminal convictions.[2]

That is simply untrue, as this Part will show. Chapter 17 lays out Bator's claims and the procedural background of *Brown*. Chapter 18 begins a review of seven collections of Justices' papers—which include two sets of notes of the critical Court conference. This examination demonstrates that the Justices did not view themselves as making new law concerning the scope of the writ. Indeed, they went out of their way not to do so. All of the Justices (except Jackson, who—egged on by his clerk William Rehnquist— sought without allies to revise existing law and narrow the writ) were working within a consensus that the substantive nature of the inquiry that a federal habeas corpus court should make into the constitutionality of prior state criminal proceedings was simply not on the table.

Throughout the Court's deliberations, the central question was the effect that a denial of certiorari from state court proceedings should have in a subsequent federal habeas corpus action. The ruling was that the requirement of filing a certiorari petition, recently imposed by *Darr v. Burford*[3] would be retained, but that the federal habeas corpus court should attribute no significance to its denial.

A secondary question was the degree to which the District Court hearing the federal habeas petition could rule on it summarily (meaning, as a practical matter, deny it)[4] simply on the basis of the state court record. Here, the Justices, unable to join a common opinion notwithstanding their lack of any substantive disagreement, wrote cloudy language leaving the decision as to whether to hold an evidentiary hearing to the District Courts' good judgment. The progress of drafts led to softening and compromise, and, ultimately, the same amorphous standard of discretion whose origins we examined in Part II.

The question of whether or not the federal courts should, in Bator's words, "redetermine the merits of federal constitutional questions decided in state criminal proceedings"[5] was not a point of contention. No one doubted that, as had been clear since *Frank*, or, at the very least since *Moore*, this was precisely their role.[6] To the extent the matter arose, the Justices' editorial changes were intended to insure that the opinions reaffirmed that role. Only Jackson, whose views (along with those of Rehnquist) are presented in Chapter 19, sought to constrict it. The resulting Court opinions are described in Chapter 20.

As Chapter 21 discusses, developments in the period surrounding the decision do not support the thesis that it worked a broadening of the writ. Contemporaries did not believe that a major change had occurred, and the long-running battles over federal habeas corpus continued, in the legislative and judicial arenas, just as they had before. Nor do statistics show that the ruling triggered a landslide of successful petitions; indeed, there is reason to believe that, by reducing the number of evidentiary hearings, its immediate impact was the opposite.

In short, as Chapter 22 describes (and as most of today's Justices recognize)[7] *Brown* fits smoothly into a line of precedent extending back to *Frank* and *Moore*. The only legal point that *Brown* permanently decided—that the denial of certiorari on direct appeal was not preclusive of federal habeas corpus review—was a logical incremental step in the evolution of the writ,[8] at most,[9] and concerned procedure not substance. *Brown* did not change the scope of the review a prisoner could obtain, but rather was designed to make sure that, whatever its scope, the review would be meaningful; the Supreme Court did not have the institutional capacity to scrutinize the merits of prisoners' Constitutional claims on certiorari, so the task was to be performed by the District Courts on habeas corpus.[10] Bator's contrary, substantive theory—that independent federal habeas corpus review of the Constitutional validity of state criminal convictions is a modern innovation attributable to *Brown*—is not only contrary to the historical evidence that has already been presented, but inconsistent with the record of *Brown* itself.

17

Backdrop to the Construction of a Piltdown Man

A. Professor Bator Meets Dr. Rorschach

When the Justices released *Brown*, "[m]ore than 40,000 words and six separate documents were required to set forth their concurrences, dissents, and separate opinions."[1] This kaleidoscopic production received withering reviews. A commentator in the journal of the Philadelphia Bar Association mourned that "that peerless wit Mr. Dooley (Finley Peter Dunne)" was no longer on the scene to do full justice to the case, and described "the number and length of opinions filed, the uncertainty as to the result, and the confusing alignment of the Justices" as follows:

> Mr. Justice Reed announced the judgment of the Court. He also handed down a 15,000-word opinion covering two—or is it three?—principal points of law. On the first point (namely, what consideration should lower courts give to a denial of certiorari by the Supreme Court), his opinion states that it is *not* the opinion of the Court. As far as anyone outside the Court can tell, one of Mr. Justice Frankfurter's *two* opinions in the case reflects the Court judgment and reasoning on this first point (although there is a vocal, if not too clearly identified, minority).
>
> On the other points, Mr. Justice Reed wrote—or at least so it seems—for himself, the Chief Justice, and Justice Minton, without reservation (excepting of course those stated or implied in the opinion itself). Mr. Justice Reed's *judgment* suited Mr. Justice Jackson, but the Reed opinion did not, so there is a Jackson opinion concurring in the judgment only.
>
> Mr. Justice Burton and Mr. Justice Clark joined in the judgment of the Court, but not in the Reed opinion in its entirety—in fact, they seem to adhere to one of Mr. Justice Frankfurter's opinions, at least on the first point of law. They did not, however, join Mr. Justice Frankfurter's second opinion (apparently dissenting on the merits), but that opinion was joined by Mr. Justice Black and Mr. Justice Douglas.
>
> Of course, Mr. Justice Black also wrote a dissent on the merits, and Mr.

Justice Douglas joined in the Black opinion too. This accounts for all the writing in the case, except that one of Mr. Justice Frankfurter's opinions has a voluminous Appendix, which seems to speak only for him.

[C]omment, in legal circles and elsewhere, has been . . . biting.

[T]here does not now seem to be any sound basis for hope that the real "last word" is any closer than it was in Mr. Dooley's day.[2]

That evaluation would seem to be the sensible response to a fragmented decision. But, as Justice Douglas later commented, the *Brown* "opinions were so long, and so discursive that one could find in them what he was looking for."[3]

Enter Professor Bator. Ten years after the decision came down, he pronounced that the Court had taken a "radical" step without "any apparent understanding" of its significance:

with only Mr. Justice Jackson disagreeing, eight of the nine Justices assumed that on federal habeas corpus federal district courts must provide review of the merits of constitutional claims fully litigated in the state-court system.

Bator claimed that in *Brown* the Court had suddenly and silently decided "that it is the purpose of the federal habeas corpus jurisdiction to redetermine the merits of federal constitutional questions decided in state criminal proceedings,"[4] rather than to assess the adequacy of the state's corrective process.

To adopt this theory has always required not only a capacity to ignore the history already presented, but also a certain willingness to suspend disbelief: the idea that a permanent revolution in the law of habeas corpus took place because of an unexamined novel assumption silently shared by eight Justices who collectively wrote six opinions in a controversial area of the law is implausible at best. This would certainly be a unique way for major doctrinal change to occur.

In any event, we now have direct evidence that the theory is wrong, as the next chapter shows. But, to make that presentation understandable, the remainder of this chapter first sets forth the legal problems that were before the Court in *Brown*.

B. The Legal Background

1. Darr v. Burford

In April, 1950, Justice Reed, writing for five members of the Court (with Justice Douglas not participating), held in *Darr v. Burford*[5] that, except in unusual circumstances,[6] a state prisoner was required to seek certiorari from the denial of state collateral relief before filing a federal habeas corpus petition.[7] At the same time, however, five of the Justices made clear in dicta their view that, this requirement having been complied with, the denial of certiorari should be given no weight by the District Court when passing upon the subsequent habeas corpus application.[8] The *Darr* opinion—inconsistent with one that had come down two years earlier[9] and rendered in a case that had not been argued orally[10]—proved very confusing to the lower federal courts,[11] some of which concluded that the District Court should proceed to examine the federal habeas corpus petition de novo, and others of which believed that the denial of certiorari was a factor of greater or lesser weight to be considered against the prisoner.[12]

The Supreme Court—as it said twice in print,[13] and as is clear throughout the records of its internal deliberations—was primarily seeking in *Brown* to resolve this problem.

2. The Decisions Below

Brown originated in five certiorari petitions granted in March, 1952:[14]

a. *Smith v. Baldi.* Although ultimately decided in a separate published opinion,[15] this case is of some significance in untangling the meaning of *Brown*. First, it represents the first post-*Brown* application of *Brown*. Second, we have the Court's own word[16] that certiorari was originally granted in this case, in tandem with the others, primarily to determine what effect should be given in federal habeas corpus proceedings to the Court's prior action in denying certiorari from state habeas proceedings.[17]

The Court acted sensibly in separating this case from the others, since it had an extensive prior history and raised a number of significant issues on the merits, but for our purposes it may be summarized rather briefly.

In January, 1948, James Smith, who had a long history of mental illness, shot and killed the driver of a taxi in which he was riding as a passenger.[18] He appeared at his arraignment without counsel, and the judge asked a lawyer who happened to be present in the courtroom to advise him. "This lawyer, who knew nothing about petitioner, advised him to enter a plea of 'not guilty.'"[19] The effect of this was that Smith lost the right to have a preliminary jury determination of sanity.[20] He eventually pleaded guilty as part of an arrangement to obtain evidence from out of state concerning his psychiatric condition (because under Pennsylvania law he was not entitled to the appointment of a defense psychiatrist), and evidence on this issue was then presented to a three-judge trial court as bearing upon sentence; although it remained in dispute when or on what basis he had been found guilty (and, implicitly, sane), this panel sentenced him to death.[21]

On direct appeal, the conviction and sentence were affirmed.[22] Smith did not seek certiorari, but filed a federal habeas corpus petition; an en banc District Court held an evidentiary hearing, but eventually the writ "was denied on the ground that the petitioner was not within the jurisdiction of the court at the time the proceeding was instituted,"[23] having been removed to the execution site.[24] After affirmance by the Third Circuit,[25] no Supreme Court review was sought.[26] "A petition for habeas corpus was then filed in the State Supreme Court. This was entertained on the merits and denied,"[27] and certiorari was denied.[28]

Smith again sought federal habeas corpus, asserting the same claims as in the state habeas petition.[29] The District Court once more convened en banc, and denied the writ on a 4–3 vote. The majority wrote:

> [I]t is the law that where remedies are available under state law and the highest state court has considered and adjudicated the merits of the relator's contentions, including a full and fair adjudication of the federal contentions raised, and the United States Supreme Court has either reviewed or declined to review the state court's decision, then the district courts will not ordinarily, upon writ of habeas corpus, re-examine the questions thus adjudicated. *Ex Parte Hawk*, 321 U.S. 114, 118 [(1944)]; . . . Parker, *Limiting the Abuse of Habeas Corpus*, 8 F.R.D. 171, 174, 175-78 [(1949)].[30]

Smith had, to be sure, met the requirements of *Darr* by filing a certiorari petition after the denial of state collateral relief, and the court would give "no legal significance" to the denial of certiorari; but, "[i]n a valid exercise of sound judicial discretion, we decline to re-examine, upon writ of habeas corpus, the questions . . . adjudicated" in the state collateral proceedings.[31] The dissenters considered this disposition "premature," and would have held a hearing.[32]

On appeal to the Third Circuit sitting en banc, a four-member majority agreed with the lower court's treatment of *Darr*, but continued:

> That [petitioner's] allegations have been decided on the merits by the highest state court is a fact to be given great weight by a district court in passing upon petitions for habeas corpus. But that fact does not relieve the federal court of the duty to pass upon the merits of the petition. The District Court exercised its "discretion" to decline to pass upon the merits. We do not think it had

such discretion, and proceed to consider whether, if factually true, the petition sets forth a violation of the federal constitution.[33]

On the merits, the majority thought that there had been no Constitutional violation, while the dissent by Chief Judge Biggs—which documented at length Smith's mental disabilities and the procedural miasma in which their consideration had been lost—argued the contrary.

At this stage, in March, 1952, the Supreme Court granted certiorari.[34]

b. *McGee v. Ekberg*. Although this case, too, ultimately formed no part of the published *Brown* decision, having been dismissed as moot in June, 1952, on the release of the prisoner,[35] it is also of significance to a proper understanding of *Brown* because it framed the issues eventually decided by the Court.

James Nel Ekberg, who had a long criminal history, was convicted in a California trial court of check fraud and weapons possession after a jury trial in which he was represented by counsel; on his pro se direct appeal, the conviction was affirmed in a reasoned opinion that systematically rejected various claims of error, including some framed in Constitutional terms.[36] According to the government, Ekberg did not seek certiorari, but rather filed a state habeas corpus petition, which was denied without opinion.[37] He sought certiorari from this decision, which was denied.[38]

Ekberg, again acting pro se, thereupon filed a petition for a writ of habeas corpus in the United States District Court for the District of California.[39] The most cogent federal claims presented in this rambling document were that Ekberg had been denied counsel of his choice, represented incompetently by trial counsel, and denied the right to call certain witnesses in his defense.[40] The petition and an application to file it in forma pauperis came before the District Judge, who denied them in an order that recited the procedural history and continued:

> Where a state court has considered and adjudicated the merits of a petitioner's contentions a federal court will not ordinarily re-examine upon writ of habeas corpus the issues thus adjudicated. The state of California affords remedies which give due process of law and there is nothing alleged which presents "exceptional circumstances of peculiar urgency" which entitle him to the issuance of the writ. *Ex parte Hawk*, 321 U.S. 114 [,117-18 (1944)]; *U.S. ex rel. Kennedy v. Tyler*, 269 U.S. 13 [,17 (1925)]. This being the situation this court should deny the right to file the petition in forma pauperis and it is so ordered.[41]

On appeal, the Ninth Circuit reversed in an opinion by Chief Judge William Denman, who, as will be seen in Chapter 21, was a prominent liberal supporter of the writ.[42] The Court of Appeals held that "special circumstances" were required only in the case of an applicant who had not exhausted his state remedies; a petitioner who had done so, and pleaded a violation of federal Constitutional rights, was entitled to have the District Court review the state court record; accordingly, the Ninth Circuit remanded the matter to the District Court for consideration on the merits.[43] In March, 1952, the Supreme Court granted the government's petition seeking review of this ruling.[44]

The remaining three cases all began as criminal prosecutions in the North Carolina courts that were challenged by federal habeas corpus petitions in the United States District Court for the District of North Carolina and then in the United States Court of Appeals for the Fourth Circuit. They were, "for the most part handled as one, particularly in the District Court."[45] This is because each case had as a central element on the merits a challenge to the jury selection system that North Carolina had implemented to replace the one that the Supreme Court had, early in 1948, brusquely struck down as racially discriminatory in *Brunson v. North Carolina*—an opinion consisting of the single word "Reversed," followed by a string citation to the Court's classic jury discrimination cases.[46]

The three cases were:

c. *Brown v. Allen*. Clyde Brown, an illiterate black youth, was arrested for the beating and rape of a white high school student.[47] He was held without charges for five days, during which time he confessed; not given a preliminary hearing until 18 days after his arrest; and not formally appointed counsel until three days after that.[48]

In connection with the trial court proceedings, which resulted in a conviction by an all-white jury and a mandatory death sentence,[49] he raised unsuccessful Fourteenth Amendment challenges to the voluntariness of his confession as well as to the allegedly racially discriminatory manner in which the grand and petit juries were selected in his case.[50] He renewed these contentions, also without success, on direct appeal to the North Carolina Supreme Court,[51] and in a petition for certiorari.[52]

His assertion of them in a federal habeas corpus petition met with a summary denial in the District Court, on the basis that the record did not reveal "any unusual situation" that would justify issuing the writ in the face of the reasoned rejection of the claims by the trial and appellate courts of the state and the Supreme Court's denial of certiorari on the same record.[53] The

Fourth Circuit affirmed in a brief opinion embracing this rationale. Deciding *Brown* and the *Speller* case described in the next section together, the panel (which included Chief Judge John J. Parker, a leading habeas opponent whom we will see again in Chapter 21), wrote:

> We think that the dismissal in both cases was clearly right [in] view of the action of the state Supreme Court upon the identical questions presented to the court below and the denial of certiorari by the Supreme Court of the United States.[54]

In March, 1952, the Supreme Court granted Brown's petition for certiorari.[55]

d. *Speller v. Allen.* Raleigh Speller, "an illiterate and feeble-minded Negro of about 46 years of age,"[56] was three times convicted of the rape of a 52-year-old white housewife and sentenced to death.[57] The first conviction was reversed because of racially discriminatory jury selection.[58] The second conviction was reversed on the basis that the defense had been denied a sufficient opportunity to investigate possible racial bias in the jury selection mechanism.[59] The third conviction was affirmed, in an opinion whose principal holding was that the trial court had acted properly when, after a full evidentiary hearing, it rejected Speller's challenge to the jury selection procedure.[60] Certiorari was denied.[61]

Speller thereupon pursued his challenge in a federal habeas corpus petition. Over the government's objections, the District Court held a hearing. This revealed, among other things, that the slips or "scrolls" containing the names of jurors that were drawn at random had dots on them showing the race of the jurors, and that of the 63 jurors summoned to attend Speller's trial four were black—6.3 percent, in a county in which 38 percent of the taxpayers were black.[62] (One of the blacks summoned actually reached voir dire, but was not selected.)[63] Following this hearing, the District Court dismissed the petition on the alternative bases, first, that a "habeas corpus proceeding is not available to the petitioner for the purpose of raising the identical question passed upon in [the state] Courts," and:

> secondly, that in any event, even if petitioner is now entitled to raise the same question passed on in the State Courts, he has failed to substantiate the charge that he did not have a trial according to due process.[64]

The Fourth Circuit affirmed in the brief opinion described at the end of the previous section,[65] and the Supreme Court granted certiorari in March, 1952.[66]

e. *Daniels v. Allen.* The cousins Lloyd Ray Daniels and Bennie Daniels, two illiterate black teenagers, were each arrested before dawn on a February morning and imprisoned on suspicion of the brutal murder of a white taxi-cab driver, a crime that had strongly outraged the local community.[67] After having been found mentally competent to stand trial, they were convicted and sentenced to death in proceedings that, they charged, had been flawed by the use of racially discriminatory procedures for the selection of their grand and petit juries, the admission of involuntary confessions that they had given while in custody, and the submission of instructions that precluded the jury from passing upon this latter issue.[68]

Their counsel was one day late in serving the record on the government, and thereby forfeited their appeal as of right.[69] The North Carolina Supreme Court:

(a) Declined to issue a discretionary writ of certiorari to allow an appeal nevertheless, but pointed out that the defendants could seek leave to file a writ of error coram nobis;[70]

(b) Denied such leave when the defendants did seek it, stating tersely that the petition did not "make a prima facie showing of substance" and was therefore "insufficient";[71] and

(c) Summarily dismissed the attempted direct appeal as untimely.[72]

The prisoners sought certiorari in the United States Supreme Court from all of these rulings.[73] The state opposed the petition on the grounds that there had been no ruling below on the Constitutional merits, and that petitioners still had an available state remedy by way of coram nobis.[74] Certiorari was denied.[75]

After a further unsuccessful coram nobis petition,[76] the prisoners sought federal habeas corpus. The warden moved to dismiss; the District Court denied the motion and heard evidence, but subsequently concluded:

that the decision overruling the respondent's motion to dismiss the writ as a matter of law upon the procedural history was erroneous, and that the motion should have been granted.[77]

The same Fourth Circuit panel that heard the prior two cases affirmed, on the grounds that habeas corpus could not be used in lieu of an appeal to assert claims of error, even Constitutional error, but was available only where there had been such a "gross violation of constitutional rights as to deny an accused the substance of a fair trial" under circumstances where "he has been unable to protect himself" by the ordinary mechanism of asserting his claims in state court.[78]

Dissenting, Judge Morris A. Soper contended that "special and unusual circumstances existed," since "the insistence by the state upon a technical and trivial procedural step" was blocking review on the merits of petitions whose contentions respecting jury selection were clearly correct—as the North Carolina Supreme Court's two reversals of Speller's convictions and the United States Supreme Court's ruling in *Brunson v. North Carolina* showed.[79] In March, 1952, the Supreme Court granted certiorari.[80]

18

The Drafting of *Brown*: The Core

The *Brown* cases were argued at the end of April, 1952.[1] Before taking the bench, apparently, Justice Burton wrote across the bottom of his law clerk's bench memo:

> It is not enough to say that fed question was presented to state court on habeas corpus and denied and then cert denied by USSC—for the factual conclusions in state ct may not have been so considered as to present the case adequately in court—and anyway cert. may have been denied for unrelated reasons (poor record, out of time etc). There is a constitutional and statutory right to have fed question passed on by fed ct.—and it is a fed ct rule that before doing so it must be passed by state cts. (including cert to USSC). Hence that routine is a qualifying routine rather than one binding on the merits, to omit a part of this routine would require explanation—but if it has been followed *no exceptional circumstances are needed for the hearing or for the decision.*[2]

The Court discussed the cases at a conference on May 3, 1952. Here, according to Justice Douglas's notes, Chief Justice Vinson stated as the:

> Question whether Denman's viewpoint or Parker's viewpoint[3] should prevail—we should work out a procedure whereby in some of the cases at least (not necessarily all) the bearings are set down. [I]t is suggested that Reed & FF who have opposing views prepare memorandum for the Conference on our precedents—.[4]

More tersely, Justice Burton recorded:

> Duel between Denman and Parker views.
> Frankfurter v. Reed
> RHJ suggests memos from both.[5]

On June 3, 1952, Justice Frankfurter circulated a memorandum beginning, "I give up."[6] He explained that he would be unable to complete his assignment—"a canvass of the issues involved in *Darr v. Burford* in light of the conflicting views that have arisen among the various circuits (both in the District Courts and the Courts of Appeals)"—before the conclusion of the Term, in light of the extensive work involved and the intervening distraction of the Steel Seizure Case.[7] He concluded by suggesting that, rather than being reargued (so as to preserve the fiction that the Court cleared its docket at the end of each Term), the cases simply be held over.

Because he "thought they might be useful in determining our course on Brother Frankfurter's suggestion," Justice Reed circulated on June 4 draft opinions in the cases, which "are not proofread and are obviously rough,"[8] being much more complete in their recitations of the procedural history than in their legal analysis. The key points were:

1. A District Court had the discretion on habeas corpus to give "such consideration to our denial" of certiorari on direct appeal "as that court feels the record justifies."[9]

2. In particular, it might rely on the denial to avoid a reexamination of the state's determination of the Constitutional issues:

> It is not necessary though they have the power for a federal court to try the merits, fact or law a second time, to assure protection of federal constitutional rights, a state trial with a right of review in this Court may furnish the necessary protection.[10]

Neither point survived the Justices' consideration. The ultimate *Brown* opinion squarely rejected the first.[11] And the second passage was modified before publication,[12] to make clear that which, according to Justice Reed, it had meant all along: that the federal court might defer to the state proceedings only on matters of fact, not law, and only if "the state process has given fair consideration to the issues and the offered evidence, and has resulted in a satisfactory conclusion."[13]

Justice Frankfurter, plainly conceiving the first problem to be the one at issue, responded on June 7 by circulating "tables [to] afford a bird's eye view of the procedural steps in three of the cases involved in our Habeas Corpus problem." He explained that, since "I had not conceived the assignment which was given to Stanley and me implied that we should rehash, more or less, what we had said in *Darr v. Burford*," he planned to compile similar procedural data:

> from the hundreds of cases in which review was sought here during the present Term of State convictions. The purpose is to ascertain what kind of issues, State or Federal, how unambiguously, and in what accessible form, they came here, in order to ascertain, with any degree of reason, what inferences may fairly be drawn from our denial of certiorari in such cases. . . . [O]nly by

such a quantitative study can we fairly deduce desirable rules of judicial administration by the Federal courts—this Court, in requiring certiorari to be applied for and the District Courts in order to ascertain the bearing of such denials by us upon federal habeas corpus jurisdiction—regardless of what we have said or have not said in the past.[14]

At the conference of June 7, 1952, there was "considerable argument" on whether or not to set the cases for reargument,[15] and it was eventually decided to do so.[16]

As the Justices reconvened in the fall, Justice Reed circulated a draft opinion dated September 26, 1952, a revision of his June 4 effort that reflected the additional legal analysis done over the summer.[17] One notable, albeit uncontroversial,[18] addition was a footnote[19] that, in language substantially similar to that contained in the final opinion,[20] rejected a statutory construction proposed by Judge Parker that would have severely limited the availability of federal habeas corpus by deeming it to be unavailable "in all states in which successive applications may be made for habeas corpus to the state courts," on the theory that in such states the petitioner could never exhaust state remedies as required by 28 U.S.C. § 2254 (1948).[21]

On October 13, 1952, as the four remaining cases were reargued, Justice Frankfurter circulated his:

> report of a study undertaken at the request of the Conference into the problem left open by *Darr v. Burford,* namely, the consequence of a denial of certiorari upon the disposition by a district court of a subsequent application for habeas corpus by a prisoner under State sentence.[22]

This consisted of a two-page covering memorandum and a lengthy appendix, presenting substantially the same empirical data that later appeared in the U.S. Reports,[23] which reported on an exhaustive survey of habeas corpus cases during a recent year. In a 23-page accompanying memorandum of the same date,[24] Justice Frankfurter argued with vigor the conclusions to be drawn from this work: (a) giving any weight to denials of certiorari would be senseless, since the papers before the Court were frequently unintelligible, and, in any event, not available to the District Court,[25] and (b) fears of abusive use of the writ were greatly exaggerated, since the prisoner had actually secured his release in only one of the 126 cases studied.[26]

On the question of how much reliance the District Court should place on prior state proceedings, the memorandum, in terms later echoed in Justice Frankfurter's published opinion,[27] responded that this was a discretionary judgment to be made on consideration of (a) the state of the available record and (b) the nature of the issue to be decided.[28] As to the record, Justice Frankfurter wrote that if:

> the record of the State proceedings is not filed or is found to be inadequate, the judge is required to decide, with due regard to efficiency in judicial administration, whether it is more desirable to call for the record or to hold a hearing. . . . When the record of the State court proceedings is before the Court, it may appear . . . that the facts . . . have been tried and adjudicated against the applicant. Unless a vital flaw be found in the process of ascertaining such facts in the State court, the District Judge will accept their determination in the State proceeding and deny the application.[29]

As to the nature of the issues, he articulated a tripartite scheme that was already well established:

> Where the dispute concerns the historical facts, the external events that occurred, a State adjudication upon them should be conclusive. On the other hand, some questions call for the exercise by the federal judge of independent judgment on what are clearly matters of law. . . . Where the ascertainment of the historical facts does not dispose of the claim but calls for interpretation of the legal significance of such facts, . . . the District Judge must exercise his own judgment on this blend of facts and their legal values. Thus, so-called mixed questions or the application of constitutional principles to the facts as found leave the duty of adjudication with the Federal Judge.[30]

On October 16, Justice Frankfurter circulated "Observations" on Justice Reed's memorandum of September 26:[31]

> This is a summary of what I get out of the memorandum after careful reading:
>
> > When a State convict applies for a writ of habeas corpus in a United States District court, that court, having informed itself of the content and meaning of the record made in the courts of the State which convicted him and on certiorari in this Court, should ordinarily deny the application without more. "Ordinarily," fairly interpreted, means that such an application should be denied without more, save in extraordinary or exceptional circumstances.
> >
> > This, together with discussion of the extraordinary circumstances alluded to, is designed to govern the exercise of discretion in the lower federal courts. It is meant to do so to the end that a minimum of interference with State administration of criminal justice may result. Putting to one side the question whether the interests of liberty to be served by the Great Writ should be subordinated to this one end, the difficulty with the rule [is that] it does not and cannot, with the clarity and definiteness appropriate to the problem, guide the exercise of discretion below. . . .

Let me put to one side those aspects of our central problem as to which there is, I assume, common ground among us: (1) The applicant for the writ in the federal district court must have exhausted his State remedies, whatever they are, though this does not mean that an applicant must have had recourse to all alternate remedies or repeated recourse to a single procedure if a State afford such repeated recourse. (2) Starting with the ruling in *Darr v. Burford*, the applicant, before he can go to a federal district court on habeas corpus, must have been refused opportunity to have the denial of his federal constitutional claim in the State court brought here for review. (3) The District Judge should derive what light he can from the *adjudication* in the State court.

Beyond these three aspects, Mr. Justice Reed and I part company, more particularly as to the legal significance which the District Judge is to give to a denial of certiorari here. . . .

Howsoever phrased, a rule presupposing that some fruitful legal conclusion is to be drawn from our denial of certiorari, as though an adjudication instead of a refusal to adjudicate were involved, will inevitably lead in the courts below to that very uncertainty and conflict to eliminate which we granted certiorari in these cases.[32]

The remainder of the memorandum elaborated on the point by showing that the District Judges in the present cases could "with equal reasonableness" have concluded that they did or did not present special circumstances justifying disregard of the Court's denial of certiorari.[33]

On October 17, 1952, Justices Reed and Frankfurter circulated a joint one-page memorandum suggesting:

that the Conference vote successively on the following two issues before voting on the results in these cases:

1. The bearing of the denial of certiorari here on what the district court should do with an application for habeas corpus.
2. The bearing of the adjudication by the State court of federal claims upon the district court's disposition of the application for habeas corpus.[34]

The cases were discussed preliminarily at the conference of October 18, 1952 (which revealed that a majority favored affirming the denial of habeas relief in each case),[35] and again more fully on October 27, 1952. Two Justices' notes record this latter conference. Justice Douglas wrote:

CJ—The bearing of the denial of cert. here on what the district court should do with an application for habeas corpus—CJ states that question as one governing this group of cases—

Black, FF, WOD, RHJ, HB & TC would give no weight to fact that we denied cert.; but there are a number of different reasons given for the conclusion. Reed & Minton think denial of cert. (though not res judicata) should be given weight—So does CJ where the federal question was made in the state record & presented here—

that case so far as the process that brought it here has been terminated—to compel the judge to have a plenary hearing in habeas corpus is unfair

—CJ would not give any weight in the case if unfairness where the issue of federal rights was not raised—

2. The bearing of the adjudication by the State court of federal claims upon the district court's disposition of the application for habeas corpus. On this Reed and F.F. as shown by their memos are in substantial agreement—Black agrees with FF's memo on this point—WOD does substantially—all agree.[36]

Justice Clark wrote:[37]

F.F.

1. Shall D.C. pay any attention to Denial? None.

Reed: Must wk out admin. syst on 3 qu=

1-No collateral relief sought in State Court-in Brown—§ 2254-as long as you can go before state judge must go there. This does not mean identical questions—Both agree -[38]

2. *Must* there be a *hearing* in Federal Court on what was done in State Court § 2244

Both say *NO*

3. Effect of former proceedings:

(1) *State record* has weight only on whatever is decided there on constitutional questions—where can get full record, *should* get full record not *always* necessary to call for record-that is discretionary

Both agree -

Differences:

Reed

1. Reed does not say res adjudicata for you can't have that in habeas corpus. DC *may give weight* to record before it including State & our record-(but his decision must not be on our denial) in examining this record he should see that same record is involved before him (*& in that case deny*)

2. What were our grounds for denial

FF on Differences:

Present Act (1867) DC authorized to *question illegal detention*

Ex parte Royal[39]—DC can come in anytime—habeas corpus more effective here than in England—old common law conception was whether court had jurisdiction (could the court try the type of case)

Johnson v. Zerbst—no counsel—then court had no jurisdiction-& habeas corpus would test it[40]

Give what weight you please to a denial of cert. see p. 15 memo 10/13/52-[41]

This discussion left Justice Frankfurter disturbed by what he considered an unduly restrictive approach to the writ, and concerned not with broadening it but with preventing a threatened narrowing of it.[42] He said so in a memorandum dated October 28, 1952:

> All things must come to an end and I should not like to be unmindful of the fact that crying over spilt milk is for children, not for grown men. . . . But since a case in this Court is not over until it is decided, I am venturing to put on paper what I did not get around to saying in yesterday's discussion regarding habeas corpus. . . .
>
> Callous and even cruel though it may seem, the fate of the four petitioners is to me a matter of little importance. What this Court may say regarding the writ of habeas corpus I deem of the profoundest importance. Put in a few words, it makes all the difference in the world whether we treat habeas corpus as just another legal remedy in the procedural arsenal of our law, or regard it as basic to the development of Anglo-American civilization and unlike other legal remedies, which are more or less strictly defined. . . . If such a conception is not merely to be rhetoric and is to be an ever-living process to be enforced, certain consequences follow which cannot be imprisoned within any such rubrics as "jurisdiction," or "habeas corpus is not a substitute for appeal," etc., etc. . . .
>
> I am not concerned with the concrete outcome of these cases—whether the judgments below are affirmed or not. I am profoundly concerned that in these days, when we boast at international conferences and otherwise through our political leaders, of habeas corpus as one of the great agencies of the Anglo-American world in safeguarding and promoting democracy,[43] this Court should not disregard the historic record, reflecting deep considerations of justice, and treat habeas corpus in a devitalizing manner as though it were construing merely one of the Rules of Civil Procedure. Marshall referred to the "obligation of providing efficient means by which this great constitutional privilege should receive life and activity." *Ex Parte Bollman*, 4 Cranch 75, 95. Congress has provided the means by the Act of February 5, 1867, 14 Stat. 385. I pray that this Court do not shrivel them because of fear of potential abuse, or even an occasional abuse which can be easily curbed without damage to the Great Writ.[44]

Justice Reed circulated draft opinions on December 4,[45] to which Justice Frankfurter responded in a memorandum dated December 19:

> The chief concern in the course we have pursued in connection with the habeas corpus cases has not been the disposition of these particular cases. . . .
>
> One vital point we have now definitively settled, namely that our denial

of certiorari has no significance in the exercise of the District Court's jurisdiction. . . .

I think I am accurate in saying that Stanley said he agreed with the views I
expressed regarding the relation of the State proceedings to proceedings in
the District Court. I am sorry to say, however, that I do not find this agreement reflected in his opinion. . . .

I have not dealt with the merits of these cases, that is, whether the judgments in these cases should be affirmed. I have not yet dealt with them even
in my own mind. I repeat, what we do with these specific cases is not the
major problem before us.[46]

Justice Frankfurter annexed a version of his memorandum of October
13, with the section dealing with the District Courts' treatment of prior
state proceedings revised to respond specifically to Justice Reed's draft. The
essence of these comments was that Justice Reed's formulations left the District Judge with too much scope to deny a habeas corpus application summarily, partially because they did not clearly reiterate the judge's duty to decide issues of law de novo, and partially because they seemed to allow the
judge too much room to make legal rulings in the absence of any factual
record at all (whether compiled in state court or at a federal habeas corpus
hearing):[47]

Mr. Justice Reed's opinion seems to me to disregard the command of Congress that the federal courts decide the legal questions raised in a petition for
habeas corpus. . . . [I]t would rub out the statute to say that the State determination of the legal question can be conclusive. Yet Mr. Justice Reed would
permit summary denial of the application if the District Judge is satisfied, "by
the record," that the State has given "fair consideration" to the issues, if the
record of the State proceedings is sufficient to make, and the District Judge
does make, the determination that "no unusual circumstances calling for a
hearing are presented," if he is satisfied that federal constitutional rights have
been protected, or, again, if he concludes that a hearing is not "proper." At
best, these expressions hardly make clear what the determination is that is to
be made.[48]

Justice Reed responded by insisting that no change in the current availability of the writ was intended, writing on December 24:

My draft opinion of December 4 was . . . not written with any purpose of
limiting access of state prisoners to the federal courts but rather to simplify
that access in situations covered by the statute.

When my memorandum in *Brown v. Allen* of September 26 was discussed at Conference with the memorandum of Justice Frankfurter, I felt that our views were not far apart on matters other than the weight to be given to our denial of certiorari. I still think this is true. . . .

There is a suggestion [in Justice Frankfurter's] Comment that my draft allows the "district judge summarily" to deny an application by accepting the rule of the state court. This was not intended by me nor do I think it can properly be said that my draft opinion does so. . . .[49]

My draft is intended to and I think does leave entirely open to the District Court to take up those unusual situations when in his views justice has not been done in the state courts. He must determine whether the record shows denial of constitutional rights; he must hold hearings if he is in doubt; and he may dismiss without a hearing if he has no doubt.[50]

When Justice Reed circulated a revised draft opinion on December 29, 1952,[51] it did not, Justice Frankfurter reported on December 31, "meet the points in my Memorandum of December 19":[52]

The uniqueness of *habeas corpus* in the procedural armory of our law cannot be too often emphasized. . . . Its history and function in our legal system and the unavailability of the writ in totalitarian societies are naturally enough regarded as one of the decisively differentiating facts between our democracy and totalitarian governments.[53]

It is inadmissible to deny the use of the writ merely because a State court has passed on a Federal constitutional issue.[54] It is equally inadmissible to leave each district judge effectively at large . . . by cloudy and confusing language as to what we expect from district judges. . . .

Is it asking too much to ask that if Brother Reed could sign, as he said he could, my formulations for guiding the district judges on pages 6–19 of my memorandum of December 19,[55] that he sign them? . . .

Let me now state explicitly why I cannot approve the revised opinion of Mr. Justice Reed on these matters. . . . I thoroughly agree that the habeas corpus procedure must be saved from abuse by excessive and repetitious applications, and I insist only that the statute does require us to insure that the State prisoner will have one opportunity to test his federal claim in the federal courts.[56] . . . I approach the problem with the same anxiety about abuse of the writ as does Mr. Justice Reed, and I have clearly delimited my standards to the one opportunity which the State prisoner is given by Congress. What I do insist is that we do not, by ambiguous or meaningless phrase, leave it open to the District Judge, if he is so disposed, to shut off that one opportunity. If we do, we would, as Mr. Justice Reed correctly infers, wipe out the practical efficacy of federal habeas corpus for State prisoners. . . .

II. It helps my understanding, if not that of a District Judge reading the opinion without libretto, to know that "the teaching" of Mr. Justice Reed's opinion is summarized in the excerpt he quotes on page 2 of his letter. I should be sorry if this were all we had been able to accomplish by two arguments and numerous circulations and conferences in these cases. But . . . should we leave resort to a hearing to the "discretion" of the District Judge without indicating some standards for the exercise of discretion?[57] On the other hand, is the statute satisfied by dismissal of an application when the State has given "fair consideration" to the issues? The congressional requirement is greater. The State court cannot have the last say when it, though on fair consideration and what procedurally may be deemed fairness, may have misconceived a federal constitutional right. . . .

V. My Memorandum certainly does not say that it is enough that the record shows that the merits received "fair consideration" in the State courts. . . . At the same time, I think often a "hearing" is unnecessary even when legal questions are involved that require a decision by the federal judge. . . .

It is at best awkward to have the Court's position on one aspect of the case—the nonsignificance of denial of certiorari here—expressed in a so-called dissenting opinion. Inasmuch as Brother Reed has said he can agree with what I have written as to the bearing of the proceedings in the State courts on the disposition of applications for the writ before the District Judge, I suggest an opinion *per curiam* to consist of the substance of what I have drafted on the general procedural issues and, since a majority of the Court is with Brother Reed on the merits, what he has written on the merits[, thus] . . . presenting in a single opinion the matters on which a majority of the Court, and therefore the Court, agree.[58]

On January 23, 1953, Justice Frankfurter circulated another draft of his opinion on the habeas issues.[59]

Also on January 23, Justice Black circulated a draft dissent on the merits.[60] Objecting to the Court's failure to review *Daniels* because of the one-day delay in serving the appeals papers, Justice Black wrote that:

the object of habeas corpus is to search records to prevent illegal imprisonments. Habeas corpus can have no higher function. To hold it unavailable under the circumstances here is to degrade it. I had thought that *Moore v. Dempsey*, 261 U.S. 86, would forbid this. Perhaps the Court's opinion overrules it. That case has stood for the principle that this Court will look straight through procedural screens to see if a man's life or liberty is being forfeited in defiance of the Constitution. I would follow that principle here.[61]

This passage provoked an immediate reaction from Justice Frankfurter. In a handwritten note also dated January 23, 1953, after praising Justice Black's "spirited piece of pithy writing," he continued, "I do beg of you, however, to cut the sentence . . . 'Perhaps the Court's opinion overrules it.'"[62] To "give needless ammunition to those who want to weaken the force of that opinion at least as a standard to which we can appeal" would, he suggested, not be "good intellectual strategy."[63]

Justice Black took the point. In a handwritten response, he thanked Justice Frankfurter and continued:

> I have never had an idea that it would be necessary to keep the line about Moore v. Dempsey—I hope it will provoke a denial—At any rate, I shall change the expression before the cases go down—.[64]

His next draft, circulated on January 28, 1953, removed the suggestion that *Moore* was anything other than good law:

> To hold [habeas corpus] unavailable under the circumstances here is to degrade it. I think *Moore v. Dempsey*, 261 U.S. 86 forbids this. That case stands for the principle that this Court will look straight through procedural screens to see if a man's life or liberty is being forfeited in defiance of the Constitution. I would follow that principle here.[65]

And in his final version, circulated on January 31, 1953,[66] which is the one that appears in print,[67] he elaborated on the point:

> To hold [habeas corpus] unavailable under the circumstances here is to degrade it. I think *Moore v. Dempsey*, 261 U.S. 86, forbids this. In that case Negroes had been convicted and sentenced to death by an all-white jury selected under a practice of systematic exclusion of Negroes from juries. The State Supreme Court had refused to consider this discrimination on the ground that the objection to it had come too late. This Court had denied certiorari. Later a federal district court summarily dismissed a petition for habeas corpus alleging the foregoing and other very serious acts of trial unfairness, all of which had been urged upon this Court in the prior certiorari petition. This Court nonetheless held that the District Court had committed error in refusing to examine the facts alleged. I read *Moore v. Dempsey, supra,* as standing for the principle that it is never too late for courts in habeas corpus proceedings to look straight through procedural screens in order to prevent forfeiture of life or liberty in flagrant defiance of the Constitution. . . . Perhaps there is no more exalted judicial function. I am willing to agree that it should not be exercised in cases like this except under special circumstances or in extraordinary situations. But I cannot join in any opinion that attempts to confine the Great Writ within rigid formalistic boundaries.

Meanwhile, the Court had been solidifying a consensus on the procedural issues that had been in the Justices' understandings but not their drafts. On January 27, Justice Frankfurter wrote to Justice Burton that his key objection to Justice Reed's draft was "I don't want District Judges to assume that merely because a federal claim has been examined in the State courts, it need not be examined even once in a federal court."[68]

On January 30, Justice Reed circulated the following brief but critical memorandum:

> At the suggestion of some of the Brethren, I am rephrasing p. 18 to read as indicated below. The added words are underscored:

> > It was under this general rule that this Court approved in Salinger v. Loisel, 265 U.S. 224, 231, the procedure that a federal judge might refuse a writ where application for one had been made to and refused by another federal judge *and the second judge is of the opinion that in the light of the record a satisfactory conclusion has been reached.* That procedure is also applicable to state prisoners. Darr v. Burford, supra, 214–215.

> > Applications to district courts on grounds determined adversely to the applicant by state courts should follow the same procedure—a refusal of the writ without more, if the court is satisfied, by the record, that the state process has given fair consideration to the issues and the offered evidence, *and has resulted in a satisfactory conclusion.* . . .[69]

The precise origins of this change, which obviated Frankfurter's objection,[70] are unclear, but it plainly had substantial support. Justices Burton and Clark, in particular, had clearly been thinking about insuring that the Court's ultimate product reflected its underlying consensus on the procedural issues.

On January 16, Justice Burton sent Justice Clark a typed draft of what was to become their brief joint statement,[71] with a handwritten covering note saying, "I am *not* circulating this but am holding it for our consideration after we see what Justice Frankfurter finally writes."[72] When Justice Frankfurter's January 23 draft arrived in Justice Clark's chambers, the latter's law clerk, Bernard Weisberg,[73] wrote a memo pointing out that, although the differences between Justices Frankfurter and Reed had narrowed, there was still considerable room for misunderstanding.[74] Substantively, there were still differences as to when District Judges must hold hearings, and how much weight they had to give to prior state proceedings.[75] As a stylistic matter, "the reader is told . . . that he may discover the views of the Court from this and Justice Reed's opinion 'jointly,'" but—although Justice Frankfurter had "the preferable position on the procedural questions"—lower court readers were likely to accept Justice Reed's formulations as authoritative, since they would be "presented as the opinion 'of the Court.'"[76]

On January 27—the date of Justice Frankfurter's letter to him objecting to the possible implication of Justice Reed's draft that the federal judge could simply defer to the state outcome—Justice Burton wrote to Justice Clark:

> It seems to me that, with some minor changes in Felix's opinion, we could afford to give weight to both of their opinions and encourage a reconciliation of their meaning by using the draft of the memorandum of our views which I showed to you.[77]

It may well be that Justice Reed's change, clearly removing from the "opinion of the Court" any implication that prior state dispositions would be preclusive, was responsive to the concerns of Justices Burton and Clark—and perhaps even necessary to retain their votes for the Reed opinion.

Regardless of its exact provenance, however, the meaning of the change is clear, and consistent with the thinking of all the Justices except Jackson (who is the subject of the next chapter). To the extent that the Justices focused on the substance of the inquiry to be made by the federal habeas court, their effort was not to broaden it, but rather to insure that the published opinions would not be wrongly read as narrowing it.

19

The Drafting of *Brown*: The Periphery

During the various interchanges between the Justices, Justice Jackson had been fairly silent (although it had been his suggestion in conference that set Justice Frankfurter and Reed off on their respective reports), but by no means idle.

In March, 1952, Justice Jackson's law clerk, William Rehnquist, wrote him a brief memo on the *McGee* case, concluding:

> In view of the generally troubled situation regarding habeas corpus in cases such as this, and also because the Court last week granted cert in a case involving closely related questions (*Daniels v. Allen*, No. 271 Misc, cert to CA 4),[1] I append hereto a sketchy survey of the law and the facts regarding habeas corpus in the District Courts. On the basis of conclusions reached from that material, I would recommend a grant here in order to consider it at the same time as No. 271, and perhaps straighten out the law on the subject.[2]

The annexed memo is entitled "HABEAS CORPUS, THEN AND NOW, Or, 'If I Can Just Find the Right Judge, Over these Prison Walls I shall Fly . . .'":[3]

> The basic problem is one of res judicata; to what extent does an adverse judgment in the state system of cts preclude a petitioner from raising anew the same questions in federal district court?
>
> *The Law.*—Recent decisions of this court contain language indicating that a federal district court may consider questions of constitutional right anew even though the state court has decided the same question adversely to the petitioner, and he has been denied cert. by this court. This approach is based on two alternative rationales: (a) Where there has been a constitutional deprivation in the state ct, the result is to actually deprive that court of jurisdiction; (b) habeas corpus represents an exception to orthodox res judicata principles, and frankly allows a collateral attack on a criminal conviction.
>
> (a) *a denial of due process by state cts ousts them of jurisdiction.* This novel concept was first advanced by Black, J, in *Johnson v. Zerbst*, 304 U.S. 458.[4] Petitioner therein was convicted in federal court and claimed a denial of counsel. The court said that denial of counsel was a denial of constitutional right, and

that such denial was sufficient to oust the court of jurisdiction. Since a judgment may always be attacked for want of jurisdiction in the rendering court, this was no variation in the ordinary restriction of collateral attack. But of course the novelty lies in the notion that denial of a right to counsel ousts the court of jurisdiction; previously jurisdiction had been confined to notions of territoriality, statutory limitations, service and process, and notice.

However, novelty per se is not a condemnation, and my feeling is that this case, confined to its facts, is right. The reason for prohibiting collateral attack is that a litigant has previously had an opportunity to present his side of the case. . . . But of course if an accused has no counsel, this "previous opportunity" is pretty meaningless . . . and only a wooden application of the theory of res judicata would foreclose petitioner.

But in succeeding cases there have been vague, uncritical allusions to this case as establishing the principle that any denial of constitutional due process goes to the jurisdiction of the court. This is a horse of a different color. Questions of validity of indictment, makeup of the jury, validity of the statute under which conviction is had, might all be questions of due process. But with counsel, there is an opportunity to litigate these before an entire system of state tribunals, and to petition this court for cert. to review the judgment. . . . Here the rationale for making an exception to ordinary restrictions of collateral attack . . . is not present. Litigation on due process and other constitutional questions must end in the same manner as litigation on any other question.

(b) *a frank exception is made in habeas corpus proceedings to the rule of res judicata.* The latest statement of this proposition is found in the opinion of Reed, J., in *Darr v. Burford,* 339 US 200. . . .

The early cases of *Frank v. Magnum,* 237 U.S. 309, and *Moore v. Dempsey,* 261 U.S. 86, are vague in their language as to the precise effect to be given a previous adjudication in the state cts. In *Frank,* the writ was denied, the majority relying at least in part on the previous state determination, although not expressly calling it res judicata. 237 U.S. at 334. *Moore* seems to reject the idea that res judicata governs, though again not in express language, on the grounds that the charge of mob domination, if true, would be such as to actually oust the trial court of jurisdiction. Thus the rationale for the decision might be said to be not that res judicata did not apply, but that mob domination goes to the jurisdiction of the court, and therefore under orthodox principles collateral attack is permissible.

Recent cases have not clarified this rule. . . . [T]he important question of the weight to be given to previous adjudication by state courts has never been squarely decided recently, and language supporting any view can be found in the opinions.

The Practice.—With only such vague standards to guide them . . . confusion [reigns] in the lower courts. . . . Where the District Judge has been receptive to claims of denial of due process presented in habeas corpus, and has not been disposed to give much weight to previous state adjudication, egregious conflicts between the state and federal systems have resulted.[5]

. . . The rationale for this strangely disturbed state of affairs . . . is apparently that the state courts do not adequately protect the rights of defendants. . . . If the judgments of state courts were otherwise final, there might be good reason for this. But they are subject to review here. All claims cannot be reviewed, but the few that are may set a standard for the guidance of state cts in similar matters. To think that state cts would deliberately or in ignorance refuse to follow Supreme Court precedents is to suggest a malady in the body politic which no additional hearing before a federal judge would cure.

I respectfully submit that the Court would perform a signal service to the federal system if they would lay down a rule which required federal district judges to observe the ordinary principles of res judicata in passing on habeas corpus petitions from those confined under state sentence. An exception could be made for the case where denial of the right of counsel made meaningless the opportunity to litigate questions in the previous proceedings, *Johnson v. Zerbst, supra.* But where the defendant has had counsel to argue all his points to the trial court, the state appellate courts, and to petition this ct for cert, it seems to me the interest in preserving some dignity in the state cts and in discouraging utterly frivolous habeas corpus petitions . . . outweigh[s] the extremely rare case where a more just result would be obtained by allowing the district judge to re-examine matters already litigated in the state ct.[6] This would [not] . . . require outright overruling of any of this court's decisions on the matter, though the language in some would have to be limited.

When the Court returned in the fall of 1952, Rehnquist composed a memo entitled *"HABEAS CORPUS, revisited":*[7]

Having submitted a lengthy memo on this subject to you last spring in connection with the cases that are to be reargued, I will not cover the same ground. You said the other day that you thought the best policy would be to completely forget about precedent and write a new ticket. There are now, as you know, two lines of activity in the court.

(1) *Reed.* From the compendious memo which he circulated at the end of last term,[8] I think he regards this problem as basically the step to be taken after *Darr v. Burford.* . . . Reed . . . seems to see . . . only the further problem of "what weight must be given to this ct's denial of cert . . ." [and] concludes that denial of cert here must be given "respectful consideration" by the federal district ct. This contributes nothing positive except a new heading in the "Words and Phrases" volumes, and has the bad result of an express invitation to confusion among the lower cts. . . . (2) FF. One of the clerks has been working most of the summer on the problem, compiling a new set of statistics for what presumably

will be a bigger and better appendix.[9] The previous statistics given in *Darr v. Burford* showed that about 500 petitions a year from prisoners in state custody were disposed of each year by the federal district cts, and that between 2 and 3% of these resulted in the prisoners being released. FF drew the conclusion that since this percentage was low, there was no conflict between state and federal systems. I submit that this conclusion misses the point—in every one of the 500 cases where a petition is disposed of, at least those in which a return must be made, the state judiciary is put on trial.[10] . . .

FF's point about this ct not being a good one to handle matters such as this, because they are essentially matters of fact, is well taken. But he proceeds to the conclusion that therefore the federal district cts must be open to them. This conclusion is valid only on the assumption that *some* federal court must be open to allow prisoners to collaterally attack a state conviction. It rests on the assumption that both history and policy make it desirable to make a special exception to the ordinary rules of res judicata. . . .

(a) History. Until 1867, only federal prisoners could use HC in federal cts, and then only to attack the validity of commitment papers.[11] When speaking loosely of the "broad scope of the great writ" it is well to remember that classical expressions on the subject dealt with England, where there is unitary jurisdiction.[12] Our problem is present here only because of the difference between the US and England—here the states have primary jurisdiction to punish criminals.

(b) Policy. One need only venture out into the halls of this Honorable Court to hear ringing phrases to the effect that where liberty is at stake traditional rules ought not to apply. I suggest that the only question really involved is, "Is this the kind of job that the federal cts can do better than the state cts?"[13] [This is not a situation where] the claim of one state will necessarily exclude the claim of another state, or of the federal government. . . . This is not to say that there should be no federal standards of due process, but only that we should trust the state cts to enforce them, as we do other federal standards.

The above is simply added reason for my hearty concurrence in your statement of last week that, whereas the denial of cert should not be held to approve the application of the law by the cts below in the sense of *stare decisis*, it should be *res judicata* so far as any further federal intervention in the case is concerned. Perhaps an exception should be made where ptr has been denied counsel . . . [and] for newly discovered evidence, raising questions which ptr *did* not and *could not have* litigated in the state proceeding. Apart from these two, apply your rule of res judicata—and no mealy mouthed talk about "respectful consideration" which would only confuse the lower cts.

While the ACLU probably would not agree, I think that this is the forward looking approach to the problem. For many years this ct exercised a strict supervision over state economic legislation, rate-making, etc. That day is now gone. . . . But the very factions which most loudly damned the old court for its position on property rights are the most vocal in urging that this ct and other federal cts strictly supervise the state cts on matters of "civil liberties" and procedural due process. This inconsistency is apparently justified on some preferred position theory. What these forces fail to recognize is that the vice of the old court was not that it imposed the wrong view on the states, but that it imposed any views at all. In the fields of liberty as well as property, the states must be left to work out their own destinies within broad limits. If innocent people are regularly sent to jail, this ct or other federal cts may intervene; but subject to that limitation, there is no more reason for making this ct or other federal cts into a "super legal-aid society" than there was for elevating the doctrine of freedom of contract into a constitutional principle. For this ct to relax the federal grip on state criminal justice would be a step in the same direction as was taken by the case which overruled *Lochner v. New York.*

Lastly, may I humbly state my hope that the opinion of the ct in these cases will be yours. Reed is so bogged down in precedent that he will be unable to reach an unequivocal result that is acceptable to either side. FF . . . is one who must set down in the opinion every nuance that comes to mind. This makes for great erudition but often damn poor law. What this problem needs is an incisive statement of new law. . . .

WRITE!!!

Around October 1, 1952, Rehnquist sent a memo headed "To The Boss; Re: Habeas Corpus."[14] Responding to Justice Reed's circulation in *Brown v. Allen* dated September 26, Rehnquist wrote that "the alternatives seem to shape up as follows":

(1) Reed
(a) previous adjudication in state cts, without more, not binding, and not even necessary to be considered
(b) previous adjudication in state cts, followed by denial of cert here—not binding upon DC, but may be "considered"
(c) *Darr v. Burford,* requiring petition for cert here as part of exhaustion of remedies, remains in effect.
Criticisms:
(a) Still pretty vague, because so enmeshed in precedents: what does "consideration" mean to the District Judge?
(b) Still does not strike at the small minority of federal judges, such as Goodman, who are causing trouble,[15] since they are apparently free to disregard previous adjudication if they so desire.
(2) Felix (as I piece it together from his clerks)[16]

(a) neither previous state adjudication nor denial of cert here have any weight whatsoever

(b) *Darr v. Burford* overruled;[17] result is to transfer this kind of litigation almost entirely to the lower federal courts, which he says are far more capable of handling it than we are.

Criticisms:

This in effect sets a one judge district ct as a reviewing tribunal for the highest ct of the state in criminal matters. A state ct is not a ct of last resort, but simply one intermediate step in a series of interminable appeals. . . .

(3) Suggestions to Restrict Collateral Attack other than Reed's

(a) Previous litigation in state cts on merits, followed by denial of cert here, is res judicata though not stare decisis. This is your idea and I think it far superior to any of the above.[18] . . . *Darr v. Burford* would have to be retained in order to prevent prisoners from circumventing the effect of this rule by not petitioning for cert.

(b) Accept Judge Parker's construction of "exhaustion of remedies" provision (8 FRD 171), rejected by Stanley, to the effect that in any state where habeas corpus is not res judicata, state remedies are always available.[19] Ptr could seek cert to review these collateral attacks in the state cts, but lower federal cts would not be available. Thus the unseemly conflict between co-ordinate courts would be eliminated, and yet a federal avenue would remain open for the exceptional case. . . .

(c) a less forthright method for cutting down this kind of litigation would be based on the fact that almost without exception these petitions to the federal ct are *in forma [pauperis]*. . . . [T]he federal cts have always required . . . a certificate of probable cause [for such litigants to take appeals]. The rule could be laid down that where the contention overruled by the federal district ct has also been decided against him on the merits in the state proceedings there is as a matter of law no probable cause. . . . [Thus,] (1) no prisoner who lost in the DC could appeal (2) the DCs themselves would feel freer in dealing with the petitions, since there would be no review of a decision adverse to the petitioner.

(d) Adopt a new policy on certs in this ct [on direct appeals]. When the contention raised is, in the opinion of six judges, free of state grounds which would preclude review,[20] this ct should deny with the notation "with prejudice to the right to bring action for federal habeas corpus."[21]

It is not clear when Justice Jackson decided that he would write an opinion (although it was probably sometime after the conference of October 27, 1952).[22] But once he did, his first step was to draft himself an extensive set of handwritten notes, headed "Habeas Corpus." Although these contain a number of thoughts that eventually found their way into his ultimate opinion, they also contain criticisms of the existing system that might have been the seeds of more radical views, e.g., "Abolishing states in interest of civil liberties"; "Any old key good enough to open jail doors. Presume innocent & court guilty of miscarriage"; "H.C. a judicial plaything in a game without rules":

> Rights of state v. individual—contrast individual elsewhere Govt. v. tax-payer—regulated—controlled—But in criminal law tie hands society—free accused. "never had it so good."[23]

Justice Jackson next produced several dated typescript drafts of an opinion, none of which he circulated. While showing significant variations, these display a pronounced trend toward narrowing and softening the legal propositions asserted, and a shift in focus from matters of substantive due process law to matters of habeas corpus procedure.

The draft of December 29, 1952 states:[24]

> It is my belief that our greatest need is not to try to cite or apply the recent decisions on this subject but rather to clear the site of many of them and to look forward rather than backward for our remedy. The only usefulness I find in most of our recent procedural precedents on this subject is that they teach us how it came about that these abuses assume such proportions. . . .[25]
>
> I can not exonerate the state courts from some responsibility for the extension of federal interference. One is sometimes shocked at the callousness with which the rights of defendants are treated, particularly where the defendant happened to be of particularly unpopular groups in the locality. We cannot claim either that federal justice is free of that. But it has been lawless procedures and savage penalties which were discreditable to the profession that originally moved the federal government into the state field. . . . [T]here were . . . cases of obtaining confession by the most brutal third degree methods of criminal and physical abuse of the person and by acts of terrorism which, given jurisdiction, no decent court could condone. There were instances of virtual denial of counsel to the accused and there were flagrant violations in some parts of the country of the federal statute which prohibits discrimination of a racial character in the selection of juries.
>
> These decisions, however . . . have left the boundaries of federal power to interfere and of the grounds upon which interference may be based so vague and indefinite that no prisoner is wholly without hope of release if he can only get his case here. . . .
>
> A considerable part of the vagueness of the effect of the Fourteenth Amendment on state trials is inherent in the subject as indicated by previous decisions. For example the *Moore v. Dempsey*, doctrine that a trial must be fair and not a mask or a form. With the development of modern methods of publicity . . . it is almost impossible to say when a fair trial has been had. . . . [Exclusion of a confession] in order not to prejudice the jury is utterly unavailing

if at his dinner table . . . he hears the content of that confession recited over the radio perhaps with extortions [*sic*] to suit the predilections of the commentator. We have stripped, by our interpretation of the same amendment, the state courts of power to protect the processes of fair trial against this kind of intrusion. I am frank to say that I do not know whether any highly publicized trial today, state or federal, could bear the scrutiny indicated in *Moore v. Dempsey.*

. . . [Additionally,] we have really reached the point where any case in which a confession is used may present a constitutional question and I again would be unable to say what questioning of a suspect would be permitted. Also, we have gone beyond the federal statute which prohibits racial discrimination in the selection of jurors and have entertained cases in which a strong minority have indicated that it is even unconstitutional for a state to attempt to select jurors on the basis of their intelligence. In *Johnson* vs. *Zerbst,* 304 U.S. 458, by a feat of interpretation the Court expanded the right to have counsel in a federal case to mean the right to be furnished counsel . . . [, which] left the whole question of the right to counsel in state court trials uncertain. Moreover there was talk in many of the opinions about the right to effective counsel. . . . The result is that we have not only a number of appeals by persons who have been convicted of minor offenses where they apparently did not have counsel, but we also have a large number of cases in which the prisoner admittedly had counsel but the claim is made that he was not effective. . . .

Another prolific source of litigation by habeas corpus has been the so-called McNabb Rule, the rule requiring immediate or semi-immediate arraignment of a prisoner after his arrest. A rule which was adopted only for federal courts and not as a constitutional matter, but in which prisoners see constitutional possibilities of its application against the state.[26]

Only after this 10-page attack on the substance of contemporary due process doctrine in the criminal procedure field, does the draft turn to matters of federal habeas corpus procedure. Although it here resembles more closely the discussion of the same subjects in his ultimate opinion,[27] the tone in the draft is notably sharper, describing "lawlessness in procedure run riot," a situation in which "there are no rules. And habeas corpus has become pretty nearly a judicial plaything in a game without rules."[28] Specifically, on the issue of the effect of the denial of certiorari:

It is true that no one outside of the Court and often those inside it do not know all of the reasons which cause six members to withhold their consent to review. Some may think the judgment below is right, others that it is wrong but of no general importance to the law, while another may believe the record not clear, that the question was [not][29] raised or preserved and still another,

[may] think the docket is sufficiently large already and wants to be off on vacation. One may even think that the question is presented and is important and is wrongly decided but still vote against grant of certiorari in fear that the ultimate decision of his brethren would strengthen or extend what he regards as a bad rule. . . .

But denial of certiorari does have all the meaning in the world in applying the doctrine of res judicata to the particular case in which it issues. It leaves standing unimpaired a final judgment which, under any rational theory of the law, is conclusive against collateral attack as to the issues it settles or could have settled had the parties raised them. . . .

Habeas Corpus goes to matters that are not apparent on the record itself. This distinction has been cavalierly cast aside in recent decisions of this court and is responsible for no small part of our present difficulty. . . .

At the risk of being a reactionary, I would revert to the former rules governing habeas corpus and certiorari. We must not forget that these rules were deemed necessary to protect it from abuse by men who took far more risks than we do to grant the writ at all. We often pay them lip service and then honor them in the breach. . . .

No petition should be entertained to raise a question which was reviewed or could have been reviewed by appeal or other process. The disregard of this old and rational limitation has caused no end of mischief. . . . Frequently no appeals are taken. . . . In other cases an appeal is attempted but defaults occur. . . . Then there are the cases in which the prisoner does appeal and does obtain from the state courts a review of his case. What possible excuse can there be for allowing the prisoner to then renew the struggle in federal court. In effect, to transfer his case on the same questions from the state courts, which has the primary function of enforcing the criminal law, to a federal judge on collateral attack upon the convictions. There is little that I can add except hearty approval to Judge Parker's comment on this subject 8 F.R.D. 171.[30] I think that his views would end unseemly conflict between coordinate courts and yet a federal avenue would remain open for the exceptional case in which the state judges have been led to violate constitutional rights.

Criminal law . . . is in disrepute and it is in many respects a disgrace to the profession. . . . A strong contributing factor to this is the law's delays, the fact that penalties are never really effective so long as the public is interested in the case. There is a great to-do about indictment and about conviction and then begin a series of appeals to intermediate courts, to courts of last resort, to this Court and then there are applications for rehearings in each of those courts and then when that is at an end, the whole process is started over again by writ of habeas corpus, habeas corpus in state courts, habeas corpus in the federal courts, appeals, rehearings, petitions for certiorari, petitions for rehearing on denial of petitions for certiorari. The whole thing is disgusting and a disgrace to the profession. Moderate penalties promptly and effectively applied after fair and calm trial reviewable once to make sure that no prejudicial error has occurred is all that a defendant, in my opinion, is entitled to. When he has had that, society is entitled to have the decrees of its courts enforced with finality.[31]

The Justice's next draft, of January 5, 1953,[32] was structurally distinctly different.[33] But it, too, while overlapping with the final version, differed from it in being far stronger in tone and substance:

> The generalities of the Fourteenth Amendment . . . provided a basis for the judicial expansion of the substantive law of habeas corpus on the premise that they are violations of due process of law. . . . [W]hen we dislike any particular practice or irregularity sufficiently we can read into the Fourteenth Amendment a constitutional prohibition of it and it thereby becomes correctable by habeas corpus. Both the courts and the profession are too familiar with this expanding concept in this field to require detailed citations or discussions of cases. While in every other field, such as taxation, regulation of business, control of activities, the power of the state over the individual has been expanded. The trend of recent times has been to limit the right of the state to enforce its criminal judgments against the individual unless those judgments in all respects meet the approval of the last federal judges to pass upon them. . . .
>
> That there has been a simultaneous trend away from an effort by this Court to enforce a rule of law in favor of a practice of deciding by the personal notions of justice of a majority of the judges is the belief of the profession and I must say I share it. . . . [The profession's view is] that we have no fixed principles and that any defendant may stand a chance of getting his liberty if he can only get his case in federal court.
>
> In seeking a way out of this bog, it is important to distinguish what is practicable from what is impossible. Gallant tilting at windmills is a pastime for judges no less ridiculous than for knights. Even if it were desirable it is too late in the day, barring some such public storm as was raised by President Roosevelt's plan to reorganize this Court, which accompanied the retreat from the use of the Fourteenth Amendment to restrict state legislation in the economic field, to now reverse the course of interpretation which warrants all manner of interference in the states' action in the criminal field.[34]

Reorganizing his material once more, Justice Jackson produced another private draft of January 13,[35] which, in its legal rulings and substantially in its language, tracks his eventual opinion.

On January 28, he finally circulated an opinion.[36] Justice Frankfurter promptly attempted—by an informal note (probably of January 28, 1953) asking Justice Jackson to detail his disagreements, in a letter dated January 29, 1953, and through marginal comments on the circulated draft—to change Justice Jackson's expressed views.[37] The only known response Frankfurter received was a note replying to the first one, reading in full:

> F.F. I can give you the answer in short form. Yours is too damned gentle—I want to make it hurt.
> Bob[38]

But just as Justice Frankfurter was unable to convince Justice Jackson, so must it have been clear to Justice Jackson that he himself would be highly unlikely to persuade any of the others—and, indeed, there is no written record of his having tried to do so. His January 28 draft—his first and only circulation to the brethren about the case—entered the U.S. Reports without material change.

Following Justice Frankfurter's circulation of his opinion on the merits on February 5,[39] the full set of opinions was duly released on February 9, 1953.

20

The *Brown* Opinions

The Court's published decision dealt with two procedural topics. First, rejecting "the position of the Fourth Circuit," it held 5–4 that a previous denial of certiorari was to be given no substantive effect by the judge ruling on a later federal habeas corpus petition.[1] Second, reiterating law whose roots we have traced to *Frank*, it ruled that in determining whether a state conviction violated the Constitution a federal habeas corpus court should, after consideration of the state court record, decide what further factual inquiries were needed in order to discharge responsibly its duty to make an independent determination of federal law, a decision that would be given a large measure of deference on appeal.[2]

While contained in two opinions (reflecting the inability of Justices Reed and Frankfurter to agree upon a single draft) all the Justices but Jackson were in accord on this second set of procedural issues. Justice Frankfurter's published discussion of these questions tracked his earlier internal writing,[3] both on the matter of the record for federal habeas corpus adjudication[4] and in elaborating upon the established distinctions between earlier state rulings on:

(a) questions of historical fact (which the federal judge could accept as binding "[u]nless a vital flaw be found in the process of ascertaining such facts"),

(b) "questions of law [which] cannot, under the habeas corpus statute, be accepted as binding," since "[i]t is precisely these questions that the federal judge is commanded to decide," and

(c) "mixed questions or the application of constitutional principles to the facts as found," where "the duty of adjudication [rests] with the federal judge," and "[t]he State court cannot have the last say when it, though on fair consideration and what procedurally may be deemed fairness, may have misconceived a federal constitutional right."[5]

Justice Reed's opinion, although more oblique, agreed.[6]

That there was no real disagreement between Justices Reed and Frank-furter respecting hearings—so that indeed "[t]he views of the Court on these questions may thus be drawn from the two opinions jointly"[7]—is shown by the fact that no Justice believed that the District Courts in the cases at hand had been required to conduct de novo review of the factual findings of the state courts regarding whether confessions had been coerced or a petitioner was sane. Thus, *Brown* not only made no new law on the scope of review, but also did not do so on the issue of when hearings were mandatory. At the same time, Justice Reed went out of his way to approve of the decision of the *Speller* District Court to hold a hearing, writing:

> This was in its discretion. *Moore v. Dempsey,* 261 U.S. 86; *Darr v. Burford,* 339 U.S. 214, cases which establish the power of federal district courts to protect the constitutional rights of state prisoners after the exhaustion of state remedies. It better enabled that court to determine whether any violation of the Fourteenth Amendment occurred.[8]

In short, Justice Frankfurter was accurate in reporting:

> The issue of the significance of the denial of certiorari raises a sharp division in the Court. This is not so as to the bearing of the proceedings in the State courts upon the disposition of the application for a writ of habeas corpus in the Federal District Courts.[9]

On the merits of the cases decided in the *Brown* opinion,[10] on the other hand, the Justices were sharply at odds. Justice Reed wrote for himself and Justices Vinson, Minton, Burton, Clark, and Jackson in denying all relief. Justice Black's dissent was joined by Justice Douglas, while Justice Frank-furter's was joined by those two Justices.

In *Brown*, the Court focused principally on the challenge to the jury se-lection procedures and held that the use of tax lists as the basis of selection for grand and petit jurors was not unconstitutionally racially discrimina-tory, notwithstanding the racially unequal distribution of wealth, the result-ing disparate impact on the composition of the jury pool, and North Car-olina's history of unconstitutional discrimination in jury selection.[11] Nor did the Court's terse review of the record respecting the confession persuade it that the statement had been involuntary.[12]

Both dissents discussed primarily the jury selection issue. (This is proba-bly because even under the procedural formulations of Justices Frank-furter[13] and Black,[14] the confession issue was one on which the district court might properly have deferred to the state's factual findings—in which case, its ultimate legal conclusion that the confession was voluntary would have been difficult to cast as reversible error.) Regarding jury selection, Justice Black concluded that there had not been a "genuine abandonment of [the] old discriminatory practices."[15] Justice Frankfurter focused his fire on the impropriety of an affirmance in a case where the Court of Appeals had—wrongly, as the Court now held—declined to reach the merits in deference to the prior proceedings.[16]

The Court disposed of *Speller* similarly. It refused to consider the additional argument that, quite apart from race, wealth discrimination in jury selection was impermissible. This claim had not been asserted below, and "[s]uch an important national asset as state autonomy in local law enforcement must not be eroded through indefinite charges of unconstitutional actions."[17]

As to *Daniels*, the Court rested its affirmance on counsel's having been one day late in serving the appeals papers. "To allow habeas corpus in such circumstances would subvert the entire system of state criminal justice and destroy state energy in the detection and punishment of crime."[18] Justice Black responded: "State systems are not so feeble."[19] Justice Frankfurter wrote that—in light of the strength of the petitioners' underlying claims—the refusal of the North Carolina Supreme Court to exercise its discretion to review the merits had resulted in a "complete . . . miscarriage of justice."[20]

The real-world outcomes of these dispositions were four executions. Within a few months, Brown and Speller were put to death in the gas chamber simultaneously,[21] as were the Daniels cousins later in the year.[22]

The decision in the companion case of *Smith v. Baldi*[23] followed a similar pattern, albeit with less fatal consequences. Again, the Court was unanimous on the issues of habeas corpus procedure.[24]

Smith argued that he was insane, that an insane person could not Constitutionally be executed, and that he was entitled to a federal court hearing on whether he was in fact insane. Rejecting this claim of entitlement, the Court quoted with approval the District Court's statement that only if:

> special circumstances prevail, should the lowest federal court reverse the highest state court in cases where the constitutional issues have been disposed on the merits by the highest state court in an opinion specifically setting forth its reasons that there has been no denial of due process of law, and where the record before the state court and the allegations in the petition for the writ before the federal court fail to disclose that the state in its prosecution departed from the constitutional requirements. That is this case.[25]

The Court then continued:

> This view of the proceedings accords with our holding in the *Brown* case, *supra*. As the trial and appellate State court records which were before the District Court show a judicial hearing, where on the plea of guilty the question of sanity at the time of the commission of the crime was canvassed, the sentence does not violate due process.[26]

The dissent, written by Justice Frankfurter for himself and Justices Douglas and Black, specifically agreed that:

> [i]t is not for this Court to find a want of due process in a conviction for murder sustained by the highest court of the State merely because a finding that the defendant is sane may raise the gravest doubts.

Rather, it contended, "the accused in this case was deprived of a fair opportunity to establish his insanity."[27]

Thus, all the Justices were in accord that—accepting Smith's legal proposition that an insane person could not be executed[28]—the Constitutional question was not whether Pennsylvania had resolved the factual issue of insanity correctly, but only whether Smith had been provided with a fair process for its resolution.[29] And that, all agreed, could properly be decided summarily.

Neither Justice Frankfurter nor any of the others mentioned that the incumbent Philadelphia District Attorney, repudiating the views of his predecessor, had filed a brief on behalf of the prisoner. Endorsing the dissent in the Court of Appeals, this urged:

> It is clear from the record, that the issues of fact raised by the petition for a writ of *habeas corpus* have not been determined either by the Supreme Court of Pennsylvania or by the United States District Court. Since substantial issues of Federal constitutional law are raised, it was incumbent on the District Court to determine the facts. . . .
>
> It is, therefore, respectfully submitted that for the reasons contained in the dissenting opinion of Chief Judge Biggs the judgment should be reversed and the cause remanded with instructions to the District Court to make findings of fact necessary for the proper determination of the Federal questions involved.[30]

Rather, as a separate and conclusive reason "why this Court should not affirm the judgment below," Justice Frankfurter highlighted an affidavit presented to the Court informing it that, subsequent to the rulings below, the government's witness on Smith's insanity "had himself been committed

. . . because of an incurable mental disease which had deprived him of 'any judgment or insight.'"[31]

Fortunately for Smith as well as for the interests of justice, within days after the Supreme Court's ruling the Pennsylvania courts ordered an inquiry into Smith's sanity, which resulted in a ruling that he was insane.[32] Eventually, in 1968, Smith was determined to be sane—and thus potentially subject to execution—at which point the Governor commuted his sentence to life imprisonment.[33] The Pennsylvania Board of Pardons reviewed the case in February, 1973, and, relying upon Smith's "excellent conduct record" in prison and the absence of any psychiatric symptoms, recommended that he be paroled as of September, 1974—a recommendation that the Governor approved.[34]

21

The Pre-Bator Context of *Brown*

None of the developments, judicial or legislative, that followed upon the release of the *Brown* decision support the view that it significantly reshaped the legal landscape. Nor did any of the contemporary antagonists over the appropriate scope of habeas corpus view it as having done so. Prior to the appearance of Bator's article, *Brown* was just another, not particularly prominent, episode in an ongoing contest that had begun long before and continues to this day. Indeed, to the extent it had any immediate impact at all, *Brown* seems to have increased the rate at which federal habeas corpus petitions by state prisoners were summarily denied.

A. *Pre*-Brown *Background*

The perceived intrusion on state criminal processes caused by federal habeas corpus review had long been the subject of complaint in certain quarters.[1]

One influential proposal for restrictions, for example, had been made a decade before *Brown*. It came from Judge John J. Parker, who, after an active career in Republican politics and five years on the Fourth Circuit, had been nominated to the Supreme Court in 1930 but rejected by the Senate on a 41–39 vote after opposition from labor unions and the NAACP. Judge Parker—who sat on the Fourth Circuit panel reviewing the North Carolina cases that were adjudicated in *Brown*, and remained a viable candidate for the Court—chaired a committee of the Judicial Conference that in 1943 persuaded that body to support a statute denying federal habeas corpus jurisdiction to state prisoners for so long as they had state collateral remedies available.[2] The effect would have been to bar federal habeas corpus entirely in any state whose courts remained theoretically open to repetitive postconviction filings—an effect that doubtless would have led many states to amend their statutes accordingly. To be sure, under such a scheme state prisoners could still file certiorari petitions raising their federal claims, but, just as with the similar post-*Brown* proposal described in the next section, this would have been of little comfort. Since the Justices lacked the district courts' capacity to review such cases, the practical (and intended) impact would have been to foreclose review—much less relief—in the overwhelming majority of cases.

Knowing this, the assembled state chief justices had, as the *Brown* opinions note,[3] resolved in the fall of 1952 that "a final judgment of a State's highest court [should] be subject to review or reversal only by the Supreme Court of the United States."[4] The rationale was that, in light of developments in the Court's jurisprudence to that point, corrective measures were needed to protect the states' autonomous decision-making authority in the criminal justice field from federal interference.

Significantly, the source of the problem leading to both proposals was generally identified as either *Moore* or *Frank*.[5]

B. *Post-*Brown *Developments*

In the aftermath of *Brown*, the opponents of generous habeas corpus review considered it one more example of their complaints, not a sea change in the law. Both Judge Parker and the state chief justices referred to it critically, but as a typical example of long-subsisting abuses.[6]

Indeed, when Attorney General Herbert Brownell spoke to the Judicial Conference following the decision, he stated that *Brown* had been correct in deciding "that the practice which permits State prisoners to apply to the lower Federal courts for relief by habeas corpus is required by the present habeas corpus statute, in particular, 28 U.S.C. 2254," and suggested various possible statutory changes.[7]

In response to these remarks, the Conference reactivated its habeas corpus committee under Judge Parker.[8] In September, 1954, the committee proposed that a subsection be added to 28 U.S.C. § 2254 providing that habeas corpus applications by state prisoners might be entertained:

> only on a ground which presents a substantial Federal constitutional question (1) which was not theretofore raised and determined (2) which there was no fair and adequate opportunity theretofore to raise and have determined and (3) which cannot thereafter be raised and determined in a proceeding in the State court, by an order or judgment subject to review by the Supreme Court of the United States on writ of certiorari.

An order denying an application for a writ of habeas corpus by a person in custody pursuant to a judgment of a State court shall be reviewable only on writ of certiorari [and the] petition for the writ of certiorari shall be filed within 30 days.[9]

This legislation—which, although more restrictive than Judge Parker's 1943 proposal, operated through essentially the same mechanism—eventually passed the House but not the Senate.[10] When it was reintroduced in 1958, Chief Justice Warren asked Justices Frankfurter, Clark, and Harlan to serve as a committee to consider it.[11] Frankfurter thereupon wrote a memorandum to the committee:

In applying *Brown v. Allen*, 344 U.S. 443 the District Courts may, barring a serious infirmity in state-court proceedings, rely on the state court record in passing on a federal habeas corpus application. The practical result of this utilization of *Brown v. Allen* is that all but a small percentage of such applications are denied upon the moving papers. During the last three years, District Courts held factual hearings on only 76 [3.5 percent] of 2,192 applications. [12]

In fact, in the aftermath of *Brown*, the percentage of petitions disposed of without hearings had increased,[13] and although Justice Frankfurter thought there was a causal connection he did not attack this effect. Indeed, he embraced it as showing that restrictive legislation was unnecessary, noting,

TABLE 3
Evidentiary Hearings by District Courts on
Habeas Corpus Applications

Fiscal Year	Percentage Disposed of after Hearing
1941	11.9
1942	24.6
1943	9.1
1944	2.9
1945	4.3
1946	6.5
1947	10.4
1948	11.3
1949	8.4
1950	10.0
1951	6.2
1952	4.9
1953	5.5
1954	3.3
1955	3.7
1956	2.7
1957	3.4

"According to a study by the Administrative Office, only .004 percent of district court time is devoted to state habeas corpus cases." Moreover, to help head off such legislation, Justice Frankfurter was willing to make the *Brown* rule "explicit by statute" so that:

> the District Court would be authorized to order a hearing on a state prisoner's habeas corpus application only in a case where the record of the state proceedings were found to be an inadequate basis for determining the merit of the constitutional claim.[14]

Thus, Frankfurter—the champion of the writ during the *Brown* deliberations, who succeeded in having the opinion written to avoid retrenchment—did not see the impact of the case as sharpening the scrutiny that the District Courts would give to state court proceedings. Rather, as he had in the past,[15] he identified the central holding of the case as its rejection of any substantive effect to the denial of certiorari, and stressed the importance of this in structural terms:

> [O]n the basis of . . . practical considerations, *Brown v. Allen* finally established that denial of certiorari by this Court in these habeas corpus cases implied no decision whatever on the merits of the case. At present about 350 of such petitions come before us per Term. Apart from all else—that is, without regard to the demands of other cases that come before the Court—we could not possibly dispose of so many cases on the merits nor would we have the facilities, time apart, to examine and ascertain the too-often hidden facts in these cases. At present, we can conscientiously deny certiorari . . . with the knowledge that the prisoner is free after our denial to seek habeas corpus in a forum equipped to ascertain the facts, *i.e.*, the District Court.
>
> The proposed measure would make certiorari the final and, for all practical purposes, exclusive federal method for review of a state prisoner's claim under the United States Constitution. A denial of certiorari would become a definitive disposition of the federal constitutional claim. But for the reasons indicated, this court could not, and therefore would not, base such a final decision on the unsatisfactory records now available here . . . [and] would be confronted with the necessity of establishing new, appropriate procedures to assure a responsible adjudication on the merits of constitutional claims. . . .
>
> But the initial and final sifting of habeas corpus claims by the federal judiciary most certainly is not the function of this Court.[16]

This view proved persuasive. Initially, only two judges, both leading liberals, had objected to the legislation, citing the problem Frankfurter identified. One of these was Chief Judge Jerome Frank of the Second Circuit.[17] The other was Chief Justice William Denman of the Ninth Circuit, the author of the *Ekberg* decision that the Court had accepted for review among the *Brown* cases and a frequent adversary of Judge Parker's on habeas matters in judicial and legislative fora both before and after the case was decided.[18] But the proposed legislation foundered in the wake of Frankfurter's memorandum, as "several members of the Supreme Court" indicated that the bill "would unduly increase the work of that Court," which "is not constituted to hear contested applications for habeas corpus" and which would respond to such legislation by referring petitions "to district judges sitting as special masters."[19]

Indeed, despite the drumbeat of criticism against federal habeas corpus for state prisoners, none of the restrictive bills was enacted into law. In fact, "the Court promptly rejected Professor Bator's thesis" in a trilogy of habeas corpus cases that:

> in 1963 confirmed *Brown* in the clearest of terms and, indeed, built upon that decision in setting down guidelines for the exercise of independent federal judgment on the merits of federal claims.[20]

And in 1966 "Congress enacted legislation that codified the essentials of *Brown*" in rejecting preclusive effects of state court determinations.[21]

In short, one can characterize *Brown* as a watershed only by shutting one's eyes to the surrounding decades of historical context. There is no evidence that anyone before Bator considered the ruling to have worked a revolutionary broadening of the writ. And for good reason. The decision was simply one episode in a long-running struggle that was under way long before the case was decided, and continued little changed thereafter.

22

Understanding *Brown*

Legally, *Brown* was an exceedingly minor event. On the issue of the federal habeas courts' reexamination of state court findings its substantive standards were deferential in the extreme, and its procedural guidelines for when hearings should be held proved ephemeral. The only enduring law that the case made—rejecting any preclusive effect for certiorari denials, so that primary responsibility for federal scrutiny of state criminal convictions would rest with the District Courts rather than the Supreme Court—was so eminently sensible as to be uncontroversial today.[1] But the pragmatic effect of that legal ruling was to assure the real-world ability of the federal court system to implement the applicable substantive standards, thereby vindicating on the ground in the second half of the twentieth century the promises of *Frank* and *Moore* in the first.

To seek to grasp *Brown* as new law is to clutch at a ghost; to understand it as the implementation of old law is to add a modest but solid stone to the fabric of a cathedral.

A. The Ghost

No evidence for the proposition that *Brown* inaugurated some new and more intrusive level of federal scrutiny of state court proceedings is to be found in the opinions themselves. "As in other appeals, the scope of review was to be *de novo* on the law"[2]—and the Court did give plenary consideration to the claims that the structure of the North Carolina jury selection system and the procedures for sanity review in Pennsylvania were unconstitutional—but "deferential on the facts,"[3] as it most certainly was. Indeed, Bator could with equal plausibility (albeit no less erroneously) have argued that *Brown* represented a return to the appropriately deferential standard of *Frank* and a repudiation of *Moore*.

In the *Brown* case itself, not even Justices Frankfurter and Black were willing to assert that the District Court should have conducted an independent review of the circumstances of the confession, notwithstanding the grave suspicions raised by those circumstances. Similarly, no Justice was willing to reexamine the state courts' sanity determinations in *Smith*, utterly wrong though they were in fact. And two people whose Constitutional rights had in all probability been denied died in North Carolina's gas chamber because the *Daniels* majority held that unless it gave preclusive effect to the one-day lateness in filing the appeals papers it "would subvert the entire system of state criminal justice and destroy state energy in the detection and punishment of crime."[4]

Just as any novel substantive aspects of *Brown* are chimerical, so did any novel procedural ones prove to be ephemeral. The case's foggy and forgiving formulations as to when federal habeas courts were required to hold hearings were replaced by more precise and demanding ones in *Townsend v. Sain*,[5] ones that were themselves replaced by equally precise but deferential ones in *Keeney v. Tamayo-Reyes*.[6] The ruling in *Daniels* precluding review due to a day's tardiness in the filing of an appeal was repudiated in *Fay v. Noia*,[7] but revived in *Coleman v. Thompson*.[8]

To attack *Brown* as a novelty that changed the direction of habeas corpus law is to spear at a cloud.

B. The Cathedral

For those who do not believe in ghosts, there is a much more sensible approach, one that views the basic contours of habeas corpus law as a legal cathedral built up over many generations by workers who have often been at odds on points of decoration but have had a common understanding of the fundamental plan.

As we have seen in Part II, in *Frank* the goverment argued that the petitioner was precluded from federal habeas corpus relief by the prior rejection of his claims by the state courts and the Supreme Court's subsequent refusal to grant writs of error. The Court rejected both positions, and held that the District Court had the power to hold a hearing to investigate the petitioner's claims of Constitutional error during the state proceedings (dividing only over whether such a hearing should have been held in the case at hand).

As we have also seen in Part II, the government made precisely the same arguments in *Moore*. They were again rejected, and, without the articulation of any new legal standards, the Court held that the District Judge was required to hold a hearing.

Thus, by the time *Darr* was decided in 1950 it was well established that neither the prior merits rulings of the state courts nor the failure of the Supreme Court to review them would preclude federal habeas review. And it was equally clear that the front line of such review was the District Court, which had some discretion—whose contours were as yet undefined—over whether or not to hold a hearing to exercise its undoubted power to consider whether the state proceedings had been infected by fundamental error.[9]

Darr, however, created doctrinal confusion and a potential practical problem. Doctrinally, the requirement that state prisoners file a certiorari petition raised the question of whether, *Frank* and *Moore* notwithstanding, some substantive significance should be given to the petition's denial. And, as a practical matter, if this were to happen, the task of reviewing state convictions for Constitutional error—under whatever standard might be applicable—would fall on the Supreme Court, not the District Courts, necessarily circumscribing such review radically. As the discussion in this Part has shown, all those involved in *Brown* clearly saw these problems, and clearly saw the legal ruling it made—to reject any preclusive effect for the denial of certiorari—as solving them.

Brown thus represented a restoration of the legal and practical *status quo ante* that *Darr* had threatened. This, no more and no less, is what the case did and should define the niche it appropriately occupies in the habeas edifice.

C. The Ghost in the Cathedral

The attempt to find in *Brown* what is not there surely owes much to now Chief Justice Rehnquist, whether one attributes it to a desire common among law clerks to believe that cases in which they participated were of special importance, an exaggeration of the extent to which his views were shared either by Justice Jackson or by the Court, to intellectual sympathy with Bator,[10] or to a more ideological distaste with the fact that *Brown* did strengthen federal habeas corpus as a practical remedy.[11] Then, too, the phenomenon that two other Justices can also see the ghost[12] demonstrates how useful it is to have an article in the Harvard Law Review to cite to buttress a position lacking in any solid support.

But there is no ghost. Nothing about *Brown* was revolutionary. The theory that independent federal habeas corpus review of the Constitutional validity of state criminal convictions is a modern innovation attributable to *Brown* is simply inconsistent with the historical evidence.

Part IV

23

Epilogue: Habeas Corpus as a Protector of Individual Liberty in a Federal System

The connection between accurate history and sound public policy is, quite properly, an attenuated one; history should be written without presentist bias, and public policy formed without being unduly constrained by the past. Nonetheless, some of the main lines of the development of the habeas corpus story since 1976, when the Court upheld several contemporary state death penalty systems,[1] may help illuminate both what the past has been and what the future should be.

In America today capital defendants systematically receive less due process than others. As we have already seen in Parts II and III, and as many current studies show, their cases are more likely than those of defendants not facing execution to have been infected by distortions arising from racism, the incompetence of defense counsel, their own mental limitations, public passion, political pressures, or jury prejudice or confusion.[2] For these reasons, the existence of a meaningful federal habeas corpus remedy for state prisoners is especially important in death penalty cases[3]—which have been the ones driving the Court's habeas corpus jurisprudence for the past quarter of a century—and they provide a particularly good lens through which to view the issues.

As the Association of the Bar of the City of New York has documented, federal habeas corpus has frequently been indispensable for Death Row inmates seeking justice. Consider some examples of successful petitions drawn from opinions published since 1980:

- A mentally deficient man gave the police two vastly different statements during 42 hours of uncounselled questioning. The later of the two confessions used words beyond the defendant's capability and,

147

unlike the first confession, distinctly recited facts which qualified defendant for the death penalty.

- The prosecution knowingly presented misleading evidence by using the same expert witness to testify at the defendant's trial that he must have been the sole triggerman, when that expert had previously testified at the codefendant's trial that the codefendant must have been the sole triggerman.

- The prosecution withheld its most crucial witness's prior statement, which corroborated evidence favorable to the defendant and would have been material in challenging the witness's trial testimony; after the federal court ordered a retrial, the charges were dropped and the defendant released.

- The prosecutor (i) deliberately withheld the fact that his chief witness had received a deal for his trial testimony, and then (ii) misled the jury by stating in his closing argument that the absence of such a deal favorably reflected upon the veracity of the witness.

- The prosecutor based his argument in favor of a death sentence on prior felony convictions that he knew did not exist, even though defense counsel agreed that they did.

- Neither defense lawyer conducted any investigation seeking evidence that might persuade the jury not to impose the death sentence, because "[e]ach lawyer . . . believed . . . the other was responsible for preparing the penalty phase."[4]

As improbable as it may at first seem, these examples are typical. A Columbia University study released in mid-2000 highlights 48 similarly stark cases that resulted in state capital prisoners succeeding on federal habeas corpus.[5] The most reliable published data show that notwithstanding the strong political, institutional, and legal pressures on the federal courts to leave undisturbed state death penalty cases (which, have, after all, already undergone state direct appeal and collateral review),[6] the federal courts felt compelled to grant habeas corpus relief (i.e., to overturn either the conviction or the death sentence) in 40 percent of the capital cases they reviewed between 1973 and 1995.[7] Thus, federal habeas corpus proceedings have served to reveal and, to some extent, to ameliorate systemic injustices.

But to mount a real attack on the arbitrary outcomes in death penalty cases would require a very great deal in the way of resources and political will. And even then, we might not succeed; it is certainly more than possible that Justice Blackmun was right in his conclusion that "the death penalty cannot be administered in accord with our Constitution."[8] Moreover, any serious exploration of that issue would raise the uncomfortable prospect of discovering that the problems endemic to capital cases are widespread in noncapital ones as well. Thus, for example, in rejecting an impeccably documented attack on the racial disparities in Georgia's death penalty system, Justice Powell wrote in the 1987 case of *McCleskey v. Kemp*:

> McCleskey's claim, taken to its logical conclusion, throws into serious question the principles that underlie our entire criminal justice system. . . . [I]f we accepted McCleskey's claim that racial bias has impermissibly tainted the capital sentencing decision, we could soon be faced with similar claims as to other types of penalty.[9]

Under the pressure of these considerations, both the courts and Congress over the past fifteen years or so have shown a consistent inclination to shoot the messenger: to respond to the unfairness revealed in capital habeas proceedings by devising mechanisms to restrict such proceedings, rather than ones to remedy the unfairness.

For an example, one need look no further than the saga of Warren McCleskey himself, which may someday come to symbolize criminal justice in the Rehnquist era. McCleskey had participated in an armed robbery in which a policeman was killed. Although he maintained that he was not the triggerman, the evidence against him at trial included a purported jailhouse confession to one Offie Evans, an inmate housed near him, in which McCleskey was said to have admitted shooting the officer.

In his original habeas corpus petition in the Georgia courts, McCleskey asserted that Evans had been deliberately sent into his cell by the government to elicit a confession; if this in fact occurred, it indisputably violated McCleskey's Sixth Amendment right to counsel. But the state denied the allegation, the prosecuting attorney stated at a deposition that he was unaware of any prior arrangement with Evans, and a set of documents represented as containing the complete prosecutor's file contained no evidence to support it. Counsel, who had tried but failed to gain any further substantiation, thereupon omitted the claim from the federal habeas corpus petition he filed following denial of relief by the state courts. That federal proceeding was the one that reached the Court in 1987, and resulted in the 5–4 decision written by Justice Powell that rejected the claim that the statistical evidence of overwhelming racial disparities in the administration of Georgia's capital punishment system made out an Equal Protection violation.

Following the decision, McCleskey again sought habeas corpus relief on his claim concerning Evans—this time armed with a 21-page account from Evans to the government of his conversations with McCleskey, a document that had not been included when the prosecution turned over to the defense what purported to be the government's "complete" file. McCleskey had obtained the report from the Atlanta police in the weeks following the Court's decision only as a result of a new interpretation of the Georgia Open Records Act by the Georgia Supreme Court.

After conducting an evidentiary hearing, including the testimony of a jailer whose identity was discovered through the document, the District Court granted habeas relief, concluding that the failure to present the claim earlier was justifiable, and that—since Evans had indeed been deliberately planted by the government—McCleskey was entitled to prevail on the merits. Without reaching the merits, the Eleventh Circuit reversed, holding that the petition should have been dismissed as an "abuse of the writ."[10] McCleskey again sought Supreme Court review.

As of that moment, the law concerning procedural missteps by counsel during habeas corpus proceedings was divided into three categories:

1. Procedural Default. These cases occurred when a prisoner had failed to properly present a claim to a state court that he later sought to assert on federal habeas corpus, and the state court had applied its own procedural rules to deny review of the merits. As a matter of comity, the Supreme Court had held,[11] the federal courts would not review such claims either, unless the petitioner surmounted the difficult hurdle of showing both "cause" for the default—i.e., "some objective factor external to the defense [that] impeded counsel's effort to comply with the State's procedural rule"[12]—and "prejudice" arising from it.

Since McCleskey had properly presented his claim to the Georgia courts, which had rejected it on the merits, the category seemingly had no application to his case.

2. Abuse of the Writ. Where a second federal petition presented a claim that had not been made previously, controlling authority required an inquiry into whether there had been subjective bad faith on the part of the petitioner, that is, whether he had deliberately withheld the newly asserted ground in an effort to multiply bites at the habeas corpus apple.[13] As noted, the District Court in McCleskey's case had held that there was no deliberate withholding, and the case proceeded to the Supreme Court to review the contrary ruling of the Eleventh Circuit.

3. Ends of Justice. In cases where a claim had previously been presented

and adjudicated on federal habeas corpus, existing doctrine required an inquiry into whether the "ends of justice" would be served by allowing its relitigation. This cloudy term had not been clarified by the Supreme Court in recent years, and apparently had nothing to do with McCleskey's case, inasmuch as his Sixth Amendment claim had not been presented in his first federal petition.

In deciding McCleskey's second appeal in 1991, the Court—without benefit of argument from the parties—simply obliterated these distinctions. Henceforth, the standard to be applied in all three situations would be that least favorable to petitioners, namely the "cause and prejudice" standard of the procedural default cases.[14]

That is a standard that falls particularly harshly on death penalty defendants. Only rarely would they have difficulty in demonstrating "prejudice," but they virtually never get that far. Attorney ineffectiveness pervades capital cases to the point of undermining the fairness of the entire system of death penalty adjudication.[15] In fact, it is the most common cause of postconviction reversals in capital cases.[16] But, even so, the courts do not tackle the problem with a realistic recognition of its extent. Rather, as mandated by the Court, they indulge in the fanciful presumption that defense lawyers were competent at trial and on direct appeal and require defendants to demonstrate that a different lawyer would have achieved a different outcome.[17] Thus, in case after case, the courts have rejected claims of ineffective assistance of counsel notwithstanding that the defense lawyer was asleep during the trial, or had never contacted the client, was addicted to cocaine, or barely cross-examined a key witness because the witness had previously been the lawyer's client.[18]

And since the Court has so far been unwilling to implement any right to counsel at all in state postconviction proceedings,[19] an attorney there can forfeit all a client's claims but the client cannot attack him or her as ineffective for having done so. Thus, deficient attorney performance almost never qualifies as "cause," meaning that, as a practical matter, the federal courts on habeas corpus almost never find "cause" for any procedural error they discern in a capital case. And, without "cause," the court does not consider "prejudice"—much less the underlying merits of the petitioner's claim of Constitutional error.

That is precisely what happened in McCleskey's case. Notwithstanding the state's deceptive response to his discovery requests (and his lawyer's obligation to assert on federal habeas corpus only those claims for which a reasonable basis existed), the majority wrote that McCleskey's attorney was at fault for not continuing to assert his claims about Offie Evans. That, however, would not make the lawyer's performance unconstitutionally ineffective because the failure took place during postconviction proceedings, where there is no right to effective counsel.

Since, therefore, McCleskey had failed to show "cause," his petition had been properly dismissed, and he should be executed—as indeed he was—regardless of whether or not the government had in fact acted unconstitutionally. "Finality," the Court said, "has special importance in the context of a federal attack on a state conviction," because "the power of a State to pass laws means little if the State cannot enforce them."[20]

This reification of the "State" as an entity with rights independent of We the People who created it has been pervasive in the recent habeas corpus jurisprudence of the Supreme Court. In creating a legalistic maze of restrictions on the availability of the habeas corpus remedy over the past two decades, the Court has repeatedly cited "federalism," but the statement of this rationale has not been accompanied by an explanation of how it justifies the results reached in the cases at hand. A stark example came a few months after *McCleskey* in *Coleman v. Thompson.*[21] There, the Court ruled that a capital prisoner whose lawyer had filed his state habeas corpus appeals papers three days late had thereby forfeited federal habeas corpus review. This decision was premised on the explicit view that the outcome represented the appropriate "allocation of costs" between the interests of the state avoiding a federal review of its conviction that might lead to an expensive retrial and those of the prisoner in not being executed pursuant to a possibly unconstitutional judgment.[22] The Court began its opinion, "This is a case about federalism."[23]

To invoke federalism to justify such results is untenable, both intellectually and practically. Intellectually, as already discussed (and as well elaborated by Justice Blackmun in his dissent in *Coleman*), the view of federalism that animated the framers supports careful federal review of state court criminal convictions, not deference to the sovereign rights of states to deprive citizens of Constitutionally protected liberty.[24] Practically, the problem is that an unrealistic reliance on the quality of justice in state judicial systems will inevitably (as in *Frank*) lead to unacceptable outcomes. These in turn will invariably produce a backlash whose certain result will be legislative or judicial action to insure more extensive habeas corpus review (as in *Moore*), and whose likely result will be to undermine public support for the criminal justice system as a whole.

But in 1995 Congress cut off funding for the postconviction defender organizations that had provided counsel to the Death Row inmates in many of the cases highlighted above.[25] There was thus considerable concern when it went to work on the habeas corpus reform statute that eventually became AEDPA. And, indeed, some of the early proposals could only be described as radical. For instance, Senator Kyl offered a provision that was designed to eliminate habeas corpus review of state convictions outright. But although Senator Lott praised this idea, on the grounds that it would solve the "problems of delay and abuse by eliminating these habeas corpus reviews of state judgments," the Senate defeated the amendment by a vote of 61 to 38.[26]

In fact, it now appears that in passing the final version of AEDPA Congress ultimately enacted a relatively modest set of reforms. Amid a welter of technical changes, the legislation seeks to speed up habeas proceedings in two basic ways: directly, by setting time limits on various litigation steps, and indirectly, by providing that the federal courts should not grant the writ unless the state proceedings "resulted in a decision that was contrary to, or involved an unreasonable application of, clearly established federal law as determined by the Supreme Court of the United States."[27]

Thus far, the Court has wisely decided to assume that in so acting Congress had learned the important lessons that history teaches about the critical role of federal habeas corpus in assuring adherence to the rule of law. The Court has read AEDPA as a Congressional decision to accomplish its purpose of speeding up habeas litigation by rewriting the procedural rules while making no fundamental alteration in the existing role of the federal courts in inquiring into state capital convictions.[28] As President Clinton said in signing the legislation, it was designed "to streamline Federal appeals for convicted criminals sentenced to the death penalty," while preserving "independent review of Federal legal claims and the bedrock constitutional principle of an independent judiciary."[29]

The episodes canvassed in this volume show why this is the way the act should be interpreted. The history of the American system of dual-level scrutiny of state incarcerations has demonstrated the practical importance of assuring that vigorous federal review actually occurs. The present can learn that lesson from the past, and should bequeath it to the future.

Notes

The following abbreviated forms are used in these notes:

Dempsey Transcript. Transcript of Record, Moore v. Dempsey, 261 U.S. 86 (1923) (No. 199) (filed October 24, 1921).

Documentary History. Documentary History of the Ratification of the Constitution (John P. Kaminski & Gaspare J. Saldino eds., 1984).

Frank Transcript. Transcript of Record, Frank v. Magnum, 237 U.S. 309 (1915) (No. 775).

M-. Citations in this form are to correspondingly numbered microfilms produced by the National Archives and Records Administration.

Milestones I. Eric M. Freedman, *Just Because John Marshall Said It, Doesn't Make It So:* Ex Parte Bollman *and the Illusory Prohibition on the Federal Writ of Habeas Corpus for State Prisoners in the Judiciary Act of 1789*, 51 Alabama Law Review 531 (2000).

Milestones II. Eric M. Freedman, *Leo Frank Lives: Untangling the Historical Roots of Meaningful Federal Habeas Corpus Review of State Convictions*, 51 Alabama Law Review 1467 (2000).

Milestones III. Eric M. Freedman, Brown v. Allen: *The Habeas Corpus Revolution That Wasn't*, 51 Alabama Law Review 1541 (2000).

Except as otherwise indicated, all the Oliver Wendell Holmes correspondence cited is to be found in the Oliver Wendell Holmes, Jr. Papers published on microfilm by University Publications of America. The originals are in the Library of Congress.

Copies of all sources cited are available on request from the reference desk of the Deane Law Library of Hofstra Law School, Hempstead, N.Y. 11550.

NOTES TO INTRODUCTION

1. 28 U.S.C. § 2254(a) (1996).
2. U.S. Const. art. VI.
3. Stated slightly more completely, as shown in Figure 1, a state criminal defendant

has the right after conviction in a state trial court to pursue a direct appeal to one or more state appellate courts, and then to seek discretionary review in the United States Supreme Court by a procedure known as certiorari. Thereafter, most states provide for some form of state postconviction review. Where such procedures exist, a defendant must utilize them before seeking the federal habeas corpus remedy.

4. Pub. L. No. 104-132, 110 Stat. 1214 (1996).

5. 8 U.S. (4 Cranch) 75 (1807).

6. U.S. Const. art. I, § 9, cl. 2.

7. First Judiciary Act, ch. 20, § 14, 1 Stat. 73, 81–82 (1789).

8. 237 U.S. 309 (1915).

9. 261 U.S. 86 (1923).

10. 344 U.S. 443 (1953).

11. The Federalist, No. 51.

NOTES TO CHAPTER 1

1. U.S. Const. art. I, § 9, cl. 2.

2. Statements by the modern Supreme Court to this effect may be found in, *e.g.*, *Felker v. Turpin*, 518 U.S. 651, 659–61, 663–65 (1996); *McCleskey v. Zant*, 499 U.S. 467, 477–78 (1991); *Wainwright v. Sykes*, 433 U.S. 72, 77–78 (1977); *Stone v. Powell*, 428 U.S. 465, 474–75 (1976). Scholars have also uncritically accepted the premise. There is a long list of examples at Milestones I, 536 n.6.

3. The current habeas corpus statute is to be found in 28 U.S.C. §§ 2241–55 (1994 & Supp. III 1997). For a discussion of its history, see Milestones I, 539 n.19.

4. 8 U.S. (4 Cranch) 75 (1807).

5. First Judiciary Act, ch. 20, § 14, 1 Stat 73, 81–82 (1789).

6. A photoreproduction of a draft of this statute in the handwriting of Oliver Ellsworth appears as the Frontispiece.

7. *Ex Parte Bollman*, 8 U.S. (4 Cranch) 75, 98 (1807).

8. *See id.* at 95 (Without statute, "the privilege itself would be lost, although no law for its suspension should be enacted.").

9. *See, e.g., Capital Traction Co. v. Hof,* 174 U.S. 1, 9–10 (1899):

The Judiciary Act of [1789], drawn by Senator (afterwards Chief Justice) Ellsworth, and passed—within six months after the organization of the government, and on the day before the first ten Amendments were proposed to the legislatures of the States—by the first Congress, in which were many eminent men who had been members of the Convention which formed the Constitution, has always been considered as a contemporaneous exposition of the highest authority.

NOTES TO CHAPTER 2

1. 2 The Records of the Federal Convention of 1787, at 334, 340–42 (Max Farrand ed., rev. ed. 1966) (reprinting entry from Convention Journal of Aug. 20, 1787 and Madison's notes based thereon).

2. *Id.*

3. *Id.* at 438.

4. *See* Address No. II of Luther Martin to the Citizens of Maryland (March 21, 1788), *reprinted in* 16 Documentary History 456:

It was my wish that the general government should not have the power of suspending the privilege of the writ of *Habeas Corpus,* as it appears to me altogether unnecessary, and that the power given to it, may and will be used as a dangerous instrument of oppression; but I could not succeed.

For an overview of Martin's role in Philadelphia and during the ratification debates, see William L. Reynolds II, *Luther Martin, Maryland, and the Constitution,* 47 Md. L. Rev. 291, 294–305 (1987).

5. Luther Martin, Genuine Information VIII (Jan. 22, 1788), *reprinted in* 15 Documentary History 434. *See also* Speech of Luther Martin to the Maryland Assembly (Nov. 29, 1787), *reprinted in* 14 *id.* at 291:

Nothing could add to the mischevious tendency of this system more than the power that is given to suspend the Act of Ha: Corpus—Those who could not approve of it urged that the power over the Ha: Corpus ought not to be under the influence of the General Government. It would give them a power over Citizens of particular States who should oppose their encroachments, and the inferior Jurisdictions of the respective States were fully competent to Judge on this important priviledge; but the Allmighty power of deciding by a call for the question silenced all opposition to the measure as it too frequently did to many others.

6. *See* 2 The Records of the Federal Convention of 1787, *supra* note 1, at 596 (reprinting Madison's copy of the committee's report of September 12, 1787).

7. For a detailed consideration, see the pathbreaking article by the late Francis Paschal, *The Constitution and Habeas Corpus,* 1970 Duke L.J. 605, at 608–17.

8. The Federalist No. 84, at 513 (Alexander Hamilton) (Clinton Rossiter ed., 1961); *see also* Speech of James Iredell to the North Carolina Ratifying Convention (July 28, 1788), *reprinted in* 4 The Debates in the Several State Conventions on the Adoption of the Federal Constitution 148 (Jonathan Elliot ed., 2d ed. 1866) [hereinafter Elliot's Debates] (Constitution "may be considered as a great power of attorney, under which no power can be exercised but what is expressly given"). For a more extended discussion, see Milestones I, 548 n.38.

9. Hamilton, *supra* note 8, at 513–14. For a fuller description of the Federalists' position on this issue, see Paul Finkelman, *James Madison and the Bill of Rights: A Reluctant Paternity,* 1990 Sup. Ct. Rev. 301, 309–13.

10. Speech of John Smilie to the Pennsylvania Ratifying Convention (Nov. 28, 1787), *reprinted in* 2 Documentary History 392.

11. Letter from Brutus II to New York Journal (Nov. 1, 1787), *reprinted in* 13 *id.* at 528. For additional examples of this argument, see Speech of George Clinton to the New York Ratifying Convention (June [27], 1788), *reprinted in* 6 The Complete Anti-Federalist 179 (Herbert J. Storing ed., 1981) and Speech of William Grayson to the Virginia Ratifying Convention (June 16, 1788), *reprinted in* 10 Documentary History 1332.

12. Speech of Patrick Henry to the Virginia Ratifying Convention (June 17, 1788), *reprinted in id.* at 1345–46.

13. A Native of Virginia, *Observations Upon the Proposed Plan of Federal Government, reprinted in* 9 Documentary History 655, 691.

14. There is a compilation of relevant primary sources at Milestones I, 551 nn.49–50.

15. *See, e.g.*, 9 Documentary History of the First Federal Congress, 1789–1791: The Diary of William Maclay and Other Notes on Senate Debates 83 (Kenneth R. Bowling & Helen E. Veit eds., 1988) (Maclay Journal entry for June 18, 1789) ("It is the fault of the best Governors when they are placed over a people to endeavour to enlarge their powers"); Broadside from A True Friend (Richmond Dec. 5, 1787), *reprinted in* 14 Documentary History 373–74:

> [I]t is unhappily in the nature of men, when collected for any purpose whatsoever into a body to take a selfish and interested bias, tending invariably towards the increasing of their prerogatives and the prolonging of the term of their function

Speech of William Grayson to the Virginia Ratifying Convention (June 21, 1788), *reprinted in* 10 *id.* at 1444 ("[P]ower . . . ought to be granted on a supposition that men will be bad"); Speech of Patrick Henry to the Virginia Ratifying Convention (June 16, 1788), *reprinted in id.* at 1321 ("Look at the predominant thirst of dominion which has invariably and uniformly prompted rulers to abuse their powers."); Speech of William Lenoir to the North Carolina Ratifying Convention (July 30, 1788), *reprinted in* 4 Elliot's Debates, *supra* note 8, at 203–04 ("[I]t is the nature of man to be tyrannical. . . . We ought to consider the depravity of human nature [and] the predominant thirst for power which is in the breast of every one.").

16. Speech of Samuel Spencer to the North Carolina Ratifying Convention (July 25, 1788), *reprinted in id.* at 68.

17. Letter from Louis Guillaume Otto to Comte de Montmorin (Oct. 20, 1787), *reprinted in* 13 Documentary History 424. *See* Letter from Montezuma to the Independent Gazetteer (Oct. 17, 1788), *reprinted in* 3 The Complete Anti-Federalist, *supra* note 11, at 53, 56:

> We do not much like that sturdy privilege of the people—the right to demand the writ of *habeas corpus*—we have therefore reserved the power of refusing it in cases of rebellion, and you know we are the judges of what is rebellion.

18. *See* Letter from Thomas Jefferson to James Madison (Dec. 20, 1787), *reprinted in* 8 Documentary History 250 ("I do not like . . . the omission of a bill of rights providing clearly and without the aid of sophisms . . . for the eternal & unremitting force of the habeas corpus laws"); Letter from Thomas Jefferson to Alexander Donald (Feb. 7, 1788), *reprinted in id.* at 354 (hoping that Constitution would be amended "by a declaration of rights which shall stipulate . . . no suspensions of the habeas corpus"); Letter from Thomas Jefferson to William Stephens Smith, (Feb. 2, 1788), *reprinted in* 14 *id.* at 500 (containing same idea).

The correspondence between Jefferson and Madison on this subject is more fully considered in Finkelman, *supra* note 9, at 329–34, which observes that Madison was skeptical about the ability of any Constitutional guarantee against suspension of the writ, however phrased, to stand up against the force of a passionate burst of public opinion.

19. *See, e.g.*, Letter of A Georgian to the Gazette of the State of Georgia (Nov. 15, 1787), *reprinted in* 3 Documentary History 240 (suggesting that Clause read: "The privilege of the Writ of Habeas Corpus shall remain, without any exceptions whatever, inviolate forever."); Dissent of the Minority of the Pennsylvania Convention (Dec. 12, 1787), *reprinted in* 2 *id.* at 630 (calling for a Bill of Rights securing "personal liberty by the clear and unequivocal establishment of the writ of *habeas corpus*").

20. Speech of James McHenry to the Maryland House of Delegates (Nov. 29, 1787), *reprinted in* 14 *id.* at 283.

21. Prior to the highly controversial decisions in *Tarble's Case*, 80 U.S. (13 Wall.) 197 (1871), and *Ableman v. Booth*, 62 U.S. (21 How.) 506 (1858), this assumption was perfectly sound. For example, state writs of habeas corpus were used in Massachusetts "on numerous occasions to test the validity of military enlistments, and in the majority of the cases the enlistees were released," William E. Nelson, *The American Revolution and the Emergence of Modern Doctrines of Federalism and Conflicts of Laws, in* Law in Colonial Massachusetts 419, 457 (Daniel R. Coquillette ed., 1984). That this seems peculiar to modern ears reflects the fact we today have forgotten that the issue became one of state-federal power only as a result of the tensions surrounding the Civil War. For lawmakers of the founding era, the question was one of the rights of the individual against the government—in this example, the right of the citizen to invoke the protection of civil against military authority. *See id.*

22. The exception was New York, which proposed an amendment:

That the writ of *habeas corpus* shall not, by any law, be suspended for a longer term than six months, or until twenty days after the meeting of the Congress next following the passing of the action for such suspension.

Resolution of the New York Ratifying Convention (July 26, 1788), *reprinted in* 1 Elliot's Debates, *supra* note 8, at 330. There is a more extended discussion at Milestones I, 555 n.59.

23. *See* Richard B. Bernstein, The Federalist *on Energetic Government, 1787–1788, in* Roots of the Republic 335, 340–41 (Steven L. Schechter ed., 1990). *See also Rhode Island v. Massachusetts,* 37 U.S. (12 Peters) 657, 729 (1838):

> [O]wing to the imbecility of congress, the powers of the states being reserved for legislative and judicial purposes, and the utter want of power in the United States to act directly on the people of the states, on the rights of the states (except those in controversy between them) or the subject matters, on which they had delegated but mere shadowy jurisdiction, a radical change of government became necessary.

I have set forth my views on this history in considerably more detail in Eric M. Freedman, *Why Constitutional Lawyers and Historians Should Take a Fresh Look at the Emergence of the Constitution from the Confederation Period: The Case of the Drafting of the Articles of Confederation,* 60 Tenn. L. Rev. 784 (1993).

24. Gordon S. Wood, *The Origins of Judicial Review Revisited, or How the Marshall Court Made More out of Less,* 56 Wash. & Lee L. Rev. 787, 791 (1999). Madison made this argument for the new Constitution explicitly at several points in The Federalist, *e.g.,* No. 10, at 84, No. 43, at 275–77 (Clinton Rossiter ed., 1961). *See also* Letter from James Madison to Thomas Jefferson (Oct. 24, 1787), *reprinted in* 12 The Papers of Thomas Jefferson 276 (Julian P. Boyd ed., 1950) (observing that the flagrant injustices of state legislatures to private individuals were critical to preparing the national mind for reform of the Confederation); Speech of Henry Lee to Virginia Ratifying Convention (June 9, 1788), *reprinted in* 9 Documentary History 1074 ("If Pandora's box were on one side of me, and a tender-law on the other, I would rather submit to the box than to the tender law."); Speech of Edmund Randolph to Virginia Ratifying Convention (June 6, 1788), *reprinted in id.* at 972–73 (denouncing unjust and oppressive legislative acts since Revolution); Speech of Jasper Yeates to Pennsylvania Ratifying Convention (Nov. 30, 1787), *reprinted in* 2 *id.* at 438–39 (By such enactments, "the government of laws has been almost superseded. . . . [But the Constitution will be] the glorious instrument of our political salvation."). *See generally* Letter XII of The Landholder to the Connecticut Courant (March 17, 1788), *reprinted in* 16 *id.* at 405 (denouncing Rhode Island tender acts).

25. *See, e.g., Coleman v. Thompson,* 501 U.S. 722, 726 (1991) (denying federal habeas corpus review because capital prisoner had filed state habeas corpus appeal three days late, in an opinion beginning, "This is a case about federalism."). *But see* Martin S. Flaherty, *More Apparent Than Real: The Revolutionary Commitment to Constitutional Federalism,* 45 Kansas L. Rev. 993, 1011–12 (1997) (by time of Declaration, patriots had already rejected a federalism based on protecting states from central control as a strategy for safeguarding liberty); Robert J. Kaczorowski, *The Tragic Irony of American Federalism: National Sovereignty versus State Sovereignty in Slavery and in Freedom,* 45 Kansas L. Rev. 1015, 1043 (1997) ("[W]hen today's state sovereignty plurality applies its state sovereignty theory of constitutional federalism, it is not enforcing the Founders' First Principles."); Eric M. Freedman, *The*

Suspension Clause in the Ratification Debates, 44 Buff. L. Rev. 451, 466 n.59 (1996) (criticizing *Coleman* for adopting a conception of federalism that "is simply the opposite of the founders'"); Akhil Reed Amar, *Of Sovereignty and Federalism*, 96 Yale L.J. 1425, 1425–26 (1987) (criticizing Court's use of "federalism" in many contexts "to thwart full remedies for violations of constitutional rights," and seeking to reclaim concept as one "designed to protect, not defeat . . . individual rights").

For a full history of *Coleman* that canvasses numerous failings during the legal process and raises haunting doubts as to whether an innocent man may have been executed, see John C. Tucker, May God Have Mercy (1997).

There is a further discussion of the case *infra* Chapter 23, text accompanying notes 21–24.

26. *See* Henry J. Bourguignon, *The Federal Key to the Judiciary Act of 1789*, 46 S.C. L. Rev. 647, 647–51 (1995) (noting that shared belief of Federalists and Antifederalists in liberty-preserving virtues of federalism, conceived of as concurrent state and federal power over as many subjects as possible, was central to many key political compromises in founding generation).

NOTES TO CHAPTER 3

1. 5 U.S. (1 Cranch) 137 (1803).

2. *See* Eric M. Freedman, *The Law as King and the King as Law: Is a President Immune from Criminal Prosecution before Impeachment?*, 20 Hast. Const. L.Q. 7, at 22 & n.47 (1992).

3. *See* 1 Political Correspondence and Public Papers of Aaron Burr 982–83 (Mary-Jo Kline & Joanne W. Ryan eds., 1983). Several detailed accounts appear in the N.Y. Eve. Post, Feb. 18, 1807, at 1, which also reports Henry Clay's much-publicized comment in the Senate on February 11 "that the late seizure of men at New Orleans, by military force, and the transportation of them to the Atlantic coast, was one of the most arbitrary and outrageous acts ever committed." Indeed, the entire sequence of events calls to mind Luther Martin's forebodings described in Chapter 2.

4. *See* 1 Charles Warren, The Supreme Court in United States History 302 (1924).

5. *See* Milton Lomask, Aaron Burr: The Conspiracy and the Years of Exile, 1805–1835, at 202 (1982).

6. *See* Jean Edward Smith, John Marshall: Definer of a Nation 355 (1996); Am. Mercury, Feb. 12, 1807, at 1 (reporting House debate).

7. *See United States v. Bollman*, 24 F. Cas. 1189 (C.C.D.C. 1807) (No. 14,622). In support of the application, the United States attorney proffered an affidavit from General Wilkinson "and a printed copy of the president's message to congress of the 22d of January, 1807," *id.* In this communication, Jefferson denounced the conspiracy and said that General Wilkinson's information placed Burr's guilt "beyond question." *See* 16 Annals of Cong. 39, 40 (1807); *see also id.* at 1008–18 (reprinting supporting documents accompanying message).

8. *See Bollman*, 24 F. Cas., at 1189. The Chief Judge, William Cranch, a Federalist, opined that there was insufficient probable cause, but was outvoted by his two Republican colleagues. Extended accounts of the proceedings appear in the National Intelligencer of Feb. 2, 1807, and Feb. 4, 1807.

9. *See Ex Parte Bollman*, 8 U.S. (4 Cranch) 75, 76 n.(a) (1807).

10. *Id.* at 79.

11. N.Y. Eve. Post, Feb. 14, 1807, at 1.

12. *Ex Parte Bollman*, 8 U.S. (4 Cranch), at 79.

13. For convenience, I have numbered counsel's arguments, and, in the two succeeding sections of text, used the same numbering to designate Marshall's responses and my own analysis. For the same reason, I have relied on the version of the argument reprinted in the United States Reports. Another version, which is very similar but perhaps preserves Goodloe's oratory slightly better, was published in two parts in the National Intelligencer of Feb. 18, 1807, and Feb. 20, 1807.

14. *Ex Parte Bollman*, 8 U.S. (4 Cranch), at 79.

15. *Id.* at 82.

16. 124 Eng. Rep. 1006 (1670).

17. *Ex Parte Bollman*, 8 U.S. (4 Cranch) at 80–81.

18. The text of Section 14 with interpolated clause numbers has been set forth *supra* Chapter 1, text accompanying note 6.

19. *Ex Parte Bollman*, 8 U.S. (4 Cranch), at 87–88.

20. "The Supreme Court shall . . . have power to issue . . . writs of mandamus, in cases warranted by the principles and usages of law, to any courts appointed, or persons holding office, under the authority of the United States." First Judiciary Act, ch. 20, § 13, 1 Stat. 73, 80 (1789).

21. U.S. Const. art. III, § 2, cl. 2:

In all Cases affecting Ambassadors, other public ministers and Consuls, and those in which a State shall be a Party, the supreme Court shall have original Jurisdiction. In all the other cases before mentioned [in U.S. Const. art. III, § 2, cl. 1], the supreme Court shall have appellate Jurisdiction, both as to Law and Fact, with such Exceptions, and under such Regulations as the Congress shall make.

The ruling in *Marbury* was that Section 13 (set forth *supra* note 20) authorized the Court to assume original jurisdiction over controversies, like the one involved there, that did not fall within the first sentence just quoted, and was therefore unconstitutional.

22. *Ex Parte Bollman*, 8 U.S. (4 Cranch), at 86.

23. That is, this case fell within the second sentence quoted from Article III *supra* note 21.

24. 3 U.S. (3 Dall.) 17 (1795).

25. *Hamilton*, 3 U.S. (3 Dall.), at 17–18. Dissenting in *Bollman*, Justice William Johnson agreed that the "case of Hamilton was strikingly similar to the pre-

sent," but argued "that the authority of it was annihilated by the very able decision in *Marbury v. Madison*," since the *Hamilton* Court had been exercising original jurisdiction. *Bollman*, 8 U.S. (4 Cranch), at 103–04 (Johnson, J., dissenting).

26. 7 U.S. (3 Cranch) 448 (1806).

27. *Id.* at 450–51, 453. Dissenting in *Bollman*, Justice Johnson reported that he had objected to the Court's disposition of *Burford*, but had "submitted in silent deference to the decision of my brethren." *Bollman*, 8 U.S. (4 Cranch), at 107 (Johnson, J., dissenting). He also reported that his *Bollman* dissent had the support of an absent Justice. *Id.* Scholars have long been hopelessly divided as to whether this was Chase or not. *See* David P. Currie, The Constitution in the Supreme Court: The First Hundred Years, 1789–1888, at 81 n.131 (1985).

28. *See Ex Parte Bollman*, 8 U.S. (4 Cranch), at 91–92.

29. *Id.* at 93–94. The elided portion of the passage contains two further responses to Harper's arguments on the role of the common law. First, Marshall asserted:

> for the meaning of the term *habeas corpus*, resort may unquestionably be had to the common law; but the power to award the writ by any of the courts of the United States, must be given by written law.

Second, responding to Harper's discussion of the contempt power, Marshall wrote:

> This opinion is not to be considered as abridging the power of courts over their own officers, or to protect themselves, and their members, from being disturbed in the exercise of their functions. It extends only to the power of taking cognisance of any question between individuals, or between the government and individuals.

It would seem to follow from this second point that the case of Comfort Sands, described *infra* Chapter 6, text accompanying notes 7–8, would have come out the same way even after *Bollman*.

30. *Bollman*, 8 U.S (4 Cranch) at 95.

31. *Id.* at 96.

32. *Id.* at 96–97.

33. *Id.* at 99.

34. *Id.*

35. *Id.* at 101.

36. *Id.* at 100.

37. *Id.* at 114.

38. *See* Supreme Court Minute Book (entries of Feb. 16–20, 1807); Letter from Buckner Thurston to Harry Innes (Feb. 18, 1807), Innes Papers, Manuscript Reading Room, Library of Congress.

39. *Ex Parte Bollman*, 8 U.S. (4 Cranch) at 125, 128–36.

40. Scholars have frequently noted Marshall's cavalier treatment of precedent, whether favorable or unfavorable. *See, e.g.*, Susan Low Bloch & Maeva Marcus, *John Marshall's Selective Use of History in* Marbury v. Madison, 1986 Wis. L. Rev. 301 (showing how Marshall invented nonexistent supporting precedent and ignored

relevant negative precedent). For an insightful summary, see Christopher L. Eisgruber, *John Marshall's Judicial Rhetoric,* 1996 Sup. Ct. Rev. 439.

41. Francis Paschal, *The Constitution and Habeas Corpus,* 1970 Duke L.J. 605, at 628. *See also* Milton Cantor, *The Writ of Habeas Corpus: Early American Origins and Development, in* Freedom and Reform, 55, 76–77 (Harold M. Hyman & Leonard W. Levy eds., 1967) ("Marshall's reasoning in *Ex Parte Bollman* was strained and evasive," nor were "the precedents cited—though Marshall was always weak in this area.").

42. These examples are drawn from actual cases described *infra* Chapter 4, sec. (B)(2) and Chapter 6, text accompanying notes 2–6.

Another such example would be a state's arrest of a foreign diplomat enjoying diplomatic immunity. Just this had occurred prior to *Bollman* in *Ex Parte Caberra,* 4 F. Cas. 964, 966 (C.C. D. Pa. 1805) (No. 2,278) (discussed *infra* Chapter 4, text accompanying note 7), and although the holding reached there—that the proviso to Section 14 precluded issuance of the writ—might have supported Marshall's opinion, the obvious undesirability of the result probably made it an unattractive case to rely upon.

43. Justice Johnson's dissent seems not to have considered these possibilities. *See Bollman,* 8 U.S. (4 Cranch), at 105 (Johnson, J., dissenting):

> To give to this clause the construction contended for by counsel, would be to suppose that the legislature would commit the absurd act of granting the power of issuing the writs of *scire facias* and *habeas corpus,* without an object or end to be answered by them.

In other words, reading the statute even more restrictively than Marshall did, his view was that a federal court had the power to issue writs of habeas corpus only if (1) the petitioner were a federal prisoner and (2) the court had an underlying action pending before it.

One wonders whether he would have taken the same position if he had foreseen the situation he would confront in *Elkison v. Deliesseline,* 8 F. Cas. 493 (C. D. S.C. 1823) (No. 4,366) (described *infra* Chapter 4, text accompanying notes 8–9).

44. *Ex Parte Bollman,* 8 U.S. (4 Cranch), at 87–88.

45. *See* Donald E. Wilkes, Jr., Federal Postconviction Remedies and Relief 61 (1996).

46. Cantor, *supra* note 41, at 75.

47. This distinction is elaborated *infra* Chapter 4, sec. B. As described there, I believe that the correct reading is precisely the opposite of the one Marshall reached.

48. *See* David P. Currie, *The Constitution in Congress: The Jeffersonians, 1801–1829,* at 31–38 (2001) Wake Forest L. Rev. 219, 249–59 (1998) (describing proceedings).

49. R. Kent Newmyer, *Chief Justice Marshall in the Context of His Times,* 57 Wash. & Lee L. Rev. 841, 844–45 (1999).

50. Paschal, *supra* note 41, at 630–32 argues that Marshall was incorrect on this point. Since, as indicated in paragraph 1(B) of text, I (unlike Paschal) believe Mar-

shall to have been correct in his conclusion that Clause [1] of Section 14 is an independent rather than an ancillary grant of power to the federal courts, I need not enter into this debate.

51. *See* Dallin Oaks, *The Original Writ of Habeas Corpus in the Supreme Court,* 1962 Sup. Ct. Rev. 153, 177–82.

52. In theory, this might change in the future if Congress were to seek to repeal the Supreme Court's statutory authority to grant habeas corpus relief. Leaving the Suspension Clause entirely aside, such a statute would seemingly violate Article III if the Supreme Court's habeas jurisdiction were original, but not if it were appellate. Recent scholarship, however, has begun to sketch out two responses. One is to suggest a reexamination of Marshall's statement that the Supreme Court's habeas corpus jurisdiction is appellate in the Constitutional sense, *see* Milestones I, 571 n.126, and the other is to make the case that, even if the jurisdiction is indeed appellate, Article III does not grant Congress unlimited control over it, *see* James S. Liebman & William F. Ryan, *"Some Effectual Power": The Quantity and Quality of Decisionmaking That Article III and the Supremacy Clause Demand of the Federal Courts,* 98 Colum. L. Rev. 696, 865–66, 882–84 (1998).

53. *See* 1 James S. Liebman & Randy Hertz, Federal Habeas Corpus Practice and Procedure, § 2.4d, at 43–46 (3d ed. 1998).

54. As the illuminating account in Wilfred J. Ritz, Rewriting the History of the Judiciary Act of 1789, 30, 35–41 (1990) demonstrates, the concept of a strict separation of roles between trial courts (primarily fact finders, tightly constricted in legal rulings) and appellate ones (primarily law declarers, tightly constricted in factual review) is a modern one. All students are indebted to Professors Wythe Holt of the University of Alabama School of Law and L. H. LaRue of Washington and Lee University School of Law for performing the extensive editorial labors necessary to bring Professor Ritz's invaluable work to publication after illness rendered him unable to complete it.

55. *See, e.g., Beglee v. Anderson,* M-1214, roll 1 (C.C. D. Tenn., Aug 5, 1812); *Smith v. Armstead,* M-931, roll 1 (C.C. D. Md., June 16, 1814); *United States v. Towson, id.* (C.C. D. Md., May 27, 1812). In both these latter cases, there is additional documentation beyond that on the microfilm in the records of the National Archives and Records Administration housed in Philadelphia. *See also United States ex rel. Wheeler v. Williamson,* 28 F. Cas. 682, 685 (E.D. Pa. 1855) (No. 16,725) (finding after hearing that return to writ, which denied custody over claimed slaves, was "evasive, if not false"); *Ex Parte Bennett,* 3 F. Cas. 204 (C.C. D. D.C. 1825) (No. 1,311) (examining anew at habeas corpus hearing witnesses who had appeared before committing magistrate); *United States v. Irvine,* M-1184, roll 1 (C.C. D. Ga., May 8, 1815) (discharging petitioner because, despite having been given opportunity, detaining officer had failed to provide proof to support statement in his affidavit that the enlistment had obtained required parental consent, *see* Act of March 16, 1802, ch. 9, § 11, 1 Stat. 135).

56. *Matter of Peters*, M-1215 (D. W. Tenn., Dec. 31, 1827). All the quotations through the end of this paragraph of text are taken from the same source.

57. Some examples appear *infra* Chapter 4, text accompanying notes 7–10.

58. Act of February 5, 1867, ch. 28, 14 Stat. 385. The background of this act, which forms the basis of the current federal habeas corpus statute, is described in Anthony G. Amsterdam, *Criminal Prosecutions Affecting Federally Guaranteed Civil Rights: Federal Removal and Habeas Corpus Jurisdiction to Abort State Court Trial,* 113 U. Pa. L. Rev. 793, 819–25 (1965).

NOTES TO CHAPTER 4

1. Wilfred J. Ritz, Rewriting the History of the Judiciary Act of 1789, at 20–22 (1990). *See* William R. Casto, *Oliver Ellsworth,* 1996 J. Sup. Ct. Hist., vol. 2, at 73, 77 ("In crafting the Judiciary Act, Ellsworth brought to bear the full extent of his remarkable ability to broker pragmatic compromises.").

2. For a modern-day example of this distinction, *see* Fed. R. App. P. 27(c) (differentiating between powers of a single Court of Appeals judge and those of the whole court to act on motions). Similarly, 28 U.S.C. §§ 2101 (c), (f) (1988) contain specific grants of authority to individual Justices of the Supreme Court.

3. *Ex Parte Bollman,* 8 U.S. (4 Cranch) 75, 99 (1807).

4. *See* William R. Casto, Correspondence, 83 Am. J. Int'l. L. 901 (1989); Wythe Holt, "*To Establish Justice": Politics, the Judiciary Act of 1789, and the Invention of the Federal Courts,* 1989 Duke L.J. 1421, at 1481–85; *supra* Chapter 1, note 9.

5. U.S. (2 Dall.) 247, 248 n.1 (Pa. 1796).

6. *See* William R. Casto, *The Federal Courts' Protective Jurisdiction over Torts Committed in Violation of the Law of Nations,* 18 Conn. L. Rev. 467, 490–95 (1986) (describing widespread concern caused by national government's inability to protect diplomats under Confederation, attention paid to this issue in Philadelphia and ratification debates, and creation by First Congress of criminal sanctions and of federal alien tort jurisdiction as Section 9 of Judiciary Act); Kenneth C. Randall, *Federal Jurisdiction over International Law Claims: Inquiries into the Alien Tort Statute,* 18 N.Y.U. J. Int'l. L. & Pol. 1, 11–28 (1985) (reviewing history, including "well publicized incidents of criminal and tortious offenses against ambassadors and other foreign dignitaries" that had occurred prior to the enactment of the Judiciary Act, noting awareness of framers that injustices to aliens could lead to war, and concluding: "it appears that the Alien Tort Statute and other provisions of the Judiciary Act concerning aliens were largely intended to avoid denying justice to aliens. That intention was consistent with the overall attempt of the framers to establish authority in the federal judiciary over actions affecting foreign relations."). *See also* Frederick W. Marks III, Independence on Trial: Foreign Affairs and the Making of the Constitution, at x (2d ed. 1986) (arguing that "the conduct of foreign affairs" under Confed-

eration was the "overriding concern" that "gave rise to the Constitution, [and] provided the winning issue in state campaigns for ratification.").

7. *See* 4 F. Cas. 964, 966 (C.C. D. Pa. 1805) (No. 2,278); *supra* Chapter 3, note 42.

8. 8 F. Cas. 493 (C. D. S.C. 1823) (No. 4,366).

9. As suggested *supra* Chapter 3, note 43, this event must have caused him to give new thought to his dissent in *Bollman*. In any event, the South Carolina statute and its enforcement provoked a great deal of controversy, both between North and South and between the United States and Great Britain, and led to two formal opinions by successive Attorneys General taking opposite positions, *compare* 2 Op. Atty. Gen. 659, 661 (1824), *reprinted in* The Constitutions and the Attorneys General 36, 38 (H. Jefferson Powell ed., 1999) (concluding law "is void, as being against the constitution, treaties, and laws of the United States, and incompatible with the rights of all nations in amity with the United States") *with* 2 Op. Atty. Gen. 426, *reprinted in id.*, at 41 (concluding the contrary). For descriptions of the political context of *Elkison*, see Paul Finkelman, *The Constitution and the Intentions of the Framers: The Limits of Historical Analysis*, 50 U. Pitt. L. Rev. 349, 386–89 (1989); Donald G. Morgan, *Justice William Johnson on the Treaty-Making Power*, 22 Geo. Wash. L. Rev. 187, 189–98 (1953). For a discussion of its international ramifications, see Jack L. Goldsmith, *Federal Courts, Foreign Affairs, and Federalism*, 83 Va. L. Rev. 1617, 1655 & n.163 (1997).

10. 44 U.S. (3 How.) 103 (1845).

11. Francis Paschal, *The Constitution and Habeas Corpus*, 1970 Duke L.J. 605, at 645.

12. 31 Car. 2, c. 2.

13. "With the sole exception of Connecticut, which passed its own unique habeas corpus statute in 1821, all of the habeas corpus acts passed in the thirteen original colonies or states were patterned after the English Act," Dallin H. Oaks, *Habeas Corpus in the States—1776–1865*, 32 U. Chi. L. Rev. 243, 253 (1965), and the act often guided courts in cases to which it did not apply directly.

14. *See Jenkes Case* [1676], 6 State Trials 1190, 1196–1205 (T. Howell comp., 1816). For a general view of the surrounding political context, see Mark Kishlansky, A Monarchy Transformed 242–62 (1996). *See also* Rollin C. Hurd, A Treatise on the Right of Personal Liberty and on the Writ of Habeas Corpus 92–103 (1858).

15. Oaks, *supra* note 13, at 252.

16. *See* Neil Douglas McFeeley, *The Historical Development of Habeas Corpus*, 30 Sw. L.J. 585, 592–93 (1976). *See also* Donald E. Wilkes, Jr., Federal Postconviction Remedies and Relief 60 (1996); Oliver H. Prince, A Digest of the Laws of the State of Georgia 921–23 (2d ed. 1837); *Remarks on the Writ of Habeas Corpus ad Subjiciendum, and the Practice Connected Therewith*, 4 Am. L. Register 257, 262–63, 276 (1856).

17. Edmund Randolph, Report on the Judiciary System (Dec. 27, 1790), *reprinted in* American State Papers: 1 Miscellaneous 21, 25, 30 (Walter Lowrie & Walter S. Franklin eds., 1834) (Miscellaneous Document no. 17). This report is considered at length in Wythe Holt's illuminating and well-documented article *"Federal Courts as the Asylum to Federal Interests": Randolph's Report, The Benson Amendment, and the "Original Understanding" of the Federal Judiciary*, 36 Buff. L. Rev. 341 (1988), and has been reprinted with a commentary in 4 Documentary History of the Supreme Court of the United States 122–67 (Maeva Marcus et al. eds., 1992).

18. Further evidence of Randolph's views is to be found in his argument in *Chisholm v. Georgia*, 2 U.S. (2 Dall.) 419, 421–22 (1793), in which he suggests that if a state were to suspend the writ in violation of the Suspension Clause, "a prisoner may be liberated by habeas corpus," which, in context, could only mean federal habeas corpus.

Professor Paschal argues in addition that Section 30 of the short-lived Judiciary Act of 1801, ch. 4, § 30, 2 Stat. 98, which unambiguously attached the proviso only to the powers granted to Justices and judges, "can only be regarded as explanatory of the Act of 1789." Paschal, *supra* note 11, at 643. The Judiciary Act of 1801 was repealed by Act of March 8, 1802, ch. 8, 2 Stat. 182, *see* Erwin C. Surrency, History of the Federal Courts 23–25 (1987).

19. Originally, the act provided that the circuit courts would consist of two Justices and the district judge, any two of whom would constitute a quorum. *See* First Judiciary Act, ch. 20, § 4, 1 Stat 73, 74–75 (1789). This was amended by the Act of March 2, 1793, ch. 22, § 1, 1 Stat. 333, 333–34, which required the attendance of only one Justice and one district judge and provided that the presence of the Justice alone was sufficient to constitute a quorum. This development is described in Wythe Holt, *"The Federal Courts Have Enemies in All Who Fear Their Influence on State Objects": The Failure to Abolish Supreme Court Circuit-Riding in the Judiciary Acts of 1792 and 1793*, 36 Buff. L. Rev. 301, 336–38 (1987), which presents the overall political context of these modifications.

20. Surrency, *supra* note 18, at 19.

21. In that year, the situation was changed by the passage of the Act of April 29, 1802, ch. 21, § 4, 4 Stat. 158 ("[W]hen only one of the judges hereby directed to hold the circuit courts, shall attend, such circuit court may be held by the judge so attending.").

22. These dates are listed individually at Milestones I, 581 n. 168.

23. *Ex Parte Everts*, 8 F.Cas. 909, 913 (C.C. S.D. Ohio 1858).

24. The minute books of this court (known as the Circuit Court for the Southern District of Georgia after 1802) are somewhat unusual in recording, and separately denominating, orders in chambers. But there is every reason to believe that petitioners everywhere regularly approached individual judges when the courts were not formally in session, *see, e.g., Nelson v. Cutter*, 17 F. Cas. 1316 (C.C. D. Ohio

1844) (No. 10,104) (opinion in vacation granting habeas discharge on basis that affidavit proffered to justify arrest of defendants for debt in diversity case was insufficient under Ohio law); *In re Keeler,* 14 F. Cas. 173 (D. Ark. 1843)(No. 7,637) (stating that "clear" power existed to grant application, presented by father to judge in chambers in vacation, to secure son's release from military, but holding application legally insufficient).

25. *Fitzgerald v. Brownlaw* (Dec. 4, 1809), M-1172. Such proceedings were conducted in chambers as a matter of course, *e.g., Billing v. Hall* (Feb. 2, 1821), *id.*; *Holbrook v. McNeil* (Mar. 18, 1839), *id.* The applicable federal statute, Act of January 6, 1800, ch. 4, § 2, 2 Stat. 5, provided that persons imprisoned on process issuing from any court of the United States were entitled to be released upon taking a prescribed oath of insolvency.

26. *United States v. Frank* (Feb. 24, 1820), M-1172.

27. That is, on suspicion that she was being illegally imported as a slave at a time when the trade had been outlawed, *see* Act of March 2, 1807, ch. 22, 2 Stat. 426; Act of April 20, 1818, ch. 91, 3 Stat. 450.

28. *United States v. Elizabeth* (Apr. 19, 1823), M-1172.

29. *United States v. Gillis and Donahue* (Feb. 10, 1824), M-1172. The District Judge wrote:

I do not think the case cognizable in the Courts of the United States, but if it should be yet it is very uncertain if any offence was committed, and if there was it is undoubtedly very uncertain & hardly capable of being ascertained who did commit it. Under such circumstances, I do not feel warranted in detaining the prisoners for trial in May.

i.e., at the next regular term of court.

30. *Bullock v. United States* (Apr. 28, 1824), M-1172. The application was for a preliminary injunction, rather than for a writ of habeas corpus, but the order of the court was that, upon petitioner's giving security in a specified sum, "the Marshal is to confine him no longer."

31. *United States v. Jarvis* (Apr. 18, 1825), M-1172.

32. *See Murray v. The Charming Betsy,* 6 U.S. (2 Cranch) 64, 118 (1804).

33. *See, e.g., United States v. X-Citement Video,* 513 U.S. 464, 469 (1994) (applying rule "that a statute is to be construed where fairly possible so as to avoid substantial constitutional questions," since "[w]e do not assume that Congress, in passing laws, intended" arguably unconstitutional results); *Public Citizen v. United States Department of Justice,* 491 U.S. 440, 465–67 (1989) (applying rule as decisive consideration where other interpretive factors resulted in "a close question"); *Edward J. DeBartolo Corp. v. Florida Gulf Coast Building and Construction Trades Council,* 485 U.S. 568, 575 (1988):

[W]here an otherwise acceptable construction of a statute would raise serious constitutional problems, the Court will construe the statute to avoid such problems unless such construction is plainly contrary to the intent of Congress. . . . This cardinal principle has its roots in Chief Justice Marshall's opinion for the Court in *Murray v. The Charming Betsy*, [6 U.S. (2 Cranch) 64, 118 (1804)], and has for so long been applied by this Court that it is beyond debate.

United States ex rel. Attorney General v. Delaware & Hudson Corp., 213 U.S. 366, 408 (1909):

> [W]here a statute is susceptible of two constructions, by one of which grave and doubtful constitutional questions arise and by the other of which such questions are avoided, our duty is to adopt the latter.

See also Immigration and Naturalization Service, 121 S. Ct. 2271, 2279–82 (2001); Note, *The Avoidance of Constitutional Questions and the Preservation of Judicial Review: Federal Court Treatment of the New Habeas Provisions*, 111 Harv. L. Rev. 1578, 1584–87 (1998) (summarizing scholarly views of the rule); Milestones I, 585 n.182 (collecting additional authority).

34. Credit for originating this suggestion belongs to Wythe Holt. *See* Holt, *supra* note 4, at 1511. Professor Holt has also been gracious enough to abandon, in light of my arguments, the reading of Section 14 he advanced in that article, *id.*, at 1496–97. *See* Wythe Holt, *Introduction: Law vs. Order, or Habeas vs. Hobbes*, 51 Ala. L. Rev. 525, 528 (2000).

35. As described in the Introduction and *supra* Chapter 3, text accompanying note 30, *Ex Parte Bollman*, 8 U.S. (4 Cranch) 75, 95 (1807) characterized the Suspension Clause as doing no more than creating an obligation on Congress to provide for the writ, since the privilege would otherwise be lost.

36. *See* Michael G. Collins, *Article III Cases, State Court Duties, and the Madisonian Compromise*, 1995 Wisc. L. Rev. 39, 102 n.178.

37. These cases are described *infra* Chapter 6.

NOTES TO CHAPTER 5

1. Letter from John Marshall to St. George Tucker (Nov. 27, 1800), *reprinted in* 6 The Papers of John Marshall 23, 24 (Charles F. Hobson et al. eds., 1990) (footnotes omitted). The quoted passage follows one in which Marshall, then Secretary of State, approves of the federal court's exercise of common-law jurisdiction in *Williams' Case*, which is described later in this chapter.

2. William R. Casto, The Supreme Court in the Early Republic: The Chief Justiceships of John Jay and Oliver Ellsworth 34–35 (1995). *See id.* at 156 ("Virtually all lawyers agreed that judges did not make the common law; they merely administered the common law that already existed in nature."); G. Edward White, *Recovering the World of the Marshall Court*, 33 John Marshall L. Rev. 781, 791–93 (2000).

3. Castro, *Supra* note 2, at 35.

4. *See* Wilfred J. Ritz, Rewriting the History of the Judiciary Act of 1789, at 28–52 (1990); *see also* G. Edward White, The Marshall Court and Cultural

Change, 1815–35, at 154–200 (1988) (vividly contrasting intellectual, procedural, and physical conditions of Marshall Court with modern ones).

5. *See, e.g.*, Julius Goebel, Jr., Antecedents and Beginnings to 1801, at 229–30 (1971); W. W. Crosskey, 1 Politics and the Constitution in the History of the United States 625 (1953).

6. As far as I am aware, the only specific mention of habeas corpus to be gleaned from the surviving records of the debate over the Judiciary Act is a note of Senator William Paterson that reads in full, "Hab. Corpus & Sovereignty of the State—," 9 Documentary History of the First Federal Congress, 1789–1791: The Diary of William Maclay and Other Notes on Senate Debates 481 (Kenneth R. Bowling & Helen E. Veit eds., 1988), a note that the series editors date in the period June 24–27, 1789. *See generally* Ritz, *supra* note 4, at 72–78 (canvassing contemporary views as to application of common law in federal court).

7. 9 First Federal Congress, *supra* note 6, at 1176 & n.34, 1178 & n.46.

8. *See* Ritz, *supra* note 4, at 98, 115, 146–48.

9. Wythe Holt, *"To Establish Justice": Politics, the Judiciary Act of 1789, and the Invention of the Federal Courts*, 1989 Duke L.J. 1421, at 1506.

10. Ritz, *supra* note 4, at 147.

11. For a more extended discussion, see Milestones I, 589–91.

12. 29 F. Cas. 1330 (C.C.D. Conn. 1799) (No. 17,708). *See also Henfield's Case*, 11 F. Cas. 1099, 1120 n.6 (C.C.D. Pa. 1793) (No. 6,360).

13. 27 F. Cas. 713 (C.C.D. Pa. 1793) (No. 16,122).

14. John D. Gordan III, United States v. Joseph Ravara: *"Presumptuous Evidence," "Too Many Lawyers,"* and a Federal Common Law Crime, in Origins of the Federal Judiciary: Essays on the Judiciary Act of 1789, at 106, 108 (Maeva Marcus ed., 1992). Gordan's masterful re-creation of the case includes a great deal of previously unpublished documentation. Several further cases are collected in Gary D. Rowe, Note, *The Sound of Silence:* United States v. Hudson & Goodwin, *the Jeffersonian Ascendancy, and the Abolition of Federal Common Law Crimes*, 101 Yale L.J. 919, at 920 n.8 (1992).

15. *See* William R. Casto, *The Federal Courts' Protective Jurisdiction over Torts Committed in Violation of the Law of Nations*, 18 Conn. L. Rev. 467, 480–81, 526 (1986) (reprinting opinion).

16. *United States v. Hudson*, 11 U.S. (7 Cranch) 32, 34 (1812) (holding that the Constitution prohibits federal courts from exercising common-law criminal jurisdiction: "The legislative authority of the Union must first make an act a crime, affix a punishment to it, and declare the Court that shall have jurisdiction of the offense.").

17. *See* Leonard W. Levy, The Emergence of a Free Press 274–81 (1985) (describing threats to freedom of expression posed by federal common-law criminal prosecutions in the period prior to *Hudson*). *See also* Gordan, *supra* note 14, at 140 (concluding that, notwithstanding historical warrant for federal criminal common-law jurisdiction, it would have become "in time, an instrument of oppression.").

For a comprehensive and scholarly analysis of *Hudson* and its political background, see Stewart Jay, *Origins of Federal Common Law* (pts. 1 & 2), 133 U. Pa. L. Rev. 1003, 1231 (1985).

18. *See* Charles Warren, *New Light on the History of the Federal Judiciary Act of 1789*, 37 Harv. L. Rev. 49, 51, 73 (1923) (arguing that *Hudson* was wrongly decided as matter of legislative intent). However, by the time the ruling came down, it commanded "strong national support," Mark A. Graber, *Federalist or Friends of Adams: The Marshall Court and Party Politics*, 12 Stud. Am. Pol. Dev. 229, 256 (1998); *see* William E. Nelson, *The American Revolution and the Emergence of Modern Doctrines of Federalism and Conflicts of Laws, in* Law in Colonial Massachusetts 419, 454–59 (Daniel R. Coquillette ed., 1984) (explaining that, although legal thinkers initially turned to common law to define jurisdiction of federal courts, this eventually produced politically unacceptable results in several areas, including that of common-law crimes).

19. Indeed, in his argument in *Ex Parte Bollman*, 8 U.S. (4 Cranch) 75, 80 (1807), Harper sought to capitalize on this difference. Arguing that the federal courts had common-law habeas corpus jurisdiction, he urged:

> This question is not connected with another, much agitated in this country, but little understood, viz., whether the courts of the United States have a common law jurisdiction to punish common law offences against the government of the United States. The power to punish offences against the government is not necessarily incident to a court. But the power of issuing writs of *habeas corpus*, for the purpose of relieving from illegal imprisonment, is one of those inherent powers, bestowed by the law upon every superior court of record, as incidental to its nature, for the protection of the citizen.

20. These cases are *Thomas v. Keeper of Debtors Apartment*, M-987 (July 4, 1822), and *Rose v. Keeper of the Gaol of the City and County of Philadelphia, id.* (Sept. 14, 1821). Their surviving documentation is described at Milestones I, 592 n.204.

21. This speculation draws support from the fact that since the prisoners were being held on federal charges, the Section 14 proviso was inapplicable under any theory, and thus the petitioners would not have gained any visible advantage from the application of state law.

22. *See* Act for the Better Securing Personal Liberty, and Preventing Wrongful Imprisonments, February 18, 1785, 2 Laws of The Commonwealth of Pennsylvania 275, § 1 (1810).

23. *See, e.g.*, Rules of the United States Circuit Court for the District of Georgia, May 28, 1790, M-1184, roll 1 (forms of practice shall be the same in law and equity cases as in the state superior court; in equity proceedings, "any one of the Judges of the Court, may in the Vacation make such Rules and Orders in any matter or cause therein, as shall be necessary to prepare the same for a final hearing"); Rules of United States Circuit Court for the District of Maryland, May 8, 1790, M-931, roll 1 (ordering that "law proceedings of this Court be conducted according to the

usage and practice of the General Court of this State, until further Order"); Rules of the United States District Court for the Southern District of New York, Feb. 4, 1800, M-886, roll 1:

> [I]n all cases not especially provided for by Rules of this Court, the Rules established for Regulating the Practice in the Supreme Court of the State, so far as the same are applicable [shall] be Rules for Regulating Practice in this Court.

24. First Judiciary Act, ch. 20, § 17, 1 Stat 73, 83 (1789).

25. An Act to Regulate Processes in the Courts of the United States, ch. 21, § 2, 1 Stat. 93 (1789).

26. *See* Eric M. Freedman, *The Law as King and the King as Law: Is a President Immune from Criminal Prosecution before Impeachment?*, 20 Hast. Const. L.Q. 7, at 18–19 & n.34 (1992).

27. An Act Providing for Regulating Processes in the Courts of the United States, ch. 36, § 2, 1 Stat. 275 (1792).

28. Charles Allan Wright, Federal Courts 424 (5th ed. 1993) (quoting *Fullerton v. Bank of United States*, 26 U.S. (4 Pet.) 604, 614 (1828)).

29. *Id.*

30. *See* An Act Further to Regulate Processes in the Courts of the United States, ch. 68, § 1 (1828).

31. It is possible that *United States v. Desfontes & Gaillard*, described *infra* Chapter 6, text accompanying note 11, fits this description.

32. *Duncan v. Dart*, 42 U.S. (1 How.) 301, 310 (1843).

33. *Ex Parte Bollman*, 8 U.S. (4 Cranch), at 93–94.

NOTES TO CHAPTER 6

1. This is particularly so because of the limitations on habeas corpus for all prisoners, whether state or federal, after conviction in criminal cases. *See Ex Parte Watkins*, 28 U.S. (3 Pet.) 193, 207–09 (1830); 1 James S. Liebman & Randy Hertz, Federal Habeas Corpus Practice and Procedure, § 2.4d, at 43–46 (3d ed. 1998).

2. All of the documents described in the text are to be found in the file of this case on M-987.

3. *See* Act of July 11, 1798, ch. 72, § 5:

> [T]he non-commissioned officers, musicians, seamen and marines, who are or shall be enlisted into the service of the United States; and the non-commissioned officers and musicians, who are or shall be enlisted into the army of the United States, shall be, and they are hereby exempted, during their term of service, from all personal arrests for any debt or contract.

4. It thereby implicitly decided not only that it was not restricted by the proviso to Section 14, but also that the writ extended to civil confinements, a question that had been left unresolved in *Ex Parte Wilson*, 10 U.S. (6 Cranch) 52 (1810), a case in which the opinion reads in full:

Marshall, C.J., after consultation with the other judges, stated that the court was not satisfied that a *habeas corpus* is the proper remedy, in a case of arrest under a civil process. Habeas corpus refused.

In *Ex Parte Randolph*, 20 F. Cas. 242, 252–53 (C.C. D. Va. 1833) (No. 11,558), District Judge Barbour reviewed the cases and decided that the writ did extend to such confinements; sitting with him as Circuit Justice, Chief Justice Marshall expressed his concurrence, *see id.* at 257.

The same question existed in England, where Parliament resolved it by a statute of 1816 explicitly extending the writ to civil confinements. *See* Barbara Wilcie Kern, *The English High Judiciary and the Politics of the Habeas Corpus Bill of 1758, in* Law as Culture and Culture as Law: Essays in Honor of John Philip Reid 147, 157 (Hendrik Hertog & William E. Nelson eds., 2000).

5. This may be found on M-987.

6. M-931, roll 1, frame 346.

7. The underlying litigation was between Cavalier Jouet and Thomas Jones, and the details recorded in the text are to be found at M-854, roll 1, frame 91, under the date of April 7, 1800.

8. For the reasons indicated *supra* Chapter 3, note 29, this use of common-law powers, although inconsistent with an interpretation of the proviso to Section 14 as applying to the whole section, might well be consistent with *Bollman.*

9. M-1214, roll 1.

10. *Cf. Ex Parte Watkins*, 28 U.S. (3 Pet.) 193, 201 (1830) (Marshall, C.J.):

The cause of imprisonment is shown as fully by the petitioner as it could appear on the return of the writ; consequently the writ ought not to be awarded, if the court is satisfied that the prisoner would be remanded to prison.

United States v. Lawrence, 26 F. Cas. 887, 891 (C.C. D.C. 1835) (No. 15,577) (Cranch, C.J.):

[B]eing perfectly satisfied that I have no authority to discharge the prisoner upon the alleged ground of insanity, if it were established; and that if brought up by habeas corpus he must be immediately remanded, it seems to me that it would be useless to issue the writ, and that it is my duty to refuse it.

Ex Parte Davis, 7 F. Cas. 45, 46 (N.D.N.Y. 1851) (No. 3,613):

[I]t is an obvious as well as an established rule that when, upon an application for habeas corpus, it appears that it would be fruitless to the petitioner if allowed, it is not to be granted.

11. M-1172, roll 2.

12. The treaty in question is the Convention of Navigation and Commerce, June 24, 1822, U.S.-Fr., 8 Stat. 278. Article 6 authorizes the consular officers of each country to apply "to the Courts, Judges and Officers competent" in local ports for the return of deserting sailors "in order to send them back and transport them out of the country," and provides that, upon proof that the wanted "men were part of said crews . . . delivery shall not be refused."

13. Almost surely, this was the Act of May 4, 1826, 4 Stat. 160, which was passed to implement the treaty described *supra* note 12. Tracking the treaty's terms, the statute provided that "on the application of a consul or vice consul of France, made in writing, stating that the person therein named has deserted from a public or private vessel of France," and on proof thereof after a hearing, "the person arrested, not being a citizen of the United States, shall be delivered up to the consul or vice consul, to be sent back to the dominions of France."

NOTES TO CHAPTER 7

1. *See Felker v. Turpin,* 581 U.S. 651, 658, 664 (1996).

2. *Id. See also Schlup v. Delo,* 513 U.S. 298, 341(1994) (Scalia, J., dissenting) (observing that Suspension Clause constrains Court's power to curtail federal habeas corpus review of state convictions); *Alexander v. Keane,* 991 F. Supp. 329, 338 (S.D.N.Y. 1998) (discussing *Felker* assumption).

3. *See* 1 James S. Liebman & Randy Hertz, Federal Habeas Corpus Practice and Procedure, § 7.2d (3d ed. 1998); Jordan Steiker, *Incorporating the Suspension Clause: Is There a Constitutional Right to Federal Habeas Corpus for State Prisoners?,* 92 Mich. L. Rev. 862, 871–74 (1994); Michael Mello & Donna Duffy, *Suspending Justice: The Unconstitutionality of the Proposed Six-Month Time Limit on the Filing of Habeas Corpus Petitions by State Death Row Inmates,* 18 N.Y.U. Rev. L. & Soc. Change 451, 465 (1990–1991). *See also Rosa v. Senkowski,* No. 97 Civ. 2468 (RWS), 1997 WL 436484, at *10–11 (S.D.N.Y. Aug. 1, 1997), *affirmed on other grounds,* 148 F.3d 134 (2d Cir. 1998). *Cf.* Henry J. Friendly, *Is Innocence Irrelevant? Collateral Attack on Criminal Judgments,* 38 U. Chi. L. Rev. 142, 170 (1970) (arguing that "it can scarcely be doubted that the writ protected by the suspension clause is the writ as known to the framers," but acknowledging that due process requires some protections for habeas rights).

4. *E.g., Buck v. Bell,* 274 U.S. 200 (1927). *See* G. Edward White, Justice Oliver Wendell Holmes: Law and the Inner Self 404–08 (1993) (summarizing modern scholarship on case). *See generally* Michael Willrich, *The Two Percent Solution: Eugenic Jurisprudence and the Socialization of American Law, 1900–1930,* 16 L. & Hist. Rev. 63, 66–67 (1998).

5. *See Lochner v. New York,* 198 U.S. 45, 75 (1905) (Holmes, J., dissenting).

6. *See Brown v. Board of Education,* 347 U.S. 483, 495 n.11 (1954); *see generally* Richard Sobel, *A Colloquy with Jack Greenberg about* Brown: *Experiences and Reflections,* 14 Const. Comment. 347, 354–57 (1997).

7. *Compare Erie R.R. Co. v. Tompkins,* 304 U.S. 64, 73 n.5 (1938), *with* Wilfred J. Ritz, Rewriting the History of the Judiciary Act of 1789, at 165–67 (1990).

8. *Cf.* Solveig Singleton, *Reviving a First Amendment Absolutism for the Internet,* 3 Tex. Rev. L. & Pol. 279, 320–21 (1999) (describing *Buchanan v. Warley,* 245 U.S. 60 (1917), which invalidated a Kentucky law segregating residential neighborhoods

notwithstanding "extensive and well-documented briefs . . . collecting the best evidence of the day from social scientists that segregation was healthy").

9. Mark Tushnet, *Interdisciplinary Legal Scholarship: The Case of History-in-Law*, 71 Chi.-Kent L. Rev. 909, 934 (1996). *See* Laura Kalman, *Border Patrol: Reflections on the Turn to History in Legal Scholarship*, 66 Fordham L. Rev. 87, 117, n.94 (1997) (commenting on this passage).

NOTES TO CHAPTER 8

1. 237 U.S. 309 (1915).

2. 261 U.S. 86 (1923).

3. *See* Note, *Mob Domination of a Trial as a Violation of the Fourteenth Amendment*, 37 Harv. L. Rev. 247, 248 (1923) ("[I]n two cases, separated by a period of nine years, presenting at least strikingly similar circumstances, the Supreme Court has reached opposite results.").

4. *See* Eric M. Freedman, *Federal Habeas Corpus in Capital Cases*, in America's Experiment with Capital Punishment: Reflections on the Past, Present and Future of the Ultimate Penal Sanction 409, 424–25 (James Acker et al. eds., 1998).

5. On the Court, this argument was originally made by Justice Brennan for the majority in *Fay v. Noia*, 372 U.S. 391, 420–23, 434 n.42 (1963). Although the authority of *Fay* was seemingly undermined by the long passage of dicta in *Coleman v. Thompson*, 501 U.S. 722, 749–51 (1991), repudiating its approach to procedural default, *see* Eric M. Freedman, *Habeas Corpus Cases Re-Wrote the Doctrine*, Natl. L.J., Aug. 19, 1991, at S6 n.21 (criticizing this decision), three Justices made clear the following year that they agreed with Justice Brennan's view of the relationship between *Frank* and *Moore*. *See Wright v. West*, 505 U.S. 277, 299 (1992) (concurring opinion of O'Connor, J., joined by Blackmun and Stevens, JJ.). *See also Wainwright v. Sykes*, 433 U.S. 72, 79 (1977) (describing the cases as "in large part inconsistent with one another").

6. This theory, which appears to have the support of three current Justices, *see Wright v. West*, 505 U.S. at 285–86 (plurality opinion of Thomas, J., joined by Rehnquist, C.J., and Scalia, J.), was previously advanced by Justice Harlan in *Fay v. Noia*, 372 U.S. at 457–58 (Harlan, J., dissenting) ("[*Moore*] cannot be taken to have overruled *Frank*; it did not purport to do so, and indeed it was joined by two Justices who had joined in the *Frank* opinion."); *see also infra* Chapter 15, note 13 (quoting additional portion of passsage).

7. *See, e.g.,* Avern Cohn, *Active Judiciary Serves Democracy*, Detroit News, Dec. 29, 1996, at B2; Susan N. Herman, *Clinton Takes Liberties with the Constitution*, Newsday, Aug. 4, 1996, at A46; Anthony Lewis, *Crime Against Justice*, N.Y. Times, July 29, 1991, at A15. All three of these authors (a federal District Judge, a law professor, and a former Supreme Court reporter for the New York Times) took the view that the Supreme Court in *Moore* overruled *Frank*, and expressed concern that

pending proposals to limit federal habeas corpus review of state criminal convictions would return the law to its prior unjust state.

8. To date, as the Second Circuit lamented in *Francis S. v. Stone*, 221 F.3d 100, 109–11 (2d Cir. 2000), the Supreme Court has been clearer about what the statute does not mean than about what it does. In *Williams v. Taylor*, 529 U.S. 362 (2000), the Court explicitly rejected the formulations of the Fourth and Fifth Circuits calling for a great deal of deference by federal habeas corpus courts to the conclusions of the state tribunals, *see id.* at 1521–22 (opinion of O'Connor, J., speaking for the Court on this point), and, as the Ninth Circuit soon recognized, *see Van Tran v. Lindsey*, 212 F.3d 1143, 1150 (9th Cir. 2000), inferentially invalidated those of the Seventh and Eleventh Circuits, *see Neeley v. Nagle*, 138 F.3d 917 (11th Cir. 1998); *Lindh v. Murphy*, 96 F.3d 856 (7th Cir. 1996) (en banc), *reversed on other grounds*, 521 U.S. 320 (1997). The Court also provided potent ammunition for the argument that the remaining Circuits would need to revisit their positions. This conclusion follows from the fact that although the Justices split 5–4 when discussing the abstract issue of statutory interpretation, they ruled 6–3 in petitioner's favor on the merits—meaning that even the more restrictive test enunciated by Justice O'Connor should as a practical matter increase the availability of federal habeas corpus relief under AEDPA beyond what the lower courts had thought safe to grant.

Indeed, vindicating the predictions of several commentators, *e.g.*, Mark Tushnet & Larry Yackle, *Symbolic Statutes and Real Laws: The Pathologies of the Antiterrorism and Effective Death Penalty Act and the Prison Litigation Reform Act*, 47 Duke L.J. 1, 4 (1997), *Williams* and the developing jurisprudence under the statute send only one affirmative message so far: the Court had shaped habeas corpus law to its liking prior to 1996, and is unwilling to read AEDPA as imposing any significant additional limitations—hence its consistent rejection of restrictive statutory readings proposed by the government. *See Immigration and Naturalization Service v. St. Cyr*, 121 S. Ct. 2271 (2001), *Artuz v. Bennett*, 531 U.S. 4 (2000); *Slack v. McDaniel*, 529 U.S. 473 (2000); *Williams v. Taylor*, 120 S. Ct. 529 U.S. 420 (2000); *Hohn v. United States*, 524 U.S. 236 (1998); *Stewart v. Martinez-Villareal*, 523 U.S. 637 (1998); *Felker v. Turpin*, 518 U.S. 651 (1996).

9. I have in mind Michael J. Klarman, *The Racial Origins of Modern Criminal Procedure*, 99 Mich. L. Rev. 48 (2000), which discusses both cases in their historical contexts and takes a viewpoint generally similar to my own.

10. *Frank v. Magnum*, 237 U.S. 309, 332 (1915).

11. Oliver Wendell Holmes, *The Profession of the Law, in* Collected Legal Papers 29, 32 (1921).

NOTES TO CHAPTER 9

1. *See* Nancy MacLean, *The Leo Frank Case Reconsidered: Gender and Sexual Politics in the Making of Reactionary Populism*, in Jumpin' Jim Crow 183, 185 (Jane Dailey et al. eds, 2000); Florence King, *Murky New View of a Southern Tragedy*,

Newsday, Feb. 2, 1988, at B9 (reviewing Mary Phagan, The Murder of Little Mary Phagan (1988)).

2. *See, e.g.,* Leonard Dinnerstein, The Leo Frank Case (Notable Trials Library ed. 1991) (containing a useful introduction by Alan Dershowitz). This book, also published in 1987 by Brown Thrasher and in 1968 by Columbia University Press, has not undergone any substantive revision since the research for it was conducted in the mid 1960's, *see id.* at ix–xi, although the 1987 and 1991 editions annex an undesignated appendix containing some important additional documentation first published by the Nashville Tennessean on March 2, 1982 (hereinafter Tenn. App.) and make the briefest of allusions to the posthumous pardon granted by the Georgia Board of Pardons, *see Georgia Pardons Victim 70 Years After Lynching*, N.Y. Times, March 12, 1986, at A16. These developments are integrated into Robert Seitz Frey & Nancy Thompson-Frey, The Silent and the Damned: The Murder of Mary Phagan and the Lynching of Leo Frank (1988), which provides at 137–45 an overview of accounts of the case in various genres. In addition, Harry Golden, A Little Girl Is Dead (1965) is based on a great deal of primary research.

In briefer works, the case has been the subject of a competent sketch, Albert S. Lindemann, The Jew Accused 235–72 (1991) and an accessible summary by Steve Oney, who is planning to publish a book on the subject. *See* Steve Oney, *Murder and Bigotry in the South: The Story of a Lynching in "Parade,"* N.Y. Times, Dec. 13, 1998, sec. 2, at 7. *See also* Don Melvin, *Sordid Old Secret Comes to Light, Gives One Pause*, Atlanta Constitution, Oct. 2, 1997, at 1G (previewing Oney's findings).

My own treatment draws most heavily upon the Dinnerstein and Golden volumes.

3. In recent years, these have included a New York musical, "Parade," *see Too Serious to Sing About?*, N.Y. Times, Dec. 12, 1998, at B7, and an off-Broadway work, "The Lynching of Leo Frank," *see* D. J. R. Bruckner, *A Story Still Painful after Repeated Tellings*, N.Y. Times, Apr. 20, 2000, at B5.

4. *See* David Mamet, The Old Religion (1997).

For a book that attempts "to understand fully the lasting cultural importance of the Frank case" by reviewing "the novels, plays, newspaper accounts, poems, web sites and songs" that have treated it, see Jeffrey Melnick, Black-Jewish Relations on Trial: Leo Frank and Jim Conley in the New South, at x (2000). My review of this work appears in the New York Law Journal of July 10, 2001, at 2.

5. The evidence in support of this theory, which includes a report from Conley's lawyer that Conley confessed to him, has been steadily growing as more evidence— notably an affidavit from a coworker witness—has emerged over the years. Following the crime, Conley was sentenced to a year on a chain gang as an accessory after the fact to the murder, on the theory that he had helped Frank dispose of the body; he had several brushes with the law in subsequent years, and died in 1962. *See* Milestones II, 1475 n.25; *see generally* Eric M. Freedman, *Innocence, Federalism, and the Capital Jury: Two Legislative Proposals for Evaluating Post-Trial Evidence of Innocence*

in Death Penalty Cases, 18 N.Y.U. Rev. L. & Soc. Change 315, 316 (1990–91) (describing "general tendency of evidence of innocence to emerge only at a relatively late stage in capital proceedings").

6. *See* Steven J. Goldfarb, *Framed*, Am. Heritage, Oct. 1996, at 108, 113. After a review of previously unexamined documents, Goldfarb concludes that "Dorsey urged witnesses to embellish their testimony, even lie under oath, to build a case against Frank," thus assuring "that Leo Frank would not receive a fair trial for a crime he almost certainly did not commit." *See also* Golden, *supra* note 2, at 65 (describing Dorsey's suppression of exculpatory X rays); Dinnerstein, *supra* note 2, at 103 (describing Dorsey's misconduct in obtaining witness statements).

7. *See* Dinnerstein, *supra* note 2, at 37, 57 (suggesting that defense lawyers "completely misjudged the nature and extent of the public hostility against Frank," and that "their trial strategy was not well planned"); Golden, *supra* note 2, at 99–102 (detailing author's view that lawyers "conduct[ed] as inept a defense of an innocent man as was ever offered in an American courtroom"); Leonard Dinnerstein, *The Fate of Leo Frank*, Am. Heritage, Oct. 1996, at 99, 108:

> [D]efense counsel . . . failed to expose the inaccuracies in Conley's testimony, and they blundered by asking him to discuss occasions when Frank had allegedly entertained young women. . . . The defense attorneys demonstrated their limitations once more by ignoring relevant constitutional questions in their original appeal to the Georgia Supreme Court.

8. The legal record concerning the pressure exerted by the crowd, as detailed in Frank's motion for a new trial (described later in this chapter), is reproduced in the Frank Transcript at 137–43, 181–95.

9. For the description of this episode by Frank's counsel as contained in their motion for a new trial, see Frank Transcript at 143 (urging that it would be "inconceivable [for] any juror, even if the verdict was not his own, to announce that it was not, in the midst of the turmoil and strife without").

10. Golden, *supra* note 2, at 197.

11. The statement, which was published in the three Atlanta newspapers on August 27, 1913, is reprinted in Golden, *supra* note 2, at 198–99.

12. Frank Transcript at 44.

13. *See Frank v. State*, 80 S.E. 1016, 1034 (Ga. 1914); Frank Transcript at 219.

14. The amended new trial motion is to be found in the Frank Transcript at 45–219. It argues that the various actions complained of were erroneous and prejudicial but cites no legal authority, state or federal. However, the grounds based on public tumult claim that the result was that the defendant did not have the fair and impartial jury trial guaranteed to him by the state's laws and Constitution, *see id.* at 140, 142, 147. The last of these claims, ground of error number 75, is further described *infra* note 21.

15. *See, e.g.*, Frank Transcript at 111–12, 117–18 (attacking admission of testimony that Frank, once in jail, refused to see Conley or detectives except in presence

or with consent of counsel). *Cf. Frank v. State*, 80 S.E. 1019, 1027 (Ga. 1914) (responding to this claim).

16. *See, e.g.*, Frank Transcript at 48–103, 106–08, 118–19, 120–24, 128–29, 135–36, 149–50. *See also id.* at 113–15 (complaining that jury was allowed to hear insinuation that Frank had made homosexual proposition to a 15-year-old black employee).

17. *See, e.g.*, Frank Transcript at 144–45 (objecting to prosecution's use in argument of defense failure to cross-examine state's witnesses concerning sexual misconduct); 166–67 (objecting to prosecution argument: "This man Frank, with Anglo-Saxon blood in his veins, a graduate of Cornell, . . . this man of Anglo-Saxon blood and intelligence, refused to meet this ignorant Negro Jim Conley . . . upon the flimsy pretext that his counsel was out of town but when his counsel returned . . . he dared not let him meet him."). *See also id.* at 167–73.

18. *See id.* at 136–37 (challenging failure to give proposed jury instructions concerning circumstantial evidence and one that no inference of wrongdoing should be drawn from failure to cross-examine government's witnesses to collateral misconduct, *cf. Frank*, 80 S.E. at 1031 (responding to this claim)); 143–44 (attacking failure to give instruction, "although no written request was formally made therefor," that jury should reject unless otherwise corroborated entire testimony of witness who knowingly swears to any falsehood, in light of the fact that, to the extent he swore to aiding Frank in the disposal of the body, Conley "admitted upon the stand that he knew he was lying in the affidavits made by him."). *See also id.* at 173 (attacking failure to give instruction, apparently also not requested at trial, that if jury found Conley to be accomplice his testimony could not be accepted without corroboration). The jury charge actually given is reproduced in *id.* at 220–24.

19. *See id.* at 146–47, 173–207.

20. *Frank v. Magnum*, 237 U.S. 309, 312 (1915). *See* Frank Transcript at 109–10, 117, 137–43, 147–48, 181–95.

21. *Frank*, 237 U.S. at 312. The passage of the amended new trial motion quoted by the Court is to be found in the Frank Transcript at 148 (ground of error number 75). The ground of error, stated in twelve paragraphs, alleges that the defendant "did not have a fair and impartial jury trial, guaranteed to him under the laws of this State, for the following reasons," *id.*, at 147.

The listed reasons include the close proximity of the crowd to the jury, *see also id.* at 181–83, 186, 192 (describing several instances of crowd members directly haranguing the jury during recesses); the court's conference with the chief of police of Atlanta and the colonel of the regiment stationed in Atlanta in the sight of the jury; the postponement of the conclusion of the case at the suggestion of the press; the disorderly conditions accompanying the reception of the verdict; the defendant's absence from the courtroom (as quoted in the next paragraph of text); and the joyous demonstration that greeted Dorsey as he left the courtroom. The ground of error concludes, "This defendant contends that the above recital shows that he did not have a fair and impartial jury trial," and refers the court to a number of affidavits detailing the events. Frank Transcript at 148. At a later point, Frank argued in a brief that this assignment of error:

> merely relates to the proposition that the trial was not a fair and impartial one. It recounts various episodes attending the trial, and incidentally states that the prisoner was not present at the rendition of the verdict, his counsel having waived his presence. It requires no argument to indicate that this was not the presentation of the constitutional question . . .

of whether due process was violated by the rendition of a verdict in his absence. *See Says Frank Verdict Was Legal Nullity,* N.Y. Times, Dec. 2, 1914, at 8. The context for this brief is further described *infra* note 43.

22. *See Frank v. State,* 80 S.E. 1016, 1034–35 (Ga. 1914). The fullest report of the contents of these affidavits is to be found in newspaper accounts, *e.g., Detailed Denial of Every Charge Made by Henslee,* Atlanta J., Oct. 21, 1913, at 1. The Georgia Supreme Court describes them only generally, and they are not in the Frank Transcript, since counsel did not include them in Frank's federal habeas corpus petition. *See Frank v. Magnum,* 237 U.S. 309, 318 (1915).

The state criticized this omission in its brief, *see* Brief of Hugh M. Dorsey, Warren Grice [for Appellee], *id.* (No. 775), at 16 and the Court majority implicitly agreed, *see Frank,* 237 U.S. at 333, 336, 344. Dissenting, Justices Holmes and Hughes asserted that petitioner had no obligation to set forth the state's evidence, *see id.,* at 349. *See infra* Chapter 10, note 31 (discussing this issue).

23. *See Frank,* 80 S.E. at 1034.

24. *See* Dinnerstein, *supra* note 2, at 79–80.

25. *Id.* at 163–65 (reprinting excerpt from appellate brief); *see id.* at 81 (reporting that oral argument centered on this issue).

26. *Frank,* 80 S.E. at 1034.

27. *Id.* at 1033–34. *See Frank v. Magnum,* 237 U.S. 309, 313–14 (1915) (accurately summarizing this passage).

28. *Frank,* 80 S.E. at 1033.

29. *See id.* at 1030–31.

30. This aspect of the case occupied the bulk of the court's opinion, *see id.* at 1019–30.

31. *Id.* at 1034–44.

32. *See Frank v. State,* 83 S.E. 233, 234 (1914) (describing procedure). *See also* Governor John M. Slaton's Commutation Order (June 21, 1915), *reprinted in* Golden, *supra* note 2, at 312, 332–34, 341 (discussing evidence presented on this motion, and observing "it is well known that it is almost a practical impossibility to have a verdict set aside by this procedure").

33. *See Frank,* 83 S.E. at 233.

34. Separate counsel were engaged to pursue this issue because the original trial lawyers "had promised Hugh Dorsey that they would not use their client's absence

during part of the judicial proceedings as a basis for future appeals [and] felt obliged to honor their pledge," Dinnerstein, *supra* note 2, at 91.

35. *See Frank v. State*, 83 S.E. 645, 648 (Ga. 1914) (setting forth all eight grounds for the demurrer). The trial court's ruling upheld the state's position in its entirety. *See id.* at 646.

36. *See id.* at 648–52.

37. *See Frank v. Magnum*, 237 U.S. 309, 317 (1915); Frank Transcript at 7; Brief of Hugh M. Dorsey, *supra* note 22, at 5.

38. *See* Frank Transcript at 7; Brief of Hugh M. Dorsey, *supra* note 22, at 7.

39. Frank Transcript at 8, 9 (Lamar, Circuit Justice 1914), *reprinted in Justice to Frank Doubted by Holmes*, N.Y. Times, Nov. 27, 1914, at 1.

40. *See* Frank Transcript at 7; Brief of Hugh M. Dorsey, *supra* note 22, at 5; *Justice to Frank Doubted by Holmes*, *supra* note 39.

41. Frank Transcript at 13 (Holmes, Circuit Justice 1914), *reprinted in Justice to Frank Doubted by Holmes*, *supra* note 39. The opinion was also published in *Holmes Denies Motion to Set Aside Verdict*, Atlanta Constitution, Nov. 27, 1914, at 5. I have so far been unable to locate a case such as that which Holmes describes in his final sentence.

42. Letter from Oliver Wendell Holmes to Lady Clare Castletown (Nov. 28, 1914); *see also infra* Chapter 10, note 38 (quoting additional portion of letter). Holmes's relationships with his various female correspondents are discussed in John S. Monagan, The Grand Panjandrum 65–94 (1988).

On Holmes's ruling, and the adverse editorial reaction to it, see Dinnerstein, *supra* note 2, at 109–110; *As Press Sees Frank Case*, N.Y. Times, Dec. 2, 1914, at 8 (quoting sampling of editorial opinions nationally).

43. *See* Memorandum from Louis Marshall to Chief Justice Edward D. White (Nov. 24, 1914), *reprinted in* 1 Louis Marshall: Champion of Liberty 299 (Charles Reznikoff ed., 1957). This memorandum summarizes Marshall's arguments to the effect that the right to be present at the reception of a jury verdict is "a part of due process, . . . which cannot be waived," and that the decision of the Georgia Supreme Court changing its rule so as to provide that a challenge on these grounds should be made by a motion for a new trial rather than a motion to set aside the verdict "was a violation of the ex post facto clause" and "in fact an attempt to evade the fundamental constitutional question, which, under the decisions of the Supreme Court of the United States, was incapable of being waived." *Id.* at 302–03. Subsequently, Marshall filed a fuller brief, substantial portions of which were reprinted in *Says Frank Verdict Was Legal Nullity*, *supra* note 21.

44. They reported this the following April in their opinion in *Frank v. Magnum*, 237 U.S. 309, 346 (1915) (Holmes & Hughes, JJ., dissenting). The reason for Holmes's change of view is not apparent, but it is possible that in the interval since the writing of his memorandum of November 25 he had read Marshall's additional filings.

In any event, it appears from the cited passage in *Frank* that these Justices wished to grant the writ of error to consider Frank's claim concerning his absence from the rendition of the verdict, apparently on the theory that this was error correctable by writ of error, but not of Constitutional magnitude, and so not cognizable on habeas corpus. This distinction is discussed further in Chapter 10.

45. *In re Frank*, 235 U.S. 694 (1914).

NOTES TO CHAPTER 10

1. The full petition is contained in the Frank Transcript at 1–9.

2. *See id.* at 8.

3. *See* Letter from Louis Marshall to Meier Steinbrink (Dec. 19, 1914), *reprinted in* Louis Marshall: Champion of Liberty 303 (Charles Reznikoff ed., 1957) (reporting that application for writ of habeas corpus had been made to District Court, and "[t]here is every likelihood that that application will be denied.").

4. Frank Transcript at 15. As far as the Frank Transcript reveals, the judge issued this opinion without receiving any written response to the petition from the government.

5. *See* Frank Transcript at 229 (Lamar, Circuit Justice 1914); *see also id.* at 21 (District Court order denying certificate). The statement in Alexander Bickel & Benno C. Schmidt, The Judiciary and Responsible Government, 1910–21, at 363 (1984) that Justice Lamar's memorandum "was widely published in the press," is correct, *see, e.g., Lamar Grants Appeal to Frank*, N.Y. Times, Dec. 29, 1914, at 1 (reprinting text of opinion). The authors' further statement that the document "is not otherwise preserved" is not correct. In addition to the printed copy in the Frank Transcript, there exists the documentation discussed *infra* note 6.

6. This draft is to be found in case file of *Frank v. Magnum*, 237 U.S. 309 (1915), in the Washington facility of the National Archives and Record Administration, Records Group 267, U.S. Supreme Court Appellate Case file No. 24519, Box 4690. The same file also contains a clean typescript version of the opinion.

7. Frank Transcript at 230. This decision "met with general newspaper acclaim," Leonard Dinnerstein, The Leo Frank Case 111 (Notable Trials Library ed. 1991).

8. *See Frank Brief Filed in Supreme Court*, N.Y. Times, Feb. 21, 1915, § 2, at 11; *Answers Frank Brief, id.* (reporting on state's brief). The Supreme Court's date stamp records Marshall's brief as having been filed on February 20, 1915, and Dorsey's on February 23.

9. *See* Appellant's Argument, *Frank v. Magnum*, 237 U.S. 309 (1915) (No. 775), at 3–8. All the arguments of Marshall's brief proceeded from record materials or legal authority; it contained no suggestion that an evidentiary hearing was needed. And Marshall told the Court on oral argument that this was "a case where there is no dispute as to the facts," *see Frank Case Appeal Arguments Ended*, N.Y.

Times, Feb. 27, 1915, at 8. In contrast, as already noted, the District Judge believed that unless he dismissed the writ there would necessarily have to be a hearing to determine whether Frank's rights had in fact been violated at trial, and, as the newspaper story just cited indicates, the state made every effort on oral argument before the Supreme Court to portray the case as turning on factual disputes.

10. *See, e.g.,* Appellant's Argument, *supra* note 9, at 82–93.

11. *See id.* at 114–31.

12. For example, as indicated at the end of Chapter 9 and further discussed *infra* note 28, Justices Holmes and Hughes thought that Frank's complaint that his rights had been violated by his absence from the rendition of the verdict presented a viable claim of legal error (and hence his application for a writ of error should have been granted), but not a viable claim of a Constitutional violation (and hence he was not entitled to habeas corpus relief on this ground). There is a comprehensive and well-documented discussion of the distinction between "jurisdictional" and "legal" errors in 1 James S. Liebman & Randy Hertz, Federal Habeas Corpus Practice and Procedure, § 2.4(d)-(e) (3d ed. 1998). *See also* Note, *The Writ of Habeas Corpus in the Federal Courts,* 35 Colum. L. Rev. 404 (1935) (surveying cases on the issue starting with *Bollman*).

13. Appellant's Argument, *supra* note 9, at 84.

14. *See id.* at 157–65. This was a considered tactical choice, based on Marshall's belief that "it would be far easier to succeed, if the Court were satisfied that a favorable decision would not finally discharge Frank," Letter from Louis Marshall to Albert D. Lasker (Jan. 30, 1915), *quoted in* Dinnerstein, *supra,* note 7, at 111.

15. Appellant's Argument, *supra* note 9, at 154.

16. *Id.* 155–57. A premise of this argument is that the requirement of "the exhaustion of remedies in the State courts cannot be said to be a jurisdictional condition precedent to the institution of habeas corpus proceedings in the Federal Courts," *id.* at 147, but is rather a discretionary doctrine of comity, *id.* at 131–33. Accordingly, in the section preceding the one from which the quote in text is drawn, *id.* at 131–54, Marshall, seeking the favorable exercise of discretion, argued at length the legal reasonableness under previously existing state law of "the most strenuous and earnest effort to obtain review," *id.* at 147, that had been made in the Georgia courts, *see id.* at 147–54.

17. *See* Brief of Hugh M. Dorsey, Warren Grice [for Appellee], *Frank v. Magnum,* 237 U.S. 309 (1915) (No. 775), at 16, 50–51.

18. *See id.* at 46–49.

19. *See id.* at 51–68, 74–81.

20. *See id.* at 71–74. While the topic heading of the brief states the proposition, neither the text nor the cases it cites support the argument, although supportive case law was available. *See* Liebman & Hertz, *supra* note 12, § 2.4d, at 54–57 (describing Supreme Court cases in wake of *Ex Parte Royall,* 117 U.S. 241 (1886), as establishing after 1892 an increasingly strict rule that Constitutional claims of state

prisoners were to be reviewed by writ of error, if meaningfully available, rather than habeas corpus).

21. The date of April 12, 1914, given in the U.S. Reports, *see Frank v. Magnum*, 237 U.S. 309 (1915), is incorrect, as the Court's Journal shows.

22. *Frank*, 237 U.S. at 331.

23. *See id.* at 334.

24. *See id.* at 328–29.

25. *See id.* at 326–27.

26. *See* Liebman & Hertz, *supra* note 12, § 2.4d, at 49 n.172 (listing Supreme Court cases granting habeas corpus review of claims previously rejected on writ of error).

27. *Id.* at 54. Credit for originating the argument in this paragraph belongs entirely Professors Liebman and Hertz. *See id.* at 53–55.

28. *See Frank*, 237 U.S. at 343. As indicated at the end of Chapter 9, the dissenters wrote that, in their view, the Court ought to have previously granted the writ of error to deal with this point. But, they continued, "we never have been impressed with the argument that the presence of the prisoner was required by the Constitution of the United States," *id.* at 346 (Holmes & Hughes, JJ., dissenting). Thus, the decision to exclude Frank from the rendition of the verdict was merely a "legal" error, not a "jurisdictional" one.

29. *See id.* at 344 (Ex Post Facto clause, "as its terms indicate, is directed against legislative action, and does not reach erroneous or inconsistent decisions by the courts").

30. *Id.* at 335. There is a further discussion of this passage in connection with the consideration of Professor Liebman's views *infra* Chapter 15, text accompanying notes 5–8.

31. *Id.* at 336. The remainder of the sentence reads, "especially not, where the very evidence upon which the determination was rested is withheld by him who attacks the finding." This disapproval of Frank's failure to include with his petition the jurors' affidavits presented by the state, *see supra* Chapter 9, note 22, is appropriately criticized as "confused" by J. S. Waterman & E. E. Overton, *Federal Habeas Corpus Statutes and* Moore v. Dempsey, 1 U. Chi. L. Rev. 307, 317–18 (1933), *reprinted in* 6 Ark. L. Rev. 8, 16–17 (1952).

32. The cited passage reads:

While it is true that upon a writ of error to a state court we cannot review its decision upon pure questions of fact, but only upon questions of law bearing upon the Federal right set up by the unsuccessful party, it equally is true that we may examine the entire record, including the evidence, if properly included therein, to determine whether what purports to be a finding upon questions of fact is so involved with and dependent upon such questions of law as to be in substance and effect a decision of the latter. That this is so is amply shown by our prior rulings.

33. The opinion in this case, which was before the Court on a railroad's writ of error from state court litigation challenging the federal constitutionality of legislatively mandated rates, states:

> So far as the findings are concerned, we have in the present case simply a general, or ultimate, conclusion of fact which is set forth in the decree of the state court; and it is necessary for us, in passing upon the Federal right which the plaintiff in error asserted, to analyze the facts in order to determine whether that which purports to be a finding of fact is so interwoven with the question of law as to be in substance a decision of the latter.

34. *Frank*, 237 U.S. at 345, 347–48 (Holmes & Hughes, JJ., dissenting).

35. *Id.* at 349.

36. *Id.* at 350.

37. *See* Oliver Wendell Holmes to the Baroness Moncheur (July 6, 1915); Oliver Wendell Holmes to John Henry Wigmore (April 22, 1915) ("I am relieved at not having the worry of the Frank case longer on my mind."); Oliver Wendell Holmes to Ellen A. (Mrs. Charles P.) Curtis (April 19, 1915); Oliver Wendell Holmes to Lady Leslie Scott (March 7, 1915) (describing question in case as "whether a trial for murder gave a man due process of law when the hostile mob was so dangerous that the Judge advised the counsel for the prisoner not to have him present or even to be present themselves when the verdict was taken").

38. *See* Letter from Oliver Wendell Holmes to Lady Clare Castletown (Nov. 28, 1914). In this letter, partially quoted *supra* Chapter 9, text accompanying note 42, the Justice expressed irritation at the public outcry that he was prepared to let a man be hanged on a seeming technicality, the public "knowing and caring nothing for the constitutional limits to our power."

39. Letter from Oliver Wendell Holmes to Lewis Einstein (April 10, 1915), *reprinted in* The Holmes-Einstein Letters 112 (James Bishop Peabody ed., 1964). Holmes also commented that he thought the opinion "is a composite performance and suffers rhetorically from being the product of two hands," Letter from Oliver Wendell Holmes to Ellen A. (Mrs. Charles P.) Curtis (April 19, 1915), and indeed Holmes and Hughes seem to have worked closely together in drafting it, *see* 1 Merlo J. Pusey, Charles Evans Hughes 289–90 (1951).

To some extent, the fact of there being a dissent at all is a measure of the strength of the dissenters' feelings on the matter. At this period, the publication of dissenting opinions was relatively rare; the Term in which *Frank* was decided saw the publication of 273 opinions for the Court and 11 dissents. *See* Walter F. Pratt, Jr., The Supreme Court under Edward Douglass White, 1910–1921, at 131 (1999).

40. Letter from Oliver Wendell Holmes to Lady Ellen Askwith (March 3, 1915).

41. Letter from Oliver Wendell Holmes to Alice Stopford Green (December 18, 1914).

42. Frank would have preferred seeking a complete pardon, but his attorneys convinced him that a commutation request would be more prudent. *See* Dinnerstein, *supra* note 7, at 117. For a more detailed discussion of the public relations campaign, see Milestones II, 1486 n.83.

43. The order is reprinted at Harry Golden, A Little Girl Is Dead 312 (1965). In a public defense of it, the Governor urged:

> Judge Roan had charged the jury that if they did not recommend to mercy the defendant, which would carry life imprisonment as a penalty, he, Judge Roan would be compelled to sentence the defendant to be hanged. This was not the law. Judge Roan overlooked the statute which gave him the discretion in the imposition of alternative penalties when the verdict was founded on circumstantial evidence. It is inconceivable that where Judge Roan doubted the guilt of the defendant at all he would have failed to impose the life sentence instead of the death sentence if he had remembered his authority to do so. . . . The imposition of the penalty had passed beyond the trial Judge, because the term of court had passed, and he asked me to prevent an injustice which might occur because of the Judge's oversight, and I exercised my power to correct a mistake when I was the only one who had the power to correct it.

John M. Slaton, *Governor Slaton's Own Defense in the Frank Case*, N.Y. World, July 4, 1915, editorial section, at 1.

44. Historians agree that this outburst had a profound effect on the Jewish community and its views on racial matters over the next several decades, *see*, e.g., Clive Webb, Fight against Fear: Southern Jews and Black Civil Rights 63 (2001), but disagree on what that impact was. *See* Mark K. Bauman, *Introduction* to The Quiet Voices: Southern Rabbis and Black Civil Rights, 1880s to 1990s, at 2–4 & n.5 (Mark K. Bauman & Berkley Kalin eds., 1997).

45. Letter from Leo M. Frank to Oliver Wendell Holmes (July 10, 1915).

46. Letter from Oliver Wendell Holmes to Lady Leslie Scott (July 13, 1915).

47. Memorandum of Talk [of Mark de Wolfe Howe] with F[elix] F[rankfurter] (Aug. 10, 1964), Oliver Wendell Holmes Papers. Although there is no particular reason to doubt the accuracy of this account, Frankfurter was 81 years old at the time of his conversation with Howe, and recounting a conversation with Holmes that would have taken place 49 years earlier.

48. While the identity of the lynchers has long been accessible in general terms, *see* Dinnerstein, *supra* note 7, at 139–42, the subject has recently become the topic of renewed interest, *see* Daphne Evitar, *Legacy of a Lynching*, Am. Law, Aug. 2000, at 27; Jonathan Turley, *Lawyers and the Lynching*, Natl. L.J., Aug. 7, 2000, at A1; Carrick Mollenkamp, *An Internet Posting Raises the Ghosts of a Notorious Crime*, Wall St. J., June 9, 2000, at 1; *see also* Michael Dorman, *2 Murders in Georgia*, Newsday, Feb. 23, 1999, at A24.

NOTES TO CHAPTER 11

1. *See* Letter from Louis D. Brandeis to Roscoe Pound (Nov. 27, 1914), *reprinted in* 3 Letters of Louis D. Brandeis 373 (Melvin I. Urofsky & David W. Levy eds., 1978): In talking with Frankfurter this morning about the Frank case and Justice Holmes' memorandum [of November 25, 1914, quoted in Chapter 9], he told me that you were convinced that Frank had not had a fair trial, and that he was not guilty, and that this was another Dreyfus case. It seems to me of great importance that you should, in a public letter, give expression to your opinion on this subject. Your standing among the lawyers of America is such that what you say men will heed, and it is important that this protest should be made by a non-Jew.

2. Letter from Louis D. Brandeis to George Sutherland (Nov. 6, 1915), *reprinted in id.* at 632.

3. Minutes of Meeting of the Executive Committee, American Bar Association (August 18, 1915), William Howard Taft Papers, Library of Congress (Reel 18).

4. W. Fitzhugh Brundage, Lynching in the New South: Georgia and Virginia, 1880–1930, at 100, 208–09 (1993).

5. *See* Robert L. Zangrando, The NAACP Crusade against Lynching, 1909–1950, at 57–58 (1980).

6. *See* David M. Levitan, *The Effect of the Appointment of a Supreme Court Justice*, 28 U. Tol. L. Rev. 37, 74 (1996); David P. Currie, *The Constitution in the Supreme Court: 1921–1930*, 1986 Duke L.J. 65, 65. *See also* Daniel J. Danelski, A Supreme Court Justice Is Appointed 181 (1964) (discussing Butler nomination); David H. Burton, Taft, Holmes, and the 1920's Court 112–14 (1998) (describing Taft nomination). *See generally* Robert C. Post, *Defending the Lifeworld: Substantive Due Process in the Taft Court Era*, 78 B.U. L. Rev. 1489, 1491–92 (1998). For an extensive analysis of Sutherland's views, see Samuel R. Olken, *Justice George Sutherland and Economic Liberty: Constitutional Conservatism and the Problem of Factions*, 6 Wm. & Mary Bill of Rights J. 1 (1997). The departures of the previous Justices are described in David N. Atkinson, Leaving the Bench: Supreme Court Justices at the End 87–93 (1999).

7. *Moore* was decided by an 8-member bench. Edward T. Sanford was sworn in as Justice Pitney's successor on February 19, 1923, the day the decision was rendered.

8. *See Justice Clarke Out of Supreme Court; To Work for League*, N.Y. Times, Sept. 5, 1922, at 1.

9. *See Callins v. Collins*, 114 S. Ct. 1127, 1130 (1994) (Blackmun, J., dissenting from denial of certiorari):

For more than 20 years I have endeavored—indeed, I have struggled—along with a majority of this Court, to develop procedural and substantive rules that would lend more than the mere appearance of fairness to the death penalty endeavor. [Footnote citing votes upholding death sentences as Court of Appeals judge omitted]. . . . I feel morally and intellectually obligated simply to concede that the death penalty experiment has failed.

10. Michal R. Belknap, Federal Law and Southern Order 8 (1987). *See* David J. Goldberg, Discontented America: The United States in the 1920's, at 92–97 (1999); Stewart E. Tolnay & E. M. Beck, A Festival of Violence: An Analysis of Southern Lynchings, 1882–1930, at 31 (1995) (noting upsurge in lynchings "during the few years following World War I, a period also characterized by a resurgence of Klan activity in the South and a rise in nativism in the country as a whole").

11. Brent Staples, *Unearthing a Riot*, N.Y. Times Magazine, Dec. 19, 1999, at 65, 67.

12. *See* Christopher Robert Reed, The Chicago NAACP and the Rise of Black Professional Leadership, 1910–1966, at 47–48 (1997) (describing Chicago race riot of July, 1919, that resulted in 38 deaths); Steven A. Holmes, *At 82 Scholar Takes On His Toughest Study of Race*, N.Y. Times, Sept. 28, 1997, at 1 (describing May, 1921 race riot in "Tulsa when mobs of whites, jealous of the economic success of blacks . . . went on a rampage, killing [more than 100] blacks, pillaging and burning buildings, [and] even dropping dynamite from airplanes"). *See generally* Leon F. Litwack, Trouble in Mind 280–319 (1999). As Chapter 12 describes, the events underlying *Moore* fell into just this pattern, and, as indicated *infra* Chapter 14, note 40, the District Judge who ruled on the federal habeas corpus petition in that case in the fall of 1921 was from Oklahoma City.

13. *See* Zangrando, *supra* note 5, at 51–71. *See also* Carolyn Wedin, Inheritors of the Spirit: Mary White Ovington and the Founding of the NAACP 197 (1998) (Ovington, who chaired the NAACP Board: "believed that, even though the bill ultimately failed to pass, the public notoriety the . . . campaign lent lynching was a prime cause of the drastic drops in these horrible numbers after 1924."); *cf.* James W. Clarke, *Without Fear or Shame: Lynching, Capital Punishment and the Subculture of Violence in the American South*, 28 Brit. J. Pol. Sci. 268, 284–85 (1998) (suggesting that "perhaps the most important reason that lynching declined is that it was replaced by a more palatable form of violence," *viz.*, capital punishment); David C. Baldus & George Woodworth, *Race Discrimination and the Death Penalty: An Empirical and Legal Overview, in* America's Experiment with Capital Punishment: Reflections on the Past, Present and Future of the Ultimate Penal Sanction 385, 386–87 (James Acker et al. eds., 1998) (adding that the replacement of lynchings by "[l]awful executions also reduced Congressional pressure for the enactment of federal anti-lynching legislation in the 1920s").

14. Note, *Mob Domination of a Trial as a Violation of the Fourteenth Amendment*, 37 Harv. L. Rev. 247, 250 (1923).

NOTES TO CHAPTER 12

1. The best historical account of these events is Richard C. Cortner, A Mob Intent

on Death (1988), which is based heavily on primary sources. Two works written relatively close to the time of the events by the Dean and an Assistant Professor at the University of Arkansas Law School, who had the benefit of assistance from various local officials, provide careful recountings of the procedural history (as well as a generally sympathetic view of the state's legal position), J. S. Waterman & E. E. Overton, *The Aftermath of Moore* v. Dempsey, 18 St. Louis L. Rev. 117 (1933), *reprinted in* 6 Ark. L. Rev. 1 (1952); J. S. Waterman & E. E. Overton, *Federal Habeas Corpus Statutes and Moore* v. Dempsey, 1 U. Chi. L. Rev. 307 (1933), *reprinted in* 6 Ark. L. Rev. 8 (1952).

2. *See Arkansas Riots Appeal Argued in Highest Court*, Wash. Post, Jan. 10, 1923, at 17 (Blacks' contention is "that they had assembled in their church at Hoop Spur to devise means as tenant farmers to relieve themselves of conditions which they asserted amounted to peonage. While so assembled, the Negroes claimed, armed white men surrounded the church and fired upon them, killing several. On behalf of the state, it is asserted the Negroes had assembled in connection with a plot to massacre white men, and that the firing was done by a posse sent to quell a riot.").

3. *See* Grif Stockley, *Scipio Africanus Jones*, Ark. Democrat-Gazette, June 8, 1999, at E1; *see also* Michael Haddigan, *Confronting the Past Conference Seeks to Revisit 1919 Race Riot*, Boston Globe, February 11, 2000, at A3 (using occasion of academic conference on riots to recount persisting racial divisions in county).

4. Inward Facts, *infra* note 5, at 27–31 (describing series of purported fund-raising schemes by this individual, Robert L. Hill, in which he "simply played upon the ignorance and superstition of a race of children"). The attempts of the authorities to return Hill to Arkansas from Kansas, where he had been arrested, led to a series of well-publicized legal and political events that ultimately resulted in his being freed rather than extradited. *See* Cortner, *supra* note 1, at 55–83. As Professor Eric W. Rise of the Criminal Justice Program of the University of Delaware detailed in a paper entitled "The NAACP, Civil Rights, and Criminal Extradition" that he presented at the 1998 meeting of the American Society for Legal History, these efforts were part of a sustained political campaign undertaken by the NAACP in the same period as its antilynching campaign, and doubtless contributed as well to public views of Southern justice.

5. The committee reported its findings in a document entitled Inward Facts About Negro Insurrection, which is contained in the record annexed to the Petition for Certiorari in *Martineau v. Arkansas*, 257 U.S. 665 (1921) (No. 525) (filed Sept. 10, 1921), at 25–32 [hereinafter cited as Martineau Record]. The quotation comes from *id.* at 27.

6. *See* Cortner, *supra* note 1, at 27–28; Fon Louise Gordon, Caste & Class: The Black Experience in Arkansas, 1880–1920, at 136–37 (1995); Jeannie M. Whayne, A New Plantation South: Land, Labor, and Federal Favor in Twentieth-Century Arkansas 75–77 (1996); O. A. Rogers, Jr., *The Elaine Race Riots of 1919*, 19 Ark. Hist. Q. 142 (1960); *see also Conference in Arkansas Re-examines 1919 Attack*, N.Y. Times, Feb. 13, 2000, at A28. For an excellent summary of the historiography, see

Jeannie M. Whayne, *Race and Class in the 1919 Elain[e] Race Riot,* Ark. Democrat-Gazette, Nov. 7, 1999, at J1.

7. *See* Carl H. Moneyhon, Arkansas and the New South, 1874–1929, at 107–08 (1997) (locating riot within framework of farmworker attempts to unionize). For a sketch of the Red Scare, see Melvin I. Urofsky, A March of Liberty 612–14 (1988).

8. *See* Cortner, *supra* note 1, at 31–32, 39–42. For descriptions of the various lawyers involved in the defense, *see* Judith Kirkpatrick, (*Extra*)*ordinary Men: African-American Lawyers and Civil Rights in Arkansas before 1950,* 53 Ark. L. Rev. 299, 364–68 (2000).

9. *See* Cortner, *supra* note 1, at 2, 15, 30.

10. *See id.* at 16–18, 86; Milestones II, 1505 n.148. As will be described below, at a subsequent point in the proceedings the cases were grouped into two sets, *Ware* and *Moore,* as indicated in the table. With respect to the *Moore* set, it was the theory of the prosecution that Frank Hicks (the brother of Ed Hicks) had fired the shots that killed Lee; the remaining defendants were charged as aiders and abetters. The transcript of the trial of Frank Hicks is to be found in the Martineau Record, Exhibit D, at 5–26. The transcript of the trial of the other *Moore* defendants is to be found in the Transcript of Record, at 27–50, *Moore v. Dempsey,* 261 U.S. 86 (1923) (No. 199) (filed October 24, 1921)[hereinafter cited as Dempsey Transcript]. *See generally* Brief for the Appellants, at 23, *Moore v. Dempsey,* 261 U.S. 86 (1923) (No. 199) (filed Jan. 8, 1923) (describing brevity of this trial).

11. *See* Cortner, *supra* note 1, at 18.

12. The text of this document is preserved, insofar as it relates to the *Moore* defendants other than Frank Hicks, in the Transcript of Record in *Moore v. Arkansas,* No. 955, at 35–40 (U.S.) (record filed May 24, 1920), which is to be found in the Washington facility of the National Archives and Record Administration, Records Group 267, U.S. Supreme Court Appellate Case File No. 27710, Box 6593. This certiorari proceeding was redesignated No. 360 when carried over from the October, 1919, to the October, 1920, Term, when the writ was denied, *see Moore v. Arkansas,* 254 U.S. 630 (1920).

Although previous scholars seem to have been unaware of the fact, the simultaneous new trial motion filed on behalf of Frank Hicks has also been preserved. It is in the Transcript of Record filed in *Hicks v. Arkansas,* No. 956, at 55–62 (U.S.) (record filed May 24, 1920), which is to be found in the Washington facility of the National Archives and Record Administration, Records Group 267, U.S. Supreme Court Appellate Case File No. 27711, Box 6593. This certiorari proceeding was redesignated No. 361 when carried over from the October, 1919, to the October, 1920, Term, when the writ was denied, *see Hicks v. Arkansas,* 254 U.S. 630 (1920). Frank Hicks's new trial motion is also to be found in the Martineau Record, Exhibit D, at 31–37.

13. Dempsey Transcript at 58–59.

14. *Id.* at 60–61.

15. *Id.* at 62.

16. *Id.* at 63.

17. *Banks v. State*, 219 S.W. 1015, 1016 (Ark. 1920) (quoting Kirby's Digest § 2409). According to Cortner, *supra* note 1, at 86, this issue was raised for the first time on oral argument of the appeal.

18. *See Hicks v. State*, 220 S.W. 308, 309 (Ark. 1920).

19. *Id.* at 309–10.

20. These are the petitions, discussed *supra* note 12, that were denied as *Moore v. Arkansas*, 254 U.S. 630 (1920) (No. 360) and *Hicks v. Arkansas*, 254 U.S. 630 (1920) (No. 361). In neither case did the state bother to file opposition papers.

NOTES TO CHAPTER 13

1. This motion was made under the Act of Mar. 3, 1911, ch. 231, § 31, 36 Stat. 1096, an ancestor of the current 28 U.S.C. § 1443 (1994), which provided:

> When any civil suit or criminal prosecution is commenced in any State court . . . against . . . any person who is denied or cannot enforce in the judicial tribunals of the State . . . any law providing for the equal civil rights of citizens of the United States, such suit or prosecution may [be removed] upon the petition of such defendant.

However, since Reconstruction the Supreme Court had construed the statute as not applying to cases "in which a right is denied by judicial action during trial," *Neal v. Delaware*, 103 U.S. 370, 386 (1880). In such cases, petitioners had to assert their federal claims in the state system, subject to ultimate Supreme Court review. *See id.* at 387.

2. Richard C. Cortner, A Mob Intent on Death 91–92 (1988).

3. *See Ware v. State*, 225 S.W. 626, 627–28 (Ark. 1920).

4. *See id.* at 628–30. Two of the Justices dissented from this last holding with respect to one of the defendants, who had not made a specific objection, *see id.* at 632.

5. These petitions have been described *supra* Chapter 12, notes 12, 20.

6. *See Hicks v. State*, 220 S.W. 208, 309 (Ark. 1920); *supra* Chapter 12, text accompanying note 18.

7. Dempsey Transcript at 77.

8. *Id.* at 71.

9. Cortner, *supra* note 2, at 99–100 (quoting the Arkansas Gazette, Nov. 16, 1920, at 1).

10. *See id.* at 105. Meanwhile, in May, the *Ware* defendants had again moved for a change of venue. In reliance upon the affidavits of several black residents of the county, the same trial judge this time granted the motion, setting the retrial in another county for October. *See id.* at 108.

11. *See id.* at 115–16.

12. Petition for Certiorari, at 2, *Martineau v. Arkansas,* 257 U.S. 665 (1921) (No. 525) (filed Sept. 10, 1921). The text of the state petition filed on behalf of Frank Hicks is to be found in the Martineau Record at 6–24. *Cf.* Cortner, *supra* note 2, at 217 n.35 (relying on text published in newspaper, probably petition of other defendants).

13. Martineau Record at 33–35.

14. *Id.* at 36–38.

15. Dempsey Transcript at 15–16. This affidavit was not attached to Frank Hicks's Chancery Court petition, but since defense counsel had it in hand and later filed it in federal court, it was doubtless annexed to the Chancery Court petition of the other defendants.

16. *See State v. Martineau,* 232 S.W. 609, 610 (Ark. 1921); Martineau Record at 53–56 (copies of orders).

17. *See Martineau,* 232 S.W. at 610.

18. *See* Cortner, *supra* note 2, at 116–17 (One effect of the state filings was to generate "the most extensive publicity the contentions of the NAACP and defense counsel had yet received in the white press of Arkansas," and an editorial representing "the first dissenting voice among the ranks of the state's white press on the handling of the Phillips County riot.").

19. Cortner, *supra* 2, at 118 (which gives the date of the argument as June 12).

20. *Martineau,* 232 S.W. at 612.

21. *See id.* at 613.

22. *Id.*

23. *See Moore v. Dempsey,* 261 U.S. 86, 92 (1923).

24. *See* Letter from H. C. McKenney [Deputy Clerk, Supreme Court of the United States] to Murphy, McHaney & Dunway [Counsel for Petitioners] (July 15, 1921). This document is to be found among the correspondence described *infra* note 26.

25. *See* Dempsey Transcript at 9. It is a plausible speculation that Holmes considered himself in the same procedural position as he had been in his November 25, 1914, ruling on Frank's similar application, which was described *supra* Chapter 9, text accompanying notes 40–42. Whatever might be thought about the petitioners' Constitutional allegations, the decision below was fully supportable on the independent state ground that the Chancellor had no jurisdiction.

26. Petition for Certiorari, *Martineau v. Arkansas,* 257 U.S. 665 (1921) (No. 525). While, as indicated *infra* note 27, this document is not of great legal significance, it has some importance as a historical source. Located in the Washington facility of the National Archives and Records Administration, Records Group 267, U.S. Supreme Court Appellate Case File No. 28480, Box 6889, it is accompanied by the Martineau Record, which contains a number of documents not otherwise accessible, and by related procedural correspondence.

27. *See* Milestones II, 1515 n.186. The certiorari petition, having been mooted

by the federal habeas proceedings described in the next chapter, was voluntarily dismissed by counsel in October. *See Martineau v. Arkansas*, 257 U.S. 665 (1921); Letter from E. L. McHaney [Counsel for Petitioner] to James D. Maher [Clerk, Supreme Court of the United States] (Sept. 27, 1921) (habeas proceedings "will supplant the Petition for Certiorari, and we will kindly ask that you dismiss the Petition for Writ of Certiorari"). This letter is among the correspondence described *supra* note 26.

28. *See* Letter from E.L. McHaney [Counsel for Petitioner] to James D. Maher [Clerk, Supreme Court of the United States] (Sept. 7, 1921) (enclosing petition, and requesting that state officers be notified of its filing "and that the contemplated executions are by virtue of the filing of the petition, automatically stayed"); Letter from William R. Stansbury [Acting Deputy Clerk, Supreme Court of the United States] to Murphy, McHaney & Dunaway [Counsel for Petitioner] (Sept. 10, 1921) (replying: "[a]s requested, I have notified the Governor, the Attorney General, and the Keeper of the Penitentiary of the filing of this petition, but the filing of such a petition does not automatically stay execution, and I have therefore not so stated in my letters to the officers above named."). This correspondence is among that described *supra* note 26. The circumstances of Stansbury's appointment to his position are described in Robert Post, *Judicial Management and Judicial Disinterest: The Achievements and Perils of Chief Justice William Howard Taft*, 1998 J. S. Ct. Hist. 50, 52–53.

NOTES TO CHAPTER 14

1. *See* United States District Court for the Eastern District of Arkansas, Law Docket Book, Book G, at 110–11 (now in the Federal Records Center, Fort Worth). One petition (No. 6247) was filed on behalf of Frank Hicks, and one (No. 6246) on behalf of the other five defendants. When the cases reached the Supreme Court, counsel stipulated that only the latter record need be printed, "and that the record in the Frank Hicks case need not be printed. We further agree that these causes may be consolidated and submitted together upon one printed record, as aforesaid, and briefs in said cause." Dempsey Transcript at 106. At the time, both cases bore Supreme Court case numbers for the October, 1921, Term, *Hicks v. Dempsey* being No. 594, and *Moore v. Dempsey*, No. 595. The former was subsequently assigned No. 198 in the October, 1922, Term and the latter No. 199.

The record of the Frank Hicks case, although not printed, remains in manuscript form in the Washington facility of the National Archives and Record Administration, where it constitutes United States Supreme Court Appellate Case File No. 28549 in Records Group 267.

2. All the quotations in the text prior to the next note are from Dempsey Transcript at 1–3.

3. *Id.* at 4. This story, which has been recounted *supra* Chapter 12, text accom-

panying note 8, may have made a particular impression on Justice Holmes, *see Moore v. Dempsey*, 261 U.S. 86, 88 (1923), because the lawyer involved was the son of one of the lawyers who argued the case in Supreme Court, where, as described later in this chapter, he narrated the tale.

4. Dempsey Transcript at 4–5.

5. All the quotations in the text prior to the next note are from *id.* at 5–7.

6. This was substantially the same as the one set forth *supra* Chapter 12, text accompanying note 13, but in place of any explicit mention of the federal Constitution was the allegation that the failure of counsel to object "was through fear of the mob for petitioners and himself." Dempsey Transcript at 7–8.

7. These events were described *supra* chapter 13, text accompanying notes 1–10. *See also* Richard C. Cortner, A Mob Intent on Death 117 (1988) (describing newspaper editorial discussing argument that state officials should have ignored chancellor's stay and executed the *Moore* defendants in order to prevent lynching of the *Ware* defendants).

8. Dempsey Transcript at 8–9.

9. *Id.* at 10.

10. *See id.* at 86–99; Cortner, *supra* note 7, at 121–25; Brief for the Appellants, at 12–14, *Moore v. Dempsey*, 261 U.S. 86 (1923) (No. 199). Justice McReynolds later referred to these as "the affidavits of two white men—low villains according to their own admissions," *Moore v. Dempsey*, 261 U.S. 86, 93 (1923) (McReynolds & Sutherland, JJ., dissenting).

11. Dempsey Transcript at 101.

12. *Cf.* Cortner, *supra* note 7, at 168–74 (detailing difficulties petitioners might have faced at a hearing).

13. Dempsey Transcript at 101, 104.

14. Brief for the Appellants, *supra* note 10, at 38.

15. *Id.* at 29. *See id.* at 38 ("The allegations of fact were never considered by the Supreme Court of Arkansas as they were by the Supreme Court of Georgia in the *Frank* case, but the opinions apparently assume that they were true. This distinction between the cases is vital.").

16. *Id.* at 36. Having read this passage, Louis Marshall commented in Letter from Louis Marshall to Walter White (March 19, 1923), NAACP Papers, Library of Congress, Box I-C-69:

The facts disclosed [in *Moore*] are shocking, but not more so than those in the Frank case. As a matter of fact in that case, as the record showed, the Presiding Judge stated that he did not believe that the guilt of Frank had been shown beyond a reasonable doubt, and when he requested Frank and his counsel to remain out of court when the jury rendered its verdict he gave as the reason that . . . he could not answer for the life of either Frank or his counsel. . . . It thus appeared clearly that the Court abdicated its powers and recognized that the mob was controlling the action of the court. The facts in

Moore v. Dempsey merely related to the attitude of the general public but did not indicate that the Judge was terrorized, as was the fact in the Frank case. . . . The distinction sought to be made between the two cases [by counsel] is scarcely justified by the record.

17. Brief for the Appellants, *supra* note 10, at 36.

18. *Id.* at 39 (quoting the statute from Crawford & Moses Digest of the Statutes of Arkansas § 3413).

19. *Id.*

20. *Id.* at 40.

21. *Id.* at 38. *See also id.* at 28 (recounting factual misstatements in Arkansas Supreme Court opinion and commenting that "the attitude of the court toward the case may be inferred" from them).

22. Both documents bear clerk's file stamps of January 8, 1923. *See also* Abstract and Brief for Appellee at 1, *Moore v. Dempsey*, 261 U.S. 86 (1923) (No. 199) ("The appellee has not been favored with any abstract or brief on behalf of the appellants").

23. *See id.* at 73–90.

24. This event has been recounted *supra* Chapter 13, text accompanying note 25.

25. Abstract and Brief for the Appellee, *supra* note 22, at 72–73 (quoting *Frank v. Magnum*, 237 U.S. 309, 326 (1915)). As indicated *supra* Chapter 10, text accompanying notes 23–27, although *Frank* had been less than explicit in its treatment of the point there was good reason to doubt that the quoted passage was as helpful to the state as its counsel probably believed when he arrived in Washington to argue the case. As the description of the oral argument of *Moore* that appears below will show, the Court's response to the argument of this issue supports that view. The Supreme Court's *Moore* opinion eventually treated the question as *Frank* had—by rejecting the argument in silence, simply reiterating the general proposition that "mere mistakes of law in the course of a trial are not to be corrected by" habeas corpus, *Moore*, 261 U.S. at 91. The surrounding passage is quoted *infra* text accompanying note 37.

26. Abstract and Brief for the Appellee, *supra* note 22, at 55.

27. *Id.* at 91–92. This ground of complaint received no sympathy from any Justice in the ultimate decision, probably on the theory, strongly implicit in the first paragraph of the dissent, that the timing of the affidavits was—like their sources—simply another factor for the District Court's consideration in determining whether to set the matter down for a hearing, rather than being a legal barrier to doing so.

28. *See* Cortner, *supra* note 7, at 152–53. These documents survive today in the form of typescripts made by a previous scholar, Arthur I. Waskow, of originals that are now lost. *See id.* at 201. Newspaper accounts of the argument included *Arkansas Riots Appeal Argued in Highest Court*, Wash. Post., Jan. 10, 1923, at 17 and *Negroes Beg Lives of Supreme Court*, N.Y. Times, Jan. 10, 1923, at 12.

29. Letter from Walter F. White to Scipio A. Jones (Jan. 12, 1923), Waskow Collection, Wisconsin State Historical Society, M76-358, Box 1, § 6 ("Ark-Trial").

30. Letter from U. S. Bratton to Walter F. White (Jan. 11, 1923), Waskow Collection, *supra* note 29.

31. Taft wrote back, simply, "I like this opinion much," a comment preserved in the copy of the opinion contained in Holmes's bound volumes in the Oliver Wendell Holmes Papers in the Library of Congress. But, in a note also preserved there, Brandeis, consistent with Taft's comment at oral argument, changed Holmes's reference in the penultimate sentence from "facts that seem incontrovertible" to the published, "facts admitted by the demurrer," *Moore v. Dempsey*, 261 U.S. 86, 92 (1923).

32. The source for this statement is a personal letter from Justice Van Devanter to Chief Justice Taft dated February 13, 1923, and found in the William Howard Taft Papers in the Library of Congress (Reel 250). It is a separate document from the one bearing the same date that is quoted in the text and cited in the next note.

33. Letter from Willis Van Devanter to William Howard Taft (Feb. 13, 1923), William Howard Taft Papers, Library of Congress (Reel 250).

34. Brandeis's views are quoted at some length *infra* Chapter 15, text accompanying notes 15–17. In a letter on the day the case was decided, Brandeis commented to Frankfurter, *in toto*, "Holmes' Arkansas Case today is a satisfaction," Letter from Louis D. Brandeis to Felix Frankfurter (Feb. 19, 1923), *reprinted in* "Half Brother, Half Son": The Letters of Louis D. Brandeis to Felix Frankfurter 136 (Melvin I. Urofsky & David W. Levy eds., 1991).

35. This has been described *supra* Chapter 10, text accompanying notes 37–39. For whatever relevance it may have, Holmes appears to have been generally stronger than at the time of *Frank*. *See* Letter from Louis D. Brandeis to Felix Frankfurter (Jan. 3, 1923), *reprinted in* "Half Brother, Half Son," *supra* note 34, at 132 ("Holmes J. felt so perky yesterday that he insisted on getting out of the carriage yesterday to walk with me from 12th & H home. And he said today that he felt better for the walk."); Letter from Louis D. Brandeis to Alice Goldmark Brandeis (Feb. 4, 1923), *reprinted in* 5 Letters of Louis D. Brandeis 87 (Melvin I. Urofsky & David W. Levy eds., 1978) ("Holmes J. . . . has finished for the printer his introduction to John Wigmore's book and read it to me. It is really good . . . and he seems in good form.").

36. Prior to the publication of the opinion, Holmes mentioned it in Letter from Oliver Wendell Holmes to Mrs. John C. (Nina L.) Gray (Jan. 20, 1923) "([J]ust now I have a case on burning themes, at which the boys have had their whack at the conference and which I must tinker to get by those who are shy and inclined to kick. I think I can keep nearly all if not perhaps get all but it will need a little diplomatic adjustment."); Letter from Oliver Wendell Holmes to Frederick Pollock (Jan. 25, 1923), *reprinted in* 2 Holmes-Pollock Letters 110 (Mark DeWolfe Howe ed., 1941) (reporting that a case "on burning themes may go over for one of the JJ. or two, to consider whether it shall be swallowed according to the majority or whether, as a child put it, they will swallow *up*.").

After the opinion was published, Holmes seems not to have alluded to it in his correspondence, although he did discuss various other contemporary cases. *See, e.g.,*

Letter from Oliver Wendell Holmes to Felix Frankfurter (Feb. 14, 1923), *reprinted in* Holmes and Frankfurter: Their Correspondence, 1912–1934, at 154 (Robert M. Mennel & Christine M. Compston eds., 1996) ("I have just sent around an opinion in a Porto Rico case [*Diaz v. Gonzalez,* 261 U.S. 102 (1923)] that gives me a mild titillation."); Letter from Alice Stopford Green to Oliver Wendell Holmes (May 6, 1923) (thanking Holmes for sending her his dissent in *Adkins v. Children's Hospital,* 261 U.S. 525 (1923)).

Indeed, he did not mention it even when a correspondent gave him an opening by asking for his views on a habeas corpus issue. *Compare* Letter from Harold J. Laski to Oliver Wendell Holmes (Feb. 11, 1923), *reprinted in* 1 Holmes-Laski Letters 482, 483 (Mark DeWolfe Howe ed., 1953) (describing case raising question of whether habeas corpus follows British flag) *with* Letter from Oliver Wendell Holmes to Harold J. Laski (March 1, 1923), *reprinted in id.* at 485 (replying, "I can say nothing profitable on the *habeas corpus* question").

37. *Moore v. Dempsey,* 261 U.S. 86, 90–92 (1923).

38. *Id.* at 93 (McReynolds & Sutherland, JJ., dissenting).

39. That is, the writ of error application to Justice Holmes and the certiorari petition that were described *supra* Chapter 13, text accompanying notes 24–28.

40. This statement was factually incorrect. The regular District Judge, a former resident of Phillips County, had recused himself on that basis, and the petition had in fact been ruled on by a District Judge from Oklahoma City. *See* Cortner, *supra* note 7, at 131. *See also supra* Chapter 11, note 12.

41. *Moore,* 261 U.S. 86, 101 (1923) (McReynolds & Sutherland, JJ., dissenting).

42. Cortner, *supra* note 7, at 159.

43. *See Ware v. State,* 252 S.W. 934 (Ark. 1923).

44. On March 1, 1924, an order was entered dismissing the action for want of prosecution. *See* J. S. Waterman & E. E. Overton, *The Aftermath of* Moore v. Dempsey, 18 St. Louis L. Rev. 117, 122 (1933), *reprinted in* 6 Ark. L. Rev. 1, 5 (1952); *see also* Letter from Charles F. Cole [Clerk, United States District Court for the Eastern District of Arkansas] to Helen Newman [Librarian, Supreme Court of the United States] (Oct. 26, 1962), William O. Douglas Papers, Library of Congress, Box 601, *Moore v. Dempsey* Folder.

45. *See* Cortner, *supra* note 7, at 166–83. Of the 67 noncapital prisoners, all but eight had been freed by the summer of 1923, *see id.* at 166, and those eight were released by the Governor in December, 1924, *see id.* at 182.

NOTES TO CHAPTER 15

1. Paul M. Bator, *Finality in Criminal Law and Federal Habeas Corpus for State Prisoners,* 76 Harv. L. Rev. 441, 485–89 (1963).

2. *Id.* at 488 n.119:

Mr. Justice Pitney makes clear that his entire reasoning is in the context of habeas corpus, which he carefully differentiates from ordinary appeal. . . . Certainly any holding that on direct review the Supreme Court does not have plenary jurisdiction . . . would have been a startling reversal of the law established by Martin v. Hunter's Lessee, 14 U.S. (1 Wheat.) 304 (1816).

3. Gary Peller, *In Defense of Federal Habeas Corpus Relitigation*, 16 Harv. C.R.–C.L. L. Rev. 579, 646–48 (1982).

4. James S. Liebman, *Apocalypse Next Time? The Anachronistic Attack on Habeas Corpus/Direct Review Parity*, 92 Colum. L. Rev. 1997, 2079–81 (1992).

5. This passage, contained in *Frank v. Magnum*, 237 U.S. 309, 345, 347–48 (1915) (Holmes & Hughes, JJ., dissenting), which discusses several of the Court's economic due process cases, has been quoted *supra* Chapter 10, text following note 31.

6. *See Frank*, 237 U.S. at 335:

> We of course agree that if a trial is in fact dominated by a mob, so that the jury is intimidated and the trial judge yields, and so that there is an actual interference with the course of justice, there is, in that court, a departure from due process of law in the proper sense of that term. And if the State, supplying no corrective process, carries into execution a judgment of death or imprisonment based upon a verdict thus produced by mob domination, the State deprives the accused of his life or liberty without due process of law.

7. *Compare Frank*, 237 U.S. at 332:

> The District Court having considered the case upon the face of the petition, we must do the same, treating it as if demurred to by the sheriff. There is no doubt of the jurisdiction to issue the writ of *habeas corpus*. The question is as to the propriety of issuing it in the present case. . . . Now the obligation resting upon us, as upon the District Court, [is] to look through the form and into the very heart and substance of the matter. . . .

with id. at 345 (Holmes & Hughes, JJ., dissenting):

> The only question before us is whether the petition shows on its face that the writ of *habeas corpus* should be denied, or whether the District Court should have proceeded to try the facts.

This decision represented a unanimous rejection of the government's argument, which has been set forth *supra* Chapter 10, text accompanying note 17, that habeas corpus could be granted only for jurisdictional defects appearing on the face of the record, and the District Court lacked power to receive oral evidence. The Supreme Court has subsequently so read *Frank. See Peyton v. Rowe*, 391 U.S. 54, 59–60 (1968) (unanimous):

> [A]t least tentatively in *Frank* . . . and more clearly in *Moore* . . . , this Court had recognized that a district court was authorized to look behind the bare record of a trial proceeding and conduct a factual hearing to determine the merits of alleged deprivations of constitutional rights.

8. Liebman, *supra* note 4, at 2080 n.503, discerns a difference "between the Court's deferential review of the mob domination issue" and its "de novo review" of Frank's claim of absence from the verdict. In truth, both were treated the same way, and given the plenary review appropriate to legal issues: in the first instance, "was the petition properly dismissed?" and in the second "does this state a constitutional claim?" All Justices agreed that the answer to this second question was no, and, as indicated *supra* Chapter 9, text accompanying notes 44–45, Justices Holmes and Hughes had wanted to grant Frank's application for a writ of error so as to review it as a nonconstitutional legal question.

My discussion is not meant to cast any doubt upon—indeed, I believe it supports—Professor Liebman's broader, and excellently documented, thesis, already described *supra* Chapter 10, text accompanying note 27, locating *Frank* at the starting point of a period of reinvigorated habeas corpus review for state prisoners responsive to the diminishing efficacy of the Court's review of their claims by writ of error.

9. *See* Comment, *Mob Domination of State Courts and Federal Review by Habeas Corpus*, 33 Yale L.J. 82, 84 (1923) (suggesting that embarrassment to foreign relations might be example).

10. Recall from *supra* Chapter 3, text accompanying note 37, that the Supreme Court had long before *Frank* established the rule that when exercising its appellate jurisdiction in habeas corpus cases it would examine the evidence and "proceed to do that which the court below ought to have done." *Ex Parte Bollman*, 8 U.S. (4 Cranch) 75, 114 (1807).

11. As recounted *supra* Chapter 14, text accompanying note 29:

Mr. Justice Holmes sharply reprimanded Attorney General Utley . . . asking him in amazement if the Attorney General meant to say that since the members of the jury, the presiding judge and every person involved in the trial had figuratively and almost literally pistols pressed against their breasts demanding conviction of the defendants, the court had no right to inquire into whether or not the men had had a fair trial. All the Attorney General could do was to hastily disclaim any such statement which he did in a very embarrassed manner.

Presumably, government counsel sensed that this was a concession he had to make—otherwise, he would have stuck to the position in his brief that the only question before the Court was whether the record showed on its face that the trial court was dominated by the mob.

12. This is the meaning of the otherwise cryptic sentence:

We shall not say more concerning the corrective process afforded to petitioners than that it does not seem to us sufficient to allow a Judge of the United States to escape the duty of examining the facts for himself.

Moore v. Dempsey, 261 U.S. 86, 92 (1923).

13. *Id.* at 101 (McReynolds & Sutherland, JJ., dissenting). As indicated *supra*

Chapter 8, note 6, the argument set forth in the text is consistent with that made by Justice Harlan in *Fay v. Noia*, 372 U.S. 391, 457–58 (1963) (Harlan, J., dissenting):

[*Moore*] cannot be taken to have overruled *Frank*; it did not purport to do so, and indeed it was joined by two Justices who had joined in the *Frank* opinion. Rather, what the Court appears to have held was that the state appellate court's perfunctory treatment of the question of mob domination . . . was not in fact acceptable corrective process and federal habeas corpus would therefore lie to consider the merits of the claim.

14. For a sketch of the relationship between Frankfurter and Brandeis, see "Half Brother, Half Son": The Letters of Louis D. Brandeis to Felix Frankfurter 3–6 (Melvin I. Urofsky & David W. Levy eds., 1991).

15. Melvin I. Urofsky, *The Brandeis-Frankfurter Conversations*, 1985 Sup. Ct. Rev. 299, 316 (conversation of July 3, 1923) (footnotes omitted).

16. *See also id.* at 315:

I wanted to have rule adopted that no case is to go down until eight days after opinion is circulated . . . Holmes was one of the seniors against that—he would be miserable for eight days—he's worry all the time. He can't wait after he circulates his opinions, to have them back and "to shoot them off."

17. *Id.* at 316–17 (footnotes omitted).

18. This is consistent with the views he expressed throughout the conversations, ranging over a number of years of the Court's work. Indeed, two days previously, he had told Frankfurter, "you must constantly bear in mind the large part played by personal considerations and inadequacy of consideration." *Id.* at 315 (conversation of July 1, 1923). *See* Philippa Strum, Louis D. Brandeis: Justice for the People 364–71 (1984) (describing how Brandeis used this insight to persuade colleagues to his viewpoint).

19. *See* Adrian Vermeule, *Judicial History*, 108 Yale L.J. 1311 (1999) (considering rationale for this prohibition); *cf. Ramdass v. Angelone*, 530 U.S.159, 167–68 (2000) (plurality opinion) (stating in dictum that a state court decision is reasonable for purposes of AEDPA when it relies on facts as stated in the controlling opinion of the United States Supreme Court, regardless of the actual facts as revealed in the Supreme Court record and briefs).

20. *See* B. F. Skinner, *"Superstition" in the Pigeon*, 38 J. Experimental Psychol. 168, 171–72 (1948).

21. *See generally* Oliver Wendell Holmes, *The Path of the Law*, 10 Harv. L. Rev. 457, 459–61 (1897).

22. The attempt to quantify, in testable terms, the degree to which Supreme Court votes are determined by precedent as opposed to the Justice's policy preferences has recently occupied a good deal of attention among social scientists, *e.g.*, Forrest Maltzman, James F. Spriggs II, & Paul J. Wahlbeck, Crafting Law on the Supreme Court (2000); Harold I. Spaeth & Jeffrey A. Segal, Majority Rule or Minority

Will: Adherence to Precedent on the U.S. Supreme Court (1999), *reviewed by* Donald R. Songer, *Book Review*, 93 Am. Pol. Sci. Rev. 983 (1999); Younksik Lim, *An Empirical Analysis of Supreme Court Justices' Decision Making*, 29 J. Leg. Stud. 721 (2000). An extensive forum on the subject appeared at 40 Am. J. Pol. Sci. 971–1082 (1996), and some of the key debaters subsequently presented their views at book length in Lee Epstein & Jack Knight, The Choices Justices Make (1998), *reviewed by* Frank B. Cross, *The Justices of Strategy*, 48 Duke L.J. 511 (1998).

For a general overview of the political science research, emphasizing how far it has yet to go to achieve a satisfactory level of explanation for judicial behavior, see Lawrence Baum, The Puzzle of Judicial Behavior (1997). *See also* Cornell Clayton & David A. May, *A Political Regime's Approach to the Analysis of Legal Decisions*, 32 Polity 233 (1999).

For an initial attempt at locating this body of work within legal norms, see Evan H. Caminker, *Sincere and Strategic Voting Norms on Multimember Courts*, 97 Mich. L. Rev. 2297 (1999).

23. *Cf. Florida v. Meyers*, 466 U.S. 380, 386 (1984) (per curiam) (Stevens, J., dissenting):

Since the beginning of the October 1981 Term, the Court has decided in summary fashion 19 cases, including this one, concerning the constitutional rights of persons accused or convicted of crimes. All 19 were decided on the petition of the warden or prosecutor, and in all he was successful in obtaining reversal of a decision upholding a claim of constitutional right.

NOTES TO CHAPTER 16

1. 344 U.S. 443 (1953).

2. The earliest Justice to accept Professor Bator's views was Justice Harlan. *See Fay v. Noia*, 372 U.S. 391, 456–63 (1963) (Harlan, J., dissenting). He was followed by several Nixon appointees, Justices Powell and Rehnquist and Chief Justice Burger. *See Schneckloth v. Bustamonte*, 412 U.S. 218, 250 (1973) (Powell, J., concurring).

3. 339 U.S. 200 (1950).

4. There is no reason to doubt that the Justices shared the premises that, although rarely articulated, still underlie the debate on the issue of hearings: (1) that the fact-finding made by a District Court is likely to shape, if not determine, the ultimate appellate resolution of the legal issues presented by a federal habeas corpus petition, and (2) that a District Judge is most unlikely to grant such a petition without a hearing. Thus, the more freedom the District Courts have to grant or deny hearings, the greater control they will have over the shape of the law and the more grants of habeas relief are likely to occur.

5. Paul M. Bator, *Finality in Criminal Law and Federal Habeas Corpus for State Prisoners*, 76 Harv. L. Rev. 441, 500 (1963).

6. *See* Gary Peller, *In Defense of Federal Habeas Corpus Relitigation*, 16 Harv. C.R.–C.L. L. Rev. 579, 662 (1982) ("By the time *Brown v. Allen* was decided, federal habeas relitigation of state court determinations of federal law was simply not an issue.").

7. Justice Kennedy's historical summary of the growth of the writ in *McCleskey v. Zant*, 499 U.S. 467, 478–80 (1991), contained in an opinion expressing the views of six Justices (all currently sitting), is consistent with the view expressed in the text. But it would appear that at least three current Justices reject that view. In *Wright v. West*, 505 U.S. 277 (1992), Justice Thomas, in lengthy dicta in an opinion in which Chief Justice Rehnquist and Justice Scalia joined, adopted the Bator thesis, *see id.* at 285–288. Justice O'Connor, "writ[ing] separately only to express disagreement with certain statements in Justice Thomas' extended discussion . . . of this Court's habeas corpus jurisprudence," *id.*, at 298, and joined by Justices Blackmun and Stevens, vigorously rejected it, *see id.*, at 297–301. The Justices have not yet resolved their differences, *see Williams v. Taylor*, 529 U.S. 362, 410–12 (2000). As further discussed *infra* Chapter 18, note 69, the evidence presented in this volume strongly supports Justice O'Connor's views.

8. *See* Barry Friedman, *A Tale of Two Habeas*, 73 Minn. L. Rev. 247, 273–77 (1988).

9. Indeed, there is strong reason to believe that it was not even that much. According to Professor Harper V. Fowler of Yale Law School, an authority on the Court's certiorari practice, this holding was merely a restatement of prior law and the dissent's contrary view was "at variance . . . with the law as applied to habeas corpus proceedings." *See* Fowler V. Harper & Arnold Leibowitz, *What the Supreme Court Did and Did Not Do During the 1952 Term*, 102 U. Pa. L. Rev. 427, 428, 432 (1954). As indicated *infra* Chapter 17, note 11, Professor Henry M. Hart, Jr., of Harvard Law School shared this view.

10. *See* 1 James S. Liebman & Randy Hertz, Federal Habeas Corpus Practice and Procedure, § 2.4(d), at 68–69 (3d ed. 1998); Henry M. Hart, Jr., *The Supreme Court, 1958 Term—Foreword: The Time Chart of the Justices*, 73 Harv. L. Rev. 84, 106–08 (1959).

NOTES TO CHAPTER 17

1. Luther A. Huston, *Suit on Juries Won by North Carolina*, N.Y. Times, Feb. 10, 1953, at 17.

2. James M. Marsh, *The "Supreme Coort": Mr. Dooley Should Take Another Look*, 16 The Shingle 179 (1953). *See Woe for the Lawyers*, Wall St. J., Feb. 13, 1953, at 6 (editorial):

There may be a "rule of law" in these cases," but the lawyers are going to be as busy as little moles digging it out. . . . Where [all the writing] leaves the learned counsels and their clients, we don't know. It left us confused.

See also Mary Frances Berry, Stability, Security And Continuity 115 (1978) ("The final decision gave little additional guidance to the bench and bar.").

3. William O. Douglas, Memorandum to the Conference at 2 (Oct. 23, 1961), Hugo L. Black Papers, Library of Congress, Box 60 Frankfurter File, 1958–64.

4. Paul M. Bator, *Finality in Criminal Law and Federal Habeas Corpus for State Prisoners*, 76 Harv. L. Rev. 441, 500 (1963).

5. 339 U.S. 200 (1950).

6. The majority pointedly did not define these, but cited *Moore* with a "Compare." *See Darr*, 339 U.S. at 210.

7. As the Judicial Conference of the United States noted in 1961:

While [*Darr*] involved a failure to seek a writ of certiorari from a decision of a state court denying postconviction relief, it [was] read by some prisoners as suggesting that they must also file petitions in the Supreme Court of the United States from the affirmance of their convictions by a state supreme court.

Report of Proceedings of the Judicial Conference of the United States 50 (1962). To avoid the resulting "useless and time consuming" filings, it recommended that the problem be fixed by statute. *Id.* The Court then rendered this course unnecessary by overruling *Darr* in *Fay v. Noia*, 372 U.S. 391, 435–38 (1963).

8. Justices Burton and Clark, concurring, wrote that "the denial should be disregarded in passing upon a subsequent application for relief." *Darr*, 339 U.S. at 219 (Burton, J., concurring). In dissenting, Justice Frankfurter, for himself and Justices Black and Jackson, wrote that "such a denial has no legal significance whatever bearing on the merits of the claim." *Id.* at 226.

Justice Reed's opinion, which on this point expressed the views only of himself, Chief Justice Vinson, and Justice Minton did not explicitly discuss the issue. It recognized the power of the District Court to "disregard our denial of certiorari," and justified the requirement that the prisoner seek certiorari on the grounds that this procedure was more respectful of the states, not on any suggestion that the Court had passed on the merits. But it did write, "It is this Court which ordinarily should reverse state court judgments concerning local criminal administration." *Id.* at 216.

Technically, as Justice Reed was later to note, *see Brown v. Allen*, 344 U.S. 443, 450 (1953), the issue of what weight the District Court should give to a denial of certiorari was not before the *Darr* Court, because the petitioner in that case had in fact never sought Supreme Court review from the state's denial of collateral relief.

9. That ruling was *Wade v. Mayo*, 334 U.S. 672, 679–82 (1948), a 5–4 decision in which Justice Reed wrote a dissent that said in substance the same thing as his majority opinion in *Darr*. *Cf. Darr*, 339 U.S. at 210 ("[W]hatever deviation *Wade* may imply from the established rule will be corrected by this decision.").

10. *See* Jan Palmer, The Vinson Court Era 28 (1990).

11. *See* Henry M. Hart, Jr., *The Supreme Court, 1958 Term—Foreword: The Time Chart of the Justices*, 73 Harv. L. Rev. 84, at 95 n.20 (1959):

The prevailing opinion in *Darr v. Burford* . . . unhappily confused the traditional doctrine in the field of federal habeas corpus for state prisoners until a divided Court straightened the matter out in *Brown v. Allen.*

12. *See Brown,* 344 U.S. at 451 n.4 (collecting cases).

13. *See id.* at 450–52; *Smith v. Baldi,* 344 U.S. 561, 565 (1953).

14. Data on the certiorari votes of the individual Justices respecting the four cases that the Court eventually decided by plenary opinion are to be found in Palmer, *supra* note 10, at 355–56.

15. *Smith v. Baldi,* 344 U.S. 561 (1953).

16. *See id.* at 565.

17. Indeed, as the next two chapters will make clear, the merits of the Constitutional claims in the individual cases were of only peripheral interest to the Court; during its internal deliberations, the focus was on procedural matters concerning habeas corpus.

18. *See* Petition for Writ of Certiorari to the United States Court of Appeals for the Third Circuit, Brief and Affidavit of Counsel at 5, *Smith v. Baldi,* 344 U.S. 561 (1953) (No. 31).

19. *Baldi,* 344 U.S. at 562.

20. *See id.* at 567.

21. *See id.* at 563, 566.

22. *Commonwealth v. Smith,* 66 A.2d 764 (Pa. 1949).

23. *Baldi,* 344 U.S. at 564.

24. *See Smith v. Warden,* 87 F. Supp. 339, 340 (E.D. Pa. 1949).

25. *See Smith v. Warden,* 181 F.2d 847 (3d Cir. 1950).

26. *See Baldi,* 344 U.S. at 564.

27. *Id. See Smith v. Ashe,* 71 A.2d 107 (Pa. 1950).

28. *Smith v. Ashe,* 340 U.S. 812 (1950).

29. *See Baldi,* 344 U.S. at 565.

30. *Smith v. Baldi,* 96 F. Supp. 100, 103–04 (E.D. Pa. 1951).

31. *Id.* at 104–05.

32. *See id.* at 106.

33. *Smith v. Baldi,* 192 F.2d 540 (3d Cir. 1951).

34. *Smith v. Baldi,* 343 U.S. 903 (1952). The case, which had been on the Miscellaneous Docket as No. 300, was given Appellate Docket No. 669 upon the grant of certiorari in the 1951 Term. When it was carried over to the 1952 Term for reargument, it was designated No. 31.

For reasons lucidly explained in Bennett Boskey, Note, *The Supreme Court's "Miscellaneous" Docket,* 59 Harv. L. Rev. 604 (1946), the Court at this period placed on a Miscellaneous Docket (a) requests for extraordinary writs, and (b) petitions for certiorari in forma pauperis. In the event that one of these latter were granted, the case was transferred to the Appellate Docket. *See* Palmer, *supra* note 10, at 23–24.

35. *See McGee v. Ekberg*, 343 U.S. 970 (1952). The release of the prisoner was reported in a pool memorandum to all the Justices, which is undated but was probably written in early June, 1952, Supplemental Memorandum re *McGee v. Ekberg* (No. 517). This survives in various copies, including one in the Harold H. Burton Papers, Library of Congress, Box 231, Briefs for Argued Cases, Book 4.

36. *See People v. Ekberg*, 211 P.2d 316, 319 (Cal. Dist. Ct. App. 1949).

37. *See* Brief in Support of Petition for Writ of Certiorari at 19, *McGee* (No. 517).

38. *Ekberg v. California*, 339 U.S. 969 (1950). The case file of this proceeding (which includes Ekberg's handwritten legal work) is currently in the Washington facility of the National Archives, Record Group No. 267, Case File 1792, Box 6217.

39. *See* Petition for Writ of Habeas Corpus, *reprinted in* Transcript of Record at 1–19, *McGee* (No. 517).

40. *See id.* at 8–11.

41. Order Denying Petition for Writ of Habeas Corpus, *reprinted in* Transcript of Record at 21, 31, *McGee* (No. 517). Noting that "there is a justiciable problem involved in this case," the District Judge thereupon issued a certificate of probable cause to appeal, *id.* at 34.

42. *See Ekberg v. McGee*, 194 F.2d 178 (9th Cir. 1951).

43. *See id.* at 180. As detailed at Milestones III, 1557 n.82, this was a correct application of then-existing Supreme Court precedent (which *Brown* was to render obsolete). A dissenting Ninth Circuit judge would have affirmed on the basis that because the "petition for the writ presented no question of substance," there had been no error in its dismissal. *See Ekberg*, 194 F.2d at 180 (Healy, J., dissenting).

44. *McGee v. Ekberg*, 342 U.S. 952 (1952). The Washington facility of the National Archives contains in Records Group 267, Box 6790, the printer's copy of the record of the lower court proceedings that was created for the Court's use as a result of this order.

45. Brief of Petitioner at 7, *Speller v. Allen*, 344 U.S. 443 (1953) (No. 22).

46. *See Brunson v. North Carolina*, 333 U.S. 851 (1948).

47. *See* Petition for Writ of Habeas Corpus, *reprinted in* Transcript of Record, at 1, 2–3, *Brown v. Allen*, 344 U.S. 443 (1953) (No. 32). The case attracted considerable local notoriety, and the Winston-Salem Journal provided updates daily for the first ten days, *see, e.g.*, *Doctors Fight to Save the Life of Girl, 17, Brutally Beaten at Her Father's Radio Shop*, Winston-Salem Journal, June 17, 1950, at 1; *Youth Admits Criminal Assault Try, id.*, June 18, 1950, at 8; *Youth Admits He Beat Girl With Rifle, Police Report, id.*, June 25, 1950, at 1; *Case Against Brown Tightens; Beaten Girl Still Unconscious, id.*, June 27, 1950, at 3.

48. *See Brown*, 344 U.S. at 476; Order Appointing Counsel for Defendant, *reprinted in* Transcript of Record at 21, *Brown* (No. 32).

49. *See* Bill Woestendick, *Jury Finds Brown Guilty of Rape; Death Penalty is Mandatory*, Winston-Salem Journal, Sept. 15, 1950, at 1.

50. The trial court heard testimony and rendered findings of fact and conclusions of law on both issues. *See* Transcript of Record at 50–53, 87–122, *Brown* (No. 32).

51. *State v. Brown*, 63 S.E.2d 99 (N.C. 1951).

52. *Brown v. North Carolina*, 341 U.S. 943 (1951). Justices Black and Douglas voted to grant review. The text of the petition is reproduced in Transcript of Record at 239–52, *Brown* (No. 32).

53. *Brown v. Crawford*, 98 F. Supp. 866, 867 (E.D. N.C. 1951).

54. *Speller v. Allen*, 192 F.2d 477, 478 (4th Cir. 1951) (citing *Darr*).

55. *Brown v. Allen*, 343 U.S. 903 (1952). At that point, the case, which had been No. 333 on the Miscellaneous Docket, was assigned Appellate Docket No. 670 in the 1951 Term; when carried over to the 1952 Term for reargument, it was designated No. 32.

56. Petition for Writ of Habeas Corpus, ¶3, *reprinted in* Transcript of Record at 2, *Speller v. Allen*, 344 U.S. 443 (1953) (No. 22).

57. *See Brown v. Allen*, 344 U.S. 443, 477 (1953); Brief of Robert A. Allen . . . Opposing Petition for Writ of Certiorari at 6, *Speller* (No. 22).

58. *See State v. Speller*, 47 S.E.2d 537 (N.C. 1948).

59. *See State v. Speller*, 53 S.E.2d 294 (N.C. 1949).

60. *See State v. Speller*, 57 S.E.2d 759 (N.C. 1950).

61. *Speller v. North Carolina*, 340 U.S. 835 (1950).

62. *See Brown v. Allen*, 344 U.S. 443, 481 (1953).

63. *See Speller v. Crawford*, 99 F. Supp. 92, 97–98 (E.D. N.C. 1951).

64. *Crawford*, 99 F. Supp. at 95, 97.

65. *Speller v. Allen*, 192 F.2d 477 (4th Cir. 1951).

66. *Speller v. Allen*, 342 U.S. 953 (1952). The case, which had been No. 274 on the Miscellaneous Docket was thereupon assigned No. 643 in the 1951 Term. When carried over to the 1952 Term for reargument, it was designated No. 22.

67. *See* Brief for Petitioners at 3, 29–30, *Daniels v. Allen*, 344 U.S. 443 (No. 20).

68. *See* Petition for Writ of Habeas Corpus, *reprinted in* Transcript of Record at 1, 3, *Daniels* (No. 20).

69. *See Brown v. Allen*, 344 U.S. 443, 484–85 (1953).

70. *See State v. Daniels*, 56 S.E.2d 2 (N.C. 1949).

71. *State v. Daniels*, 56 S.E.2d 646, 647 (N.C. 1949).

72. *State v. Daniels*, 57 S.E.2d 653 (N.C. 1950). The court wrote, "We have carefully examined the record filed in this case and find no error therein. . . . [T]he judgment of the lower court is affirmed and the appeal is dismissed," *id.* at 654.

73. *See* Petition for Writ of Certiorari to the Supreme Court of North Carolina and/or to the Superior Court, Pitt County, North Carolina, at 1–2, *Daniels v. North Carolina*, 339 U.S. 954 (1950) (No. 412 Misc.). This document is to be found in the Washington facility of the National Archives and Record Administration, Record Group 267, Entry 21. In addition to reasserting the prior grounds for relief,

this petition challenged the rulings designated (a) and (b) in the text as Equal Protection violations. *See id.* at 11–12, 13–15.

74. The government argued that since the ruling designated (b) in the text: merely held that the petition was insufficient, there is no reason why the Petitioners cannot now avail themselves of this remedy [coram nobis] if they will file a proper and sufficient petition. . . . The Respondent, therefore, contends that the Petitioners have never exhausted their remedies [and the North Carolina Supreme Court] has, therefore, not passed upon the constitutional issues. Brief of the State of North Carolina, Respondent, Opposing Petition for Writ of Certiorari at 28, *Daniels v. North Carolina,* 339 U.S. 954 (1950) (No. 412 Misc.).

Petitioners' response was that, even assuming that the ruling of the North Carolina Supreme Court was procedural rather than substantive, repetitive resort to the state courts was not required. *See* Reply Brief of Petitioners in Support of Petition for Writ of Certiorari at 10, *Daniels* (No. 412 Misc.). Both of these documents are to be found in the Washington facility of the National Archives, Record Group 267, Entry 21.

75. *Daniels v. North Carolina,* 339 U.S. 954 (1950).

76. *See State v. Daniels,* 59 S.E.2d 430 (N.C. 1950). The court ruled that the issues sought to be pursued were presented to and passed upon by the trial court, so that the prisoners were improperly attempting to use coram nobis as a substitute for an appeal, rather than for its intended purpose of correcting errors not appearing in the record.

77. *Daniels v. Crawford,* 99 F. Supp. 208, 212 (E.D. N.C. 1951). The Court considered in the alternative the possibility that it was entitled to intervene notwithstanding the prior state rulings "where it appears clearly that there has been such a gross violation of a defendant's constitutional rights as amounts to a denial of even the substance of a fair trial," but, reviewing the contentions made and their handling by the North Carolina courts, concluded that "[i]t is difficult to believe that any impartial person would conclude" that this was such a case. *Id.* at 213.

78. *Daniels v. Allen,* 192 F.2d 763, 767–68 (4th Cir. 1951).

79. *Id.* at 772 (Soper, J., dissenting).

80. *Daniels v. Allen,* 342 U.S. 941 (1952). The case, which was No. 271 on the Miscellaneous Docket, was then transferred to the Appellate Docket and assigned No. 626. When carried over to the 1952 Term for reargument, it was designated No. 20.

NOTES TO CHAPTER 18

1. The account in this chapter and the next is based upon a review of the collected papers of Hugo L. Black, Harold H. Burton, William O. Douglas, and Robert H. Jackson in the Library of Congress; the papers of Felix Frankfurter, which are physically divided between the Harvard Law Library and the Library of

Congress, but available on microfilm; the papers of Stanley Reed in the Margaret I. King Library of the University of Kentucky; and the papers of Tom C. Clark at the Tarlton Law Library of the University of Texas. Its purpose is not to report every reference to *Brown* in the document sets indicated, but rather to make a fair presentation of the points that are central to the present inquiry. When, as is frequently the case, the same document exists in several of these collections, I have cited to only one of them, but I have reviewed all the copies for annotations.

Because of the frequent use of these papers by sometimes-careless researchers and the fact that *Brown* was in fact five cases, each bearing more than one number and four of which were heard in two Terms, the documents referred to may be found by future students in file locations slightly different from those described here. As indicated above, they are also available from the reference desk of the Deane Law Library of Hofstra Law School.

2. Bench Memorandum, *McGee v. Ekberg* (No. 517) (dated 4/27/52) (original emphasis). This document is to be found in the Harold H. Burton Papers, Library of Congress, Box 231, Briefs for Argued Cases, Book 4.

3. These have been set forth *supra* Chapter 17.

4. Conference Memorandum, *McGee* (No. 517) (dated 5/3/52). This document is to be found in the William O. Douglas Papers, Library of Congress, Box 210, Argued Cases Memos. *See generally* Forrest Maltzman & Paul J. Wahlbeck, *Inside the Supreme Court: The Reliability of the Justices' Conference Records*, 58 J. Pol. 528 (1996) (studying conference records of four Justices, including Douglas, for 1967–68 Terms and finding them "substantially accurate and reliable").

5. Conference Note Dated 5/3/52 re Nos. 517, 626, 643, 670, 669. This document is to be found in the Burton Papers, Library of Congress, Box 231, Briefs for Argued Cases, Book 4. On his copy of the Conference List for May 3, 1952, Justice Burton also noted of the habeas cases, "All go over for memos from SR & FF." This document is to be found in the Burton Papers, Library of Congress, Box 235, Conference Sheets, March–June 1952.

6. Memorandum from Felix Frankfurter to the Brethren (June 3, 1952). A number of copies of this document survive. One is to be found in the Hugo L. Black Papers, Library of Congress, Container 314, Habeas Corpus Folder.

7. *Youngstown Sheet and Tube Co. v. Sawyer*, 343 U.S. 579 (1952). Justice Frankfurter noted in his memorandum, "Certiorari in that case was granted the same day, on May 3, that the *Habeas Corpus* cases were assigned for reports."

8. Memorandum from Stanley Reed to the Conference re Nos. 517, 626, 643, 670 & 669 (June 4, 1952). Copies of this document, a covering memorandum to the draft opinion cited *infra* note 9, survive in many locations, including the Tom C. Clark Papers at the Tarlton Law Library of the University of Texas, Box A19.

9. Memorandum by Mr. Justice Reed, *McGee v. Ekberg* (No. 517), at 22 ([June 4, 1952]). Among the surviving copies of this document is one in the Tom C. Clark Papers at the Tarlton Law Library of the University of Texas, Box A19.

10. *Id.* at 28 (footnote citing *Darr* omitted).

11. This is described *infra* Chapter 20, text accompanying note 1.

12. An account appears later in this chapter.

13. *Brown v. Allen*, 344 U.S. 443, 463 (1953).

14. Memorandum from Felix Frankfurter to The Brethren (June 7, 1952). Among the surviving copies is one in the Hugo L. Black Papers, Library of Congress, Supreme Court Case File, October Term 1952, Habeas Corpus Folder.

15. Diary Entry (June 7, 1952), Harold L. Burton Papers, Library of Congress, Reel 3 ("we voted after considerable argument to set down habeas corpus & Kerdoff [*sic*] cases for reargument in fall"); *see Kedroff v. St. Nicholas Cathedral*, 343 U.S. 972 (1952); Letter from Robert H. Jackson to Felix Frankfurter (July 12, 1952), Felix Frankfurter Papers, Library of Congress, Container 69 (recalling that Chief Justice Vinson "was very much upset . . . that the habeas corpus cases went over the term"). The disputed issue was surely whether to set the cases for reargument or simply hold them over as Justice Frankfurter had suggested; there was plainly no realistic prospect of writing a decision in the two days before the Court began its summer recess on June 9, 1952.

16. *See Daniels v. Allen*, 343 U.S. 973 (1952).

17. Memorandum by Mr. Justice Reed, *Brown v. Allen*, No. 670 (Sept. 26, 1952). This document survives in many locations, including the Tom C. Clark Papers at the Tarlton Law Library of the University of Texas, Box A19. It elaborates, *id.* at 8–16, on the discussion regarding the effect to be given to a denial of certiorari, but this was cut back before publication, presumably after Justice Reed discovered in the conference of October 27 (described later in this chapter) that he was outvoted on the issue. His draft of December 4, 1952 (also noted later in this chapter) covers the issue substantially as his final opinion does.

18. As indicated *infra* note 38, there was a consensus on this point in conference. Justice Jackson initially considered taking a different view, but decided not to do so. *See infra* Chapter 19, notes 19, 30.

19. Memorandum by Mr. Justice Reed, *supra* note 17, at 6 n.4.

20. *See Brown v. Allen*, 344 U.S. 443, 447 n.2, 448 n.3, 449–50 (1953).

21. *See* John J. Parker, *Limiting the Abuse of Habeas Corpus*, 8 F.R.D. 171, 176 (1949).

22. Memorandum from Felix Frankfurter to the Conference re Nos. 20, 22, 31 and 32 (Oct. 13, 1952). Numerous copies of this document survive, including one in the Tom C. Clark Papers at the Tarlton Law Library of the University of Texas, Box A19.

23. *See Brown*, 344 U.S. at 514–32 (Appendix to opinion of Frankfurter, J.).

24. Memorandum of Mr. Justice Frankfurter re *Daniels v. Allen*, No. 20 (Oct. 13, 1952). There is a copy in, among other places, the Tom C. Clark Papers at the Tarlton Law Library of the University of Texas, Box A19.

25. The substance of this argument, somewhat shortened and toned down,

eventually appeared in his opinion in *Brown v. Allen*, 344 U.S. 443, 489–97 (1953) (opinion of Frankfurter, J.) *See also* Supplemental Memorandum of Mr. Justice Frankfurter re *Daniels v. Allen*, No. 20 (October 22, 1952) ("put[ting] on a single page what seem to me to be the controlling data" in support of this position). There is a copy in, among other places, the Tom C. Clark Papers at the Tarlton Law Library of the University of Texas, Box A19.

26. *See Brown*, 344 U.S. at 526 (Appendix to opinion of Frankfurter, J.). *See also id.* at 510 (opinion of Frankfurter, J.) Figures:

showing that during the last four years five State prisoners, all told, were discharged by federal district courts, prove beyond peradventure that it is a baseless fear, a bogeyman, to worry lest State convictions be upset by allowing district courts to entertain applications for habeas corpus on behalf of prisoners under State sentence.

27. *See Brown*, 344 U.S. at 498–510 (opinion of Frankfurter, J.).

28. Memorandum, *supra* note 24, at 17–23. As stated *supra* Chapter 15, text accompanying note 9, I believe that just this rule had already been established in *Frank*, and Frankfurter probably thought so too, *see infra* Chapter 19, note 22.

29. Memorandum, *supra* note 24, at 22–23.

30. *Id.* at 20, 23.

31. Observations by Mr. Justice Frankfurter on Memorandum of Mr. Justice Reed in *Brown v. Allen* (Oct. 16, 1952). There is a copy in, among other places, the Tom C. Clark Papers at the Tarlton Law Library of the University of Texas, Box A19.

32. *Id.* at 3–4.

33. *Id.* at 5–11.

34. Memorandum from Stanley Reed and Felix Frankfurter to the Conference re Habeas Corpus Cases (Oct. 17, 1952). There is a copy in, among other places, the Tom C. Clark Papers at the Tarlton Law Library of the University of Texas, Box A19.

35. The evidence is to be found in annotations by Justice Burton in the margin of his copy of the list circulated on October 17, 1952, of cases to be conferenced on October 18. The document is in the Harold H. Burton Papers, Library of Congress, Box 248 (List No. 1, Sheet 4).

36. Conference Memorandum, *Daniels v. Allen* (No. 20) (dated 10-27-52). This document is to be found in the William O. Douglas Papers, Library of Congress, Box 222, Argued Cases Office and Conference Memos.

37. These handwritten notes are to be found in Box A-19 of the Tom C. Clark Papers at the Tarlton Law Library of the University of Texas.

38. Put slightly more formally, this appears to be a consensus that, as the Court eventually held, *see Brown v. Allen*, 344 U.S. 443, 447–50 (1953), the requirement of exhaustion of state remedies contained in 28 U.S.C. § 2254 does require the pursuit of any state postconviction remedies that might be available for the presentation of Constitutional issues not previously tendered to the state courts, but not

repetitive state filings on the same question. *See Wilwording v. Swenson*, 404 U.S. 249, 250 (1971).

39. The reference is to *Ex Parte Royall*, 117 U.S. 241 (1886).

40. *See Johnson v. Zerbst*, 304 U.S. 458, 465–68 (1938) (relying on *Frank* to hold that denial of counsel at trial could be attacked by federal habeas corpus since violation of the Sixth Amendment "stands as a jurisdictional bar to a valid conviction and sentence"). The *Johnson* decision was well grounded, because, as discussed *supra* Chapter 10, *Frank* confirmed the already-established meaning of "jurisdiction" in the law of habeas corpus as a synonym for fundamental error—a meaning that, as described *infra* Chapter 19, was unknown to clerk Rehnquist.

41. At the cited page, Frankfurter had presented data showing that "[i]n less than 10% of the cases did the applicant file any papers which would serve to indicate to the District Court what questions were before the Supreme Court." The same material appears at *Brown v. Allen*, 344 U.S. 443, 523 (1953) (Appendix to opinion of Frankfurter, J.).

42. In view of subsequent developments, there is every reason to believe that his objection was to a suggestion (recorded just before the second paragraph numbered 2 in Justice Clark's note) that he considered as cutting back on the existing independent authority of the federal habeas court to investigate the state proceedings. As the account given later in this chapter will reveal, Justice Reed disclaimed any such purpose, and the *Brown* opinion was written to incorporate this understanding.

43. Professors Derrick A. Bell, Jr., of New York University Law School and Mary L. Dudziak of the University of Southern California Law School have forcefully called attention to the importance of Cold War propaganda considerations in the federal government's enforcement of racial equality during this period. *See* Mary L. Dudziak, Cold War Civil Rights: Race and the Image of American Democracy (2000); Derrick A. Bell, Jr., Brown v. Board of Education *and the Interest-Convergence Dilemma*, 93 Harv. L. Rev. 518, 524 (1980). Similarly, as indicated *infra* note 53, the Court's consideration of *Brown v. Allen* took place against a Cold War background, and was closely intertwined chronologically—and, surely, psychologically—with its consideration of the most salient case of the Term, the espionage prosecution against Julius and Ethel Rosenberg. *See* Milestones III, 1574 n.167 (providing detailed chronology).

Throughout that lengthy litigation, *see Rosenberg v. United States*, 346 U.S. 273, 277–85 (1953) (recounting procedural history through defendants' execution on June 19, 1953), Justice Frankfurter (like Justice Black) "voted to review the *Rosenberg* cases at every opportunity," William Cohen, *Justice Douglas and the* Rosenberg *Case: Setting the Record Straight*, 70 Cornell L. Rev. 211, 214 (1985). *See* Melvin I. Urofsky, Felix Frankfurter 119–24 (1991).

44. Memorandum From Felix Frankfurter to the Brethren re Nos. 20, 22, 31 and 32, at 1, 5–6 (Oct. 28, 1952). There is a copy in, among other places, the Tom C. Clark Papers at the Tarlton Law Library of the University of Texas, Box A19.

45. One of these covered *Smith v. Baldi*, and the other one the remaining cases. Copies of these drafts are to be found in, among other places, the Tom C. Clark Papers at the Tarlton Law Library of the University of Texas, Box A19.

46. Memorandum From Felix Frankfurter to the Brethren re Nos. 20, 22, 31 and 32, at 1–2 (Dec. 19, 1952). There is a copy in, among other places, the Tom C. Clark Papers at the Tarlton Law Library of the University of Texas, Box A19.

47. *See, e.g., id.* at 9 ("Congress has placed no obstacles in the way of a hearing such as Mr. Justice Reed seems to suggest"), 10:

Nor does Mr. Justice Reed give appropriate guidance to the District Judge as to the circumstances in which it is "proper" to hold a hearing. His opinion seems to me to authorize whatever the District Judge happens to be disposed to do.

12:

The District Judge is not told what to do if the record is silent on the relevant questions, and certainly a reasonable District Judge could read the language . . . to mean that he did not need to go beyond whatever record is available.

48. *Id.* at 14 (footnotes omitted).

49. At this point, Justice Reed quotes the unrevised version of the passage that, as will be seen below, he was to revise on January 30, which "summarizes the teaching of the opinion."

50. Memorandum from Stanley Reed to the Conference re Nos. 32, 22 & 20, at 1–2, 4 (Dec. 24, 1952). Among the many surviving copies of this document is one in the Tom C. Clark Papers at the Tarlton Law Library of the University of Texas, Box A19.

51. A copy may be found, among other places, in the Tom C. Clark Papers at the Tarlton Law Library of the University of Texas, Box A19.

52. Memorandum from Felix Frankfurter to the Brethren re Nos. 20, 22, 31 and 32, at 1 (Dec. 31, 1952). A copy may be found, among other places, in the Tom C. Clark Papers at the Tarlton Law Library of the University of Texas, Box A19.

53. During the same period, Justice Douglas was emphasizing the same idea in public, pointedly observing: "Due process, as well as bullets, helps win . . . wars against Communism." William O. Douglas, *A Crusade for the Bar: Due Process in a Time of World Conflict*, 39 A.B.A. J. 871, 875 (1953) (address delivered to the American Law Institute, May 20, 1953), *reprinted as* William O. Douglas, *A Challenge to the Bar*, 28 Notre Dame Law. 497 (1953); William O. Douglas, *Address Before the American Law Institute*, 12 Law. Guild Rev. 145 (1953); William O. Douglas, *Some Antecedents of Due Process*, 2 Kan. L. Rev. 1 (1953).

54. At this point, Justice Reed wrote across his copy, which is to be found in the Stanley Reed Papers, Margaret I. King Library, University of Kentucky, Box 147, "Why? No reason not to." *See infra* note 56 (discussing the meaning of this note).

55. The material referred to is that which later appeared in more elaborate form in Justice Frankfurter's opinion in *Brown v. Allen*, 344 U.S. 443, 501–08 (1953)

(opinion of Frankfurter, J.). For some possible responses to Justice Frankfurter's question, see *infra* note 70.

56. Justice Reed underlined the word "test" in his copy, which is to be found in the Stanley Reed Papers, Margaret I. King Library, University of Kentucky Library, Box 147, and wrote in the margin: "That is meant—not a hearing fn p 13 of Comment says no." The reference is to a passage in Justice Frankfurter's December 19 memorandum, which, in substantially the same language as that appearing in his opinion in *Brown v. Allen*, 344 U.S. 443, 504 (1953) (opinion of Frankfurter, J.), authorizes District Judges to dispose of habeas corpus proceedings summarily when the record is sufficiently clear for them to do so. In other words, as the two Justices recognized in emphasizing the common ground between them (and as clerk Rehnquist recognized in making the criticisms of Reed's position that appear *infra* Chapter 19, text accompanying note 8), there was no disagreement that the prisoner was entitled to an independent ruling on the Constitutional merits from the federal court. The sparring was over the criteria that would entitle the applicant to a plenary hearing. The eventual resolution of this issue is described *infra* Chapter 20, text accompanying note 2.

57. In his copy, Justice Reed underlined "discretion," and wrote in the margin "must be left to discretion as defined on p 2 of my memo," again a reference to the unrevised version of the passage that, as described later in this chapter, was to be modified on January 30.

58. Memorandum, *supra* note 52, at 1–6, 8.

59. A copy of this draft with a covering memorandum may be found, among other places, in the Tom C. Clark Papers at the Tarlton Law Library of the University of Texas, Box A19. The key change was the addition of the paragraph that now appears as the first paragraph of Justice Frankfurter's opinion in *Brown v. Allen*, 344 U.S. 443, 503 (1953) (opinion of Frankfurter, J.), dealing with the effect on federal habeas corpus of procedural defaults at the state level. In his covering memorandum, Justice Frankfurter said, "I have heretofore written nothing about this aspect of the general problem because I stupidly had not realized it bothered some of the Brethren," Memorandum from Felix Frankfurter to The Brethren (Jan. 23, 1953), a statement that can be explained only by the assumption that he had not yet turned his mind to the merits of the cases (especially *Daniels,* which centered on just that issue).

60. A copy of this draft, applying to *Brown, Speller,* and *Daniels,* may be found, among other places, in the Tom C. Clark Papers at the Tarlton Law Library of the University of Texas, Box A19.

61. *Id.* at 5–6.

62. Letter from Felix Frankfurter to Hugo L. Black (Jan. 23, 1953). This document is to be found in the Hugo L. Black Papers, Library of Congress, Container 315, *Brown v. Allen* Folder.

63. *Id.* This concern that the Court's opinion as it then stood could be read as weakening the preexisting investigatory powers of the federal habeas corpus court illustrates how far off the mark Professor Bator's thesis is.

64. Letter from Hugo L. Black to Felix Frankfurter, Felix Frankfurter Papers, Part I, Reel 66, Frame 00038. The document is undated, but, on the basis of the chronology set forth in this paragraph of text, was surely written sometime between January 23 and January 28, 1953.

65. A copy of this version may be found, among other places, in the Tom C. Clark Papers at the Tarlton Law Library of the University of Texas, Box A19.

66. A copy of this version may be found, among other places, in the Tom C. Clark Papers at the Tarlton Law Library of the University of Texas, Box A19. The quoted passage appears at 6–7.

67. *See Brown v. Allen*, 344 U.S. 443, 553–54 (1953) (Black, J., dissenting).

68. Letter from Felix Frankfurter to Harold H. Burton (Jan. 27, 1953), Felix Frankfurter Papers, Part III, Reel 1, Frame 260.

69. Memorandum from Stanley Reed to the Conference re Nos. 32, 22 & 20 (January 30, 1953). A copy may be found, among other places, in the Tom C. Clark Papers at the Tarlton Law Library of the University of Texas, Box A19.

Reflecting Justice Reed's change, the published passage in *Brown v. Allen*, 344 U.S. 443, 462–64 (1953) (appearing under the heading "Right to a Plenary Hearing") reads:

Applications to district courts on grounds determined adversely to the applicant by state courts should follow the same principle—a refusal of the writ without more, if the court is satisfied, by the record, that the state process has given fair consideration to the issues and the offered evidence, and has resulted in a satisfactory conclusion. Where the record of the application affords an adequate opportunity to weigh the sufficiency of the allegations and the evidence, and no unusual circumstances calling for a hearing are presented, a repetition of the trial is not required. . . . However, a trial may be had in the discretion of the federal court or judge hearing the new application. A way is left open to redress violations of the Constitution. . . . *Moore v. Dempsey,* 261 U.S. 86. Although they have the power, it is not necessary for federal courts to hold hearings on the merits, facts or law a second time when satisfied that federal constitutional rights have been protected. It is necessary to exercise jurisdiction to the extent of determining by examination of the record whether or not a hearing would serve the ends of justice. (footnotes omitted)

As Justice O'Connor summarizes in a portion of her opinion in *Williams v. Taylor,* 529 U.S. 362 (2000) that expresses the views of the Court, the meaning of the phrase "and has resulted in a satisfactory conclusion" has been the subject of some disagreement among subsequent Justices. *See id.* at 410–12. In his three-Justice opinion in *Wright v. West,* 505 U.S. 277, 287 (1992), Justice Thomas suggested that "a satisfactory conclusion" might mean a reasonable one as opposed to a correct one. Justice O'Connor, in an opinion also expressing the views of three Justices, convincingly rebutted this view, correctly pointing out that the passage relates to determinations of fact, not questions of law or mixed questions of law and fact. *See id.* at 299–302. The history presented here—clearly showing that the phrase was added precisely to obviate concerns that the opinions might be read to narrow the federal courts' duty to review the latter categories of question de novo—strongly supports Justice O'Connor's position.

70. An outsider can only speculate as to why at this point the Justices could not agree on a draft. But the fact is probably best explained by some combination of tense interpersonal relations on the Court, *see* Melvin I. Urofsky, *Conflict among the Brethren: Felix Frankfurter, William O. Douglas and the Clash of Personalities and Philosophies on the United States Supreme Court,* 1988 Duke L.J. 71; the normal investment of people in prose compositions to which they have devoted much work, *see* William O. Douglas, Memorandum to the Conference, at 2 (Oct. 23, 1961), Hugo L. Black Papers, Library of Congress, Box 60, Frankfurter File, 1958–64 (implicitly attributing form of *Brown* opinions to this factor); and an unwillingness to labor further on this long-running project. With respect to this last point, it may be relevant that the Justices knew that they would soon be confronting a climactic appeal from the Rosenbergs.

71. *See Brown v. Allen,* 344 U.S. 443, 487–88 (1953) (opinion of Burton and Clark, JJ.) The iterations of this document are detailed in Milestones III, 1587 n.213. But the various drafts reflected only minor tinkering and no substantive change. In all versions, the authors clearly rejected the idea of giving any weight to the denial of certiorari and considered the Reed and Frankfurter opinions to be consistent with each other on the remaining procedural issues.

72. Letter from Harold H. Burton to Tom C. Clark re ##32, 22 & 20, Habeas Corpus (Jan. 16, 1953). This document and the enclosed typescript opinion are to be found in the Tom C. Clark Papers at the Tarlton Law Library of the University of Texas, Box A19.

73. For a brief sketch of Weisberg's later career, which culminated in appointment as a United States Magistrate Judge in Chicago in 1985, see *Obituary,* Chi. Daily L. Bull., Jan. 17, 1994, at 3.

74. Memorandum from B[ernard] W[eisberg] to Mr. Justice [Clark]. This memorandum, to be found in the Tom C. Clark Papers at the Tarlton Law Library of the University of Texas, Box A19, is undated, but, on the basis of the chronology set forth in the text, was undoubtedly written sometime between January 23 and January 27, 1953.

75. Just as Frankfurter had done in his memorandum of December 31, Weisberg pointed specifically to the then-unamended version of the passage that Justice Reed was to alter on January 30.

76. Memorandum, *supra* note 74, at 1–2.

77. Letter from Harold H. Burton to Tom C. Clark (Jan. 27, 1953). There is a copy in the Tom C. Clark Papers at the Tarlton Law Library of the University of Texas, Box A19.

NOTES TO CHAPTER 19

1. This statement serves to date the document, which does not bear a date, with some precision. Certiorari was granted in *Daniels* on March 3, 1952, *Daniels v. Allen*, 342 U.S. 941 (1952), and in *McGee* on March 10, 1952, *McGee v. Ekberg*, 342 U.S. 952 (1952).

2. Certiorari Memorandum, *McGee v. Ekberg* (No. 517, O.T. 1951), Robert H. Jackson Papers, Library of Congress, Legal File, Supreme Court—O.T. 1952, Case Nos. 32, 22, 20, 31, *Brown v. Allen*, etc., Folder #2.

3. This document, bearing the notation Appendix to No. 517, is to be found annexed to *id.* It has been previously noted in Saul Brenner, *The Memos of Supreme Court Law Clerk William Rehnquist: Conservative Tracts or Mirrors of his Justice's Mind?*, 76 Judicature 77, 80–81 (1992) and David J. Garrow, *The Rehnquist Reins*, N.Y. Times Magazine, Oct. 6, 1996, at 65, 66. *See also* Larry W. Yackle, *The Habeas Hagioscope*, 66 S. Cal. L. Rev. 2331, 2343 (1993). *See generally* William H. Rehnquist, *Who Writes the Decisions of the Supreme Court?*, 74 U.S. News & World Rep. 74 (1957). I have silently corrected some obvious typographical errors.

4. *See supra* Chapter 18, note 40 (describing case). As recapitulated there, Rehnquist's statement, like the argument built thereon, is simply wrong as a matter of law and history. In American habeas corpus jurisprudence, the term "jurisdictional defect" has never been restricted to the sorts of issues described in the final sentence of this paragraph of text but has always meant "fundamental error." *Compare Custis v. U.S.*, 511 U.S. 484, 494–96 (1994) (Rehnquist, C.J.) (restating his theory), *with id.* at 508–10 (Souter, J.) (answering argument).

5. The next paragraph of the memorandum, elided here, discusses the *Wells* litigation, described by Justice Jackson in *Brown v. Allen*, 344 U.S. 443, 537 n.11 (1953) (Jackson, J., concurring in the result). *See also infra* note 15 and accompanying text.

6. This position closely resembles the one that Bator later took. *See* Paul M. Bator, *Finality in Criminal Law and Federal Habeas Corpus for State Prisoners*, 76 Harv. L. Rev. 441, 458 (1963).

7. This document is to be found in the Robert H. Jackson Papers, Library of Congress, Legal File, Supreme Court—O.T. 1952, Case Nos. 32, 22, 20, 31, *Brown v. Allen*, etc., Folder #2. Again, obvious typographical errors have been silently corrected.

8. This reference indicates that the memorandum was written prior to Justice Reed's circulation of September 26, 1952.

9. Supporting the dating suggested *supra* note 8, this reference makes clear that the memorandum was, in any event, written before Justice Frankfurter's circulation of October 13, 1952.

10. For the form in which Justice Jackson ultimately incorporated this thought into his opinion, see *Brown v. Allen*, 344 U.S. 443, 533 (1953) (Jackson, J., concurring in the result).

11. I have, of course, already set forth in Part I my disagreement with this proposition.

12. *But cf. Ex Parte Watkins*, 28 U.S. (3 Pet.) 193, 202 (1830) (Marshall, C.J.):
The writ of habeas corpus is a high prerogative writ, known to the common law, the great object of which is the liberation of those who may be imprisoned without sufficient cause. It is in the nature of a writ of error, to examine the legality of the commitment.

13. Bator eventually made exactly this argument in his article as well. *See* Bator, *supra* note 6, at 441–54.

14. This document is to be found in the Robert H. Jackson Papers, Library of Congress, Legal File, Supreme Court—O.T. 1952, Case Nos. 32, 22, 20, 31, *Brown v. Allen*, etc., Folder #2.

The document is undated, so the dating given in the text is conjectural, but, for the following reasons, I believe it to be correct within a few days. The document begins "Reed, J., circulated this yesterday afternoon," and describes material appearing at "p. 6–8 of Stanley's memo." That material appears in the indicated location of Justice Reed's memorandum in *Brown v. Allen* dated September 26, 1952, a Friday. Justice Clark's copy of that memorandum, found in the Tom C. Clark Papers at the Tarlton Law Library of the University of Texas, Box A19, bears a pencil annotation indicating its receipt on September 30, 1952. Assuming that all chambers received the circulation on that day, then Rehnquist was writing on October 1, 1952.

15. The reference is to Judge Louis E. Goodman of the Northern District of California, who sat on the *Wells* case, *see supra* note 5.

Following the publication of the initial print of the *Brown* opinion on February 9, 1953, Judge Goodman wrote Justice Jackson a letter referring to note 11 of his opinion and saying, that, as "one of the first judges who, in published writings, called attention to the mounting abuse of the writ," he was "somewhat shocked to find myself, not by name of course, singled out as an aider of abusive habeas corpus practice"; he urged that his conduct had been entirely in accord with governing Circuit and Supreme Court authority. *See* Letter from Louis E. Goodman to Robert H. Jackson (Feb. 16, 1953), Robert H. Jackson Papers, Library of Congress, Legal File, Supreme Court—O.T. 1952, Case Nos. 32, 22, 20, 31, *Brown v. Allen*, etc., Folder #3.

Justice Jackson replied:
I think the footnote to which you call my attention unconsciously does you an injustice. Fortunately, the Reporter's Office had not prepared the final text for the United States Reports and I am adding to the footnote, after the citation of the *Wells* case, the following:
The opinions of the District Judge show that he was well aware of the difficulties presented by the procedure, but felt he had no alternative in the

light of this Court's decisions. Indeed, he has contributed the lessons of his own experience in this field in Goodman, Use and Abuse of the Writ of Habeas Corpus, 7 F.R.D. 313.

Letter from Robert H. Jackson to Louis E. Goodman (Feb. 19, 1953), which is to be found in the same file location.

16. Consistent with the dating already suggested, this reference also implies that the document was written before Justice Frankfurter laid out his views in his memorandum of October 13, 1952.

17. If, as is plausible, this is what Justice Frankfurter wished to do, he did not so indicate in his formal circulations. As already recounted in Chapter 18, these did not seek to persuade the brethren to abandon the requirement that would-be habeas petitioners first file a certiorari petition, but only to insure that the denials of such petitions would not be given any substantive effect. This is consistent with the approach that both Justice Reed and Justice Jackson took in modifying their various drafts; all the Justices made substantial efforts to moderate positions that they knew lacked internal support.

18. Next to this paragraph, Justice Jackson wrote "yes."

19. Next to this paragraph, Justice Jackson wrote "yes." He incorporated the thought in an early draft of his opinion, *see infra* text accompanying note 30, but abandoned it thereafter. As indicated in the next sentences of text, the consequence of its adoption would have been that, in a state permitting successive postconviction filings in state court, the prisoner would never be able to file a federal habeas corpus in District Court—only a petition seeking certiorari from the denial of state remedies. The Court's rejection of this suggestion has been described *supra* Chapter 18, text accompanying notes 18–21.

20. Recalling from the discussion of *Frank, supra* Chapter 10, text accompanying note 26, that an independent and adequate state ground would bar review on direct appeal but not on federal habeas corpus, this appears to mean, "when the vote to deny certiorari is not based on the existence of adequate and independent state grounds."

See Letter from William O. Douglas to Jerome N. Frank (Sept. 27, 1956):

You state in your letter [of September 11 about pending habeas corpus legislation, *see infra* Chapter 21, text accompanying note 17] that you assume we are too busy to scrutinize carefully all the certs coming to us from State courts denying relief. I do not think that is true. We look at all these things very closely. The difficulty is that there are often persuasive grounds for believing that the State court judgment rests on an adequate State ground. Some here are sticklers on that point. Others of us are more liberal in that regard. But nonetheless a lot of cases get impaled on that barrier. So we do not get to the merits. That leaves open the avenue of relief through the Federal courts.

Copies of both letters are to be found in the William O. Douglas Papers, Library of Congress, Box 583, Habeas Corpus Law Folder.

21. Justice Jackson never gave serious consideration to this suggestion, consistently maintaining his view that habeas corpus was the appropriate vehicle for the assertion of errors that did not and could not have been made part of the record before the Court on certiorari. *See Brown v. Allen*, 344 U.S. 443, 546–47 (1953). *Cf. Coleman v. Balkcom*, 451 U.S. 949, 956–57, 963 (1981) (Rehnquist, J., dissenting from the denial of certiorari) (proposing that the Court grant certiorari from the state court's denial of postconviction relief in a capital case where "the issues presented are not substantial" and petitioner had not "made any showing in the Georgia courts that he was deprived of any rights secured to him by the United States Constitution" so "that this Court may deal with all of petitioner's claims on their merits" and thereby preclude federal habeas review should the petitioner lose); *Coleman v. Kemp*, 778 F.2d 1487, 1543 (llth Cir. 1985) (granting same petitioner federal habeas relief), *cert. denied*, 476 U.S. 1164 (1986).

22. The inference regarding timing is based on the fact that no typed draft emerged until December, and the hypothesis that it would be inefficient to begin working on such a project until after one had heard the views of the brethren in conference. In addition, the notes described in the next sentence of text contain the Justice's research responding to the point "FF says Frank v. Magnum and Moore v. Dempsey authority for considering on h.c. same issue as on cert.," and so were written at some point after Justice Jackson had heard this from Justice Frankfurter.

23. Opinion notes re Habeas Corpus, Robert H. Jackson Papers, Library of Congress, Legal File, Supreme Court—O.T. 1952, Case Nos. 32, 22, 20, 31, *Brown v. Allen*, etc., Folder #1.

24. Draft Opinion, Nos. 20, 22, 31 & 32 (dated 12/29), Robert H. Jackson Papers, Library of Congress, Legal File, Supreme Court—O.T. 1952, Case Nos. 32, 22, 20, 31, *Brown v. Allen*, etc., Folder #2. Like all of his notes and drafts, this one appears to be Justice Jackson's own work, with only tangential incorporation of Rehnquist's ideas and research.

25. The paragraph omitted at this point consists substantially verbatim of the paragraph labeled "History" from Rehnquist's memo of the fall of 1952.

26. Draft Opinion, *supra note 24*, at 1–10.

27. *See Brown v. Allen*, 344 U.S. 443, 540–48 (1953) (Jackson, J., concurring in the result).

28. Draft Opinion, *supra* note 24, at 11–12.

29. This word is not in the original document; the interpolation is purely mine.

30. As indicated, *supra* note 19, and consistent with the progression of his drafts toward more moderate views, Justice Jackson deleted this suggestion from later drafts.

31. Draft opinion, *supra* note 24, at 13–20.

32. Draft Opinion, Nos. 20, 22, 31 & 32 (dated 1/5/53), Robert H. Jackson Papers, Library of Congress, Legal File, Supreme Court—O.T. 1952, Case Nos. 32, 22, 20, 31, *Brown v. Allen*, etc., Folder #3.

33. Most obviously, it deleted the long introductory attack on the substance of

contemporary due process jurisprudence in the criminal procedure field, although, as will be seen below, remnants of the thought persisted for the nonce. But the overall focus of this draft, most of which is not quoted here because of its similarity to the ultimate opinion, is on habeas corpus procedure as such.

34. Draft Opinion, *supra* note 32, at 1–3, 7–8. Noting the shallow roots of *Darr v. Burford* as described *supra* Chapter 17, text accompanying notes 5–12, this draft also contains a proposal, later dropped, that the prisoner be given the option of either seeking certiorari from the highest state court (and be precluded by an adverse result from seeking habeas corpus) or forgoing certiorari at that point and applying to the federal district court for habeas corpus. Draft Opinion, *supra*, at 11.

35. Draft Opinion, Nos. 20, 22, 31 & 32 (dated 1/13), Robert H. Jackson Papers, Library of Congress, Legal File, Supreme Court—O.T. 1952, Case Nos. 32, 22, 20, 31, *Brown v. Allen*, etc., Folder #3.

36. Among the surviving copies is one in the Tom C. Clark Papers at the Tarlton Law Library of the University of Texas, Box A19.

37. These documents are all to be found in the Robert H. Jackson Papers, Library of Congress, Legal File, Supreme Court—O.T. 1952, Case Nos. 32, 22, 20, 31, *Brown v. Allen*, etc., Folder #3.

38. This document is to be found in the Felix Frankfurter Papers, Harvard Law School, Part I, Reel 66, Frame 00028.

39. There is a copy in the Tom C. Clark Papers at the Tarlton Law Library of the University of Texas, Box A19.

NOTES TO CHAPTER 20

1. *See Brown v. Allen*, 344 U.S. 443, 491, 497 (1953) (opinion of Frankfurter, J.) (expressing the "position of the majority upon that point," *Brown*, 344 U.S. at 452). The view of the Fourth Circuit as expressed by Judge Parker has been described *supra* Chapter 17. The section of Justice Reed's opinion for the Court stating the minority viewpoint on this issue, *see Brown*, 344 U.S. at 456–57, had the support of Justice Minton and Chief Justice Vinson, neither of whom wrote separately. Justice Jackson urged a broader rule of preclusion, *see Brown*, 344 U.S. at 543–45 (Jackson, J., concurring), which would have foreclosed the petitioners before the Court.

2. *See id.* at 463–64 (opinion of the Court per Reed, J.); *id.* at 500 (opinion of Frankfurter, J.).

3. *See supra* Chapter 18, text accompanying notes 29–30.

4. *See Brown*, 334 U.S. at 503–04 (opinion of Frankfurter, J.).

5. *Id.* at 506–08. The Court has continued to apply this framework until recently, *see Thompson v. Keohane*, 516 U.S. 99, 102 (1995), but has not specifically ruled on whether it survives AEDPA.

6. *See Brown*, 344 U.S. at 463–65.

7. *Id.* at 497 (opinion of Frankfurter, J.).

8. *Id.* at 478.

9. *Id.* at 497 (opinion of Frankfurter, J.).

10. That is, *Brown, Speller,* and *Daniels.* As noted *supra* Chapter 18, *Ekberg* had previously been dismissed as moot, and *Smith v. Baldi* was decided in a separate published opinion.

11. *See Brown,* 344 U.S. at 467–74.

12. *See id.* at 475–76.

13. *See id.* at 504–08 (opinion of Frankfurter, J.).

14. *See id.* at 554 (Black, J., dissenting).

15. *Id.* at 551 (Black, J., dissenting). Justice Black took a similar approach to *Speller,* adding that he would consider on the merits the challenge to a wealth-based jury selection system. *See id.* at 551–52.

16. *See id.* at 556 (Frankfurter, J., dissenting). Since the Court of Appeals had decided *Speller* in the same opinion as *Brown,* Justice Frankfurter labeled this section of his merits dissent as applicable to *Speller* as well. *See id.* at 554–55.

17. *Id.* at 480–81.

18. *Id.* at 485.

19. *Id.* at 553 (Black, J., dissenting). He then continued with the passage about the inconsistency of the Court's ruling with *Moore,* which has been set forth *supra* Chapter 18, text accompanying note 67.

20. *Brown,* 344 U.S. at 559 (Frankfurter, J., dissenting).

21. *See* Barron Mills, *Clyde Brown, Speller Pay With Lives for Crimes,* Winston-Salem J., May 30, 1953, at 1.

22. *See Cousins Die In Gas Chamber For Killing Pitt Cab Driver,* The News and Observer [Raleigh, N.C.], Nov. 7, 1953, at 1.

23. 344 U.S. 561 (1953).

24. *See id.* at 565. The Court was also unanimous in rejecting Smith's substantive claim that he had a Constitutional right to the appointment of a psychiatrist. *Id.* at 568. This decision was repudiated in *Ake v. Oklahoma,* 470 U.S. 68, 85 (1985). Justice Rehnquist dissented.

25. *Smith,* 344 U.S. at 569–70 (quoting *Smith v. Baldi,* 96 F. Supp. 100, 103 (E.D. Pa. 1951)).

26. *Smith,* 344 U.S. at 570.

27. *Id.* at 571–72 (Frankfurter, J., dissenting).

28. This presented no difficulty in the case at hand because Pennsylvania law so provided, *see id.* at 568–69, 571, and thus it was not necessary to rule whether the Constitution so required.

29. *See Ford v. Wainwright,* 477 U.S. 399, 406 (1986).

30. Brief of the District Attorney for the City and County of Philadelphia at 3, *Smith v. Baldi,* 344 U.S. 561 (1953) (No. 31). *See* Earl Selby, *Dilworth Will Intercede in High Court for Killer,* Philadelphia Eve. Bull., Apr. 16, 1952, at 1 (describing pros-

ecutor's decision as "an action believed to be almost without precedent" and detailing issues in case). This brief was filed for its persuasive effect only, since the litigation on the government's side was conducted by the Attorney General of Pennsylvania.

31. *Smith*, 344 U.S. at 572 (Frankfurter, J., dissenting).

32. *See 1951 Mental Health Act Applies to Prisoner Awaiting Execution*, [Philadelphia] Legal Intelligencer, Mar. 24, 1953, at 1 (reprinting ruling and sanity commission report on which it was based). The question at this point was present competency to be executed, not whether Smith had been sane at the time of the crime or his guilty plea, but the findings cast strong doubt on the earlier determinations. *See* Michael von Moschzisker, *An Old Murder Case Returns to the Courts*, Philadelphia Eve. Bull., June 18, 1968, at 68 ("Technically [the commission] was to determine the condition of the man five years after the crime, but the real effect was to recheck the original diagnosis of the court psychiatrist, who had been found to be not well himself."); Earl Selby, *Insanity Ruling Saves Life of Cabbie's Killer*, Philadelphia Eve. Bull., Mar. 23, 1953, at 1 (publishing Smith's diagram of a "supernatural efficacious transmitter" that, by shooting out a "telepathic electro-magnetic beam," prevented his mind from "rotating normally," thereby causing his troubles).

33. *See Shafer Commutes Slayer's Sentence*, Philadelphia Eve. Bull., Nov. 19, 1968, at 35.

34. *In re Application of Smith*, No. 9994 (Pa. Bd. Pardons, Feb. Sess. 1973).

NOTES TO CHAPTER 21

1. Indeed, such complaints began within a decade of the 1867 statutory expansion of the writ that was noted *supra* Chapter 3, text accompanying note 58. *See* William M. Wiecek, *The Great Writ and Reconstruction: The Habeas Corpus Act of 1867*, 36 J. S. Hist. 530, 544 (1970). For a more extensive account of the tangled maneuverings over habeas corpus from the early 1940's through the late 1960's than appears in this chapter, see Larry W. Yackle, *The Habeas Hagioscope*, 66 S. Cal. L. Rev. 2331, 2341–48 (1993).

2. *See* Report of the [1943] Judicial Conference of Senior Circuit Judges 22–25 (1944); Report of the [1945] Judicial Conference of Senior Circuit Judges 18 (1946); John W. Winkle, III, *Judges as Lobbyists: Habeas Corpus Reform in the 1940s*, 68 Judicature 263, 266–67, 272 (1985). As noted in Chapter 18, in *Brown v. Allen*, 344 U.S. 443, 447–50 (1953), the Court unanimously rejected Judge Parker's argument that the 1948 revisions to 28 U.S.C. § 2254 embodied this rule. For biographical sources on Parker, see Milestones III, 1611 n.286.

3. *See Brown*, 344 U.S. at 451 n.5 (opinion of the Court); *id.* at 539 & n.13 (Jackson, J., concurring in the result).

4. *Id.* (setting forth text of resolution).

5. *See, e.g., Brown*, 344 U.S. at 533 n.4 (Jackson, J., concurring in the result) (noting both cases).

6. *See Habeas Corpus: Hearings Before Subcommittee No. 3 of the Committee on the Judiciary,* House of Representatives, 84th Cong., 1st Sess. at 10–11 (1955) (Parker testimony); *Report of the Special Committee on Habeas Corpus to the Conference of Chief Justices* at App. 8–10 (June 1953). There is a copy of this latter document in the Robert H. Jackson Papers, Library of Congress, Box 120, Habeas Corpus file.

7. *See* Report of the Judicial Conference of the United States 40 (1953).

8. *See id.* at 26.

9. Annual Report of the Proceedings of the Judicial Conference of the United States 22–23 (1955).

10. *See* Annual Report of the Judicial Conference of the United States 34 (1956).

11. *See* Letter from Felix Frankfurter to Tom Clark and John Harlan (Sept. 29, 1958), Felix Frankfurter Papers, Part III, Reel 6, Frame 728.

12. Memorandum for the Committee on Proposed Habeas Corpus Legislation at 3 (Nov. 3, 1958), Felix Frankfurter Papers, Part III, Reel 6, Frame 422.

13. *See infra* Table 3. The figures therein are taken from S. Rep. No. 2228 at 30 (85th Cong. 2d Sess.) (Aug. 6, 1958) (to accompany H.R. 8361).

14. Memorandum, *supra* note 12, at 3, 7–8.

15. *See* Letter from Felix Frankfurter to Sherman Minton (May 28, 1954), Felix Frankfurter Papers, Part III, Reel 2, Frame 441.

16. Memorandum, *supra* note 12, at 5–6. The problem of the distribution of business between the Supreme Court and the lower federal courts had been of concern to Frankfurter since the mid-1920's. *See* Edward A. Purcell, Jr., *Reconsidering the Frankfurterian Paradigm: Reflections on Histories of the Lower Federal Courts,* 24 L. & Soc. Inquiry 679 (1999) (analyzing Felix Frankfurter & James L. Landis, The Business of the Supreme Court (1928)).

17. *See* Letter from Jerome N. Frank to William O. Douglas (Sept. 11, 1956). There is a copy in the William O. Douglas Papers, Library of Congress, Box 583, Habeas Corpus Law folder.

18. *See, e.g.,* Letter from John J. Parker to William Denman (May 16, 1956) (defending proposed restrictive legislation against objections raised by Denman; copied to Senate Judiciary Committee, Supreme Court, and Judicial Conference). There is a copy in the William O. Douglas Papers, Library of Congress, Box 583, Habeas Corpus Law folder.

19. Annual Report of the Proceedings of the Judicial Conference of the United States [for 1959] 313 (1960).

20. Yackle, *supra,* note 1 at 2347 (citing *Townsend v. Sain,* 372 U.S. 293 (1963), *Fay v. Noia,* 372 U.S. 391 (1963), and *Sanders v. United States,* 373 U.S. 1 (1963)).

21. *Id.* at 2347–48 (citing 1966 revision of 28 U.S.C. § 2254(a)). *See* 1 James S. Liebman & Randy Hertz, Federal Habeas Corpus Practice and Procedure, § 2.4(d), at 64 (3d ed. 1998) (concluding that "the 1966 amendments either confirmed or left intact what the caselaw had long established."). This, of course, was not the end

of the story. Like the combatants in World War I, succeeding waves of warriors continued to do battle over the same narrow terrain—and are doing so still. *See* Larry W. Yackle, *Recent Congressional Action on Federal Habeas Corpus: A Primer*, 44 Buff. L. Rev. 381 (1996); *see also* Mark Tushnet & Larry Yackle, *Symbolic Statutes and Real Laws: The Pathologies of the Antiterrorism and Effective Death Penalty Act and the Prison Litigation Reform Act*, 47 Duke L.J. 1, 37–47 (1997).

NOTES TO CHAPTER 22

1. *See* 1 James S. Liebman & Randy Hertz, Federal Habeas Corpus Practice and Procedure, § 2.4(d), at 68–69 (3d ed. 1998). For this reason, those seeking to narrow habeas review have sought in more recent years to constrict the ability of habeas corpus petitioners to appeal from the District Courts to the Circuit Courts of Appeals. *See* 28 U.S.C. § 2253(c) (1994 & Supp. II 1996); *Hohn v. United States*, 524 U.S. 236, 256, 263–64 (1998) (Scalia, J., dissenting) (claiming Court is defying this provision).

2. Liebman & Hertz, *supra* note 1, § 2.4d, at 69. *See Brown v. Allen*, 344 U.S. 443, 458 (1953) (federal habeas courts should give rulings of the state courts on the Constitutional law issues "the weight that federal practice gives to the conclusion of a court of last resort of another jurisdiction on federal constitutional law issues").

3. Liebman & Hertz, *supra* note 1, § 2.4d, at 69.

4. *Brown*, 344 U.S. at 485. *Cf.* William J. Brennan, Jr., *Federal Habeas Corpus and State Prisoners: An Exercise in Federalism*, 7 Utah L. Rev. 423, 430–32, 437–38, 441–42 (1961) (attacking this outcome).

5. 372 U.S. 293, 312–19 (1963) (announcing "the appropriate standard—which must be considered to supersede, to the extent of any inconsistencies, the opinions in *Brown v. Allen*").

6. 504 U.S. 1, 5–8 (1992) (overruling *Townsend*). In 1996, Congress created its own statutory standards for mandatory, but not discretionary, hearings. *See* 28 U.S.C. § 2254 (e) (2) (1994 & Supp. II 1996); *Jones v. Vacco*, 126 F.3d 408, 417 n.2 (2d Cir. 1997); *see also Burris v. Parke*, 116 F.3d 256, 258–59 (7th Cir. 1997); *Jones v. Wood*, 114 F.3d 1002, 1113 (9th Cir. 1997).

7. 372 U.S. 391, 425–26, 433–35 (1963) (Brennan, J.) (granting habeas relief to applicant who had filed no state appeal at all). As indicated *supra* Chapter 17, note 7, the same case also took the step that the *Brown* Court had been unwilling to take, and overruled *Darr*. *See Fay*, 372 U.S. at 435–38.

8. 501 U.S. 722, 749–51 (1991) (holding habeas relief precluded by three-day lateness in filing appeal from denial of state postconviction remedies). The case is discussed *supra* Chapter 2, note 25 and *infra* Chapter 23, text accompanying notes 21–24.

9. As indicated *supra* Chapter 19, note 22, this is just what Justice Frankfurter told his colleagues during the *Brown* deliberations.

10. The fact that some parts of Professor Bator's argument were so clearly in tune with clerk Rehnquist's thinking, *see supra* Chapter 19, notes 6, 13, doubtless made Chief Justice Rehnquist readier to believe the parts relating to the importance of *Brown*.

11. *See* Jordan Steiker, *Innocence and Federal Habeas*, 41 UCLA L. Rev. 303, 319 (1993) (observing that *Brown* remains important because, although "as a theoretical matter," it was "simply a codification of pre-*Brown* habeas law," it eventually led in practice to more habeas relief).

12. *See supra* Chapter 16, note 7 (discussing views of Justices Rehnquist, Thomas, and Scalia in *Wright v. West*, 505 U.S. 277, 285–88 (1992)).

NOTES TO CHAPTER 23

1. *See Gregg v. Georgia*, 428 U.S. 153 (1976).

2. *See* Eric M. Freedman, *Federal Habeas Corpus in Capital Cases*, in America's Experiment with Capital Punishment: Reflections on the Past, Present and Future of the Ultimate Penal Sanction 409, 424–25 (James Acker et al. eds., 1998).

3. *See* 1 James S. Liebman & Randy Hertz, Federal Habeas Corpus Practice and Procedure, § 2.6 (3d ed. 1998).

4. *See* Association of the Bar of the City of New York, *The Crisis in Capital Representation*, 51 Rec. Assoc. Bar City of N.Y. 169, 177–81 (1996) (citing many additional examples).

5. *See* James S. Liebman, Jeffrey Fagan, et al., A Broken System: Error Rates in Capital Cases, 1973–1995, at App. D (2000).

6. Tellingly, the same study shows, *id.* Part II at 5–6, that of every 100 death sentences imposed, at least 47 were reversed by the state courts prior to federal habeas review, either on direct appeal or in state collateral proceedings—which demonstrates the importance of maintaining vigorous review at the state as well as at the federal level.

7. *See id.* at 6. Combining these statistics with those in the foregoing note, the study finds that of the original 100 death sentences, 68 were overturned (47 at the state level and 21 at the federal level), *id.* This 68 percent figure compares with a total reversal rate of perhaps 15 percent in noncapital cases, *see id.*, at 8–9.

8. *Callins v. Collins*, 114 S. Ct. 1127, 1137 (1994) (Blackmun, J., dissenting from denial of certiorari). A fragment of this eloquent, comprehensive, and thoughtful opinion has been previously quoted *supra* Chapter 11, note 9.

9. *McCleskey v. Kemp*, 481 U.S. 279, 315–16 (1987).

10. *See McClesky v. Kemp*, 890 F.2d 342 (11th Cir. 1991).

11. *See Wainwright v. Sykes*, 433 U.S. 72 (1977).

12. *Murray v. Carrier*, 477 U.S. 478, 488 (1986).

13. *See Sanders v. United States*, 373 U.S. 1 (1963); *Fay v. Noia*, 372 U.S. 391 (1963).

14. *See McCleskey v. Zant*, 499 U.S. 467 (1991).

15. *See, e.g.*, James S. Liebman, *The Overproduction of Death*, 100 Colum. L. Rev. 2030, 2102–08 (2000); Stephen B. Bright, *Counsel for the Poor: The Death Sentence Not for the Worst Crime but for the Worst Lawyer*, 103 Yale L.J. 1835 (1994); Ira P. Robbins, *Toward a More Just and Effective System of Review in State Death Penalty Cases*, 40 Am. U. L. Rev. 1 (1990) (reporting results of American Bar Association Study); Michael Mello & Paul J. Perkins, *Closing the Circle: The Illusion of Lawyers for People Litigating for Their Lives at the* Fin de Siècle *in* Acker, *supra* note 2, at 245, 260–82; Note, *The Eighth Amendment and Ineffective Assistance of Counsel in Capital Trials*, 107 Harv. L. Rev. 1923 (1994); Association of the Bar, *supra* note 4, at 183–87; *Illusory Justice*, St. Petersburg Times, Jul. 22, 2000, at A16.

16. *See* Liebman, Fagan, et al., *supra* note 5, at 5.

17. *See Strickland v. Washington*, 466 U.S. 668 (1984); Association of the Bar of the City of New York, *Legislative Modification of Habeas Corpus in Capital Cases*, 44 Rec. Assoc. Bar City of N.Y. 849, 862 n.28 (1989).

18. *See* Steve Mills, Ken Armstrong, et al., *Flawed Trials Lead to Death Chamber; Bush Confident in System Rife With Problems*, Chicago Tribune, June 11, 2000, at 1; Stephen B. Bright, *Death in Texas*, 23 The Champion 16 (1999). Numerous similar examples are documented in the sources cited *supra* note 15.

19. *See Murray v. Giarratano*, 492 U.S. 1 (1989).

20. *Zant*, 499 U.S. at 491.

21. 501 U.S. 722 (1991).

22. *Id.* at 754.

23. *Id.* at 726.

24. *See supra* Chapter 2. Note 25 thereof discusses *Coleman* specifically.

25. *See* Association of the Bar, *supra* note 4, at 188–91, 200–05.

26. *See* Larry W. Yackle, *Recent Congressional Action on Federal Habeas Corpus: A Primer*, 44 Buff. L. Rev. 381, 398–401 (1996).

27. 28 U.S.C. § 2254(d) (Supp. II 1996).

28. *See supra* Chapter 8, note 8.

29. President's Statement on Antiterrorism Bill Signing, 1996 WL 203049 (April 24, 1996).

Index

About the Author

Eric M. Freedman is a Professor of Law at Hofstra University School of Law, where his courses include Legal History, the Death Penalty, and Constitutional Law. He is a graduate of the Phillips Exeter Academy, Yale College, and Yale Law School, and earned a Master's Degree in History from Victoria University of Wellington, New Zealand, while holding a Fulbright Scholarship there. In addition to writing and lecturing frequently on habeas corpus for scholarly and general audiences, Professor Freedman is active nationally as a capital defense litigator and consultant.